PRAISE FOR *CHRIST KITCHEN:*

Loving Women Out of Poverty

Jan Martinez has taken two towns, Sychar and Spokane; two meeting places, Jacob's Well and Christ's Kitchen; and Jesus, and skillfully woven them into a stunning tapestry of hope for women in poverty. Read this, and thank God for this companion in the faith who has made it her vocation to mentor women out of poverty and into a life full of hope. *Christ Kitchen: Loving Women Out of Poverty* is a delightful work of art—spiritual theology at its best.

—Eugene H. Peterson, professor of spiritual theology, Regent College, Vancouver BC; translator of *The Message.*

Before meeting Christ, I, like the Samaritan woman in the Gospel of John, harbored a silent scream within: *If only someone would tell me . . .* Tell me what? What I knew not! Yes, my thirsty soul somehow knew there was something to know that I knew not, Someone to meet that I'd met not, something to heal that had healed not, and a spiritual purpose and dynamic that I knew not!

This book documents the silent life screams of broken, mangled, misused women. As the result of Jan's own encounter with evil treatment and her healing through the living Christ, she has been able to help so many women match the torn, jagged pieces of their experiences with the giving grace of a mending, merciful, and transforming God.

Once Jan knew the Jesus who "healed her broken image and changed her everything," she put pen to paper and wrote a book that must be read. Her passionate insistence to make sure that all who come within the orbit of her life encounter the healer, transformer, and friend whose name is Christ brings a practical life challenge for good and for God to all—men and women alike.

Buy this book, read this book, and allow this book to read you. When you are finished, you will wonder what on earth you were doing going shopping!

—Jill Briscoe, popular international Bible teacher and author of over forty books, including *8 Choices That Will Change a Woman's Life* and *Out of the Storm and Into God's Arms*

Dr. Jan Bowes Martinez has just written the single most helpful book on modern mission to our poor, particularly women, that I have read. It is the perfect Christian extension and application of Kristof and WuDunn's recent *Half the Sky.*

—Dale Bruner, professor emeritus, theology department, Whitworth University; biblical commentator; author of *Matthew: A Commentary, A Theology of the Holy Spirit: The Pentecostal Experience and the New Testament Witness,* and *The Gospel of John: A Commentary*

Jan Martinez has a story to tell, a story of how God called her to get involved with women living in poverty only a few miles from her comfortable home, which culminated in the founding of Christ Kitchen, a business that helps women to find employment and to be found by Christ at the same time. But Jan does more than tell her story; she invites us to follow Christ, just as she did, which might require us to leave behind the safety we cherish and give ourselves to the people God cherishes so much. Jan writes with energy, insight, and polish. It is rare to read a book about such a vital subject written in such a vital style. Her book both disturbed and inspired me; I suspect it will do the same for you. I highly recommend it.

—Gerald L. Sittser, professor of theology, Whitworth University;
author of *A Grace Disguised* and *Water From a Deep Well*

It could not be more appropriate for Jan Martinez to see the Samaritan woman of John's gospel as a metaphor for Christ Kitchen of Spokane. Like Jesus, who engaged a social outcast at the public well and ended up eating with her in her home, Jan has engaged women at the social margins of Spokane. And she has introduced many to the extravagant love of Jesus, turning grace, love, and forgiveness into the fine art of employment, and enjoyment. This is a great book—unique, biblically grounded, and set in Spokane—with global implications.

—Raymond J. Bakke, chancellor of Bakke Graduate University; author of *A Theology as Big as the City*

Jan Martinez is an entrepreneur who is putting her faith into action. By gathering groups of women who reach across socio-economic boundaries to provide access to opportunity through redemptive relationships, she models a creative approach to empowering the poor that really works. Read this book if you want to be inspired to join God's overarching mission to redeem the world. Prepare to be personally transformed by the experience.

—Arloa Sutter, executive director of Breakthrough Urban Ministries;
author of *The Invisible: What the Church Can Do to Find and Serve the Least of These*

Walking beside psychotherapist Dr. Jan Martinez in her razor-raw-edged book, *Christ Kitchen: Loving Women Out of Poverty* (think Oswald Chambers meets Anne Lamott here), is a chance for us average, middle-class Christians to walk beside her and her Spokane, Washington nonprofit in the trenches. Down the roads of Samaria or along the brutally mean streets of any impoverished neighborhood in America, we meet and learn how to truly greet, love, and minister to those who, for whatever reasons, find themselves living there. This book will change the way you think about poverty and those who grow up in it. And you'll be the richer for it.

—Ronna Snyder, author of *Hot Flashes from Heaven*

Christ Kitchen

Loving Women Out of Poverty

Jan Martinez

Deep River
BOOKS

Christ Kitchen: Loving Women Out of Poverty
© 2013 by Jan Martinez
All rights reserved.

Published by
Deep River Books
Sisters, Oregon
www.deepriverbooks.com

Some names have been changed to protect privacy.

ISBN 10: 1937756920
ISBN 13: 9781937756925

Library of Congress: 2013943345
Printed in the United States of America

Design by Robin Black, Inspirio Design

Dedication

To the women at Christ Kitchen,
whose passion for Christ inspires me,
whose honesty fills these pages,
whose joy and simplicity focuses me,
whose courage makes me strong.

Acknowledgments

This book has been in process for a long time. It has been quite literally prayed into existence by many faithful souls. I am indebted to those who read initial drafts and to my mentors who wrote endorsements: Eugene Peterson, Jill Briscoe, Dale Bruner, Jerry Sittser, Arloa Sutter, Ronna Snyder, and Ray Bakke. I am thankful to Jill Briscoe for suggesting that women of faith in every town across the country should start a Christ Kitchen and for publishing my article about it years ago. I am also thankful to Deep River Books for taking a chance on a new author.

There are so many people who have supported, encouraged, and prayed for me and for Christ Kitchen throughout these years. I am grateful to all the volunteers who grace our doors, bringing their time, support, casseroles, and love for the women. I owe a debt of gratitude to the Christ Clinic/Christ Kitchen Board of Directors for backing this wacky "bean thing" from its inception and to Danielle Riggs for being my friend and on-site prayer partner. I am particularly thankful for my Bible study, Linda Koeske, Pam Brownlee, and Patty Seebeck, whose encouragement I needed so often and whose patient support saw me through each phase. I am deeply indebted to Jane Larson for her precious friendship, her intense love for Samaritans, and for not letting me give up on writing this book.

My deepest appreciation goes to Sarah Johnson, my sister and mentor, who has been on this road with me longer than any, who taught me what a true disciple looks like, who loves me no matter what. Through my children, Jake and Rosie, I learned the meaning of sacrificial love, and I am indebted to them for patiently allowing the women of Christ Kitchen to share my life. I am most grateful to my husband, Felix, for his enduring love and support. He has stood by me in the darkness. His steadfastness has taught me to be strong and persevere, his joy brightens my life, and his partnership has allowed Christ Kitchen to flourish.

Contents

Appendix C

Introduction

This is a story from the fourth chapter of John's gospel about the Samaritan woman who encounters Jesus at the well near her home. She reminds me of the women I work with in our mission to low-income women in Spokane, Washington. She is tough and street-smart, funny and caring, deeply wounded, and disconcertingly honest. She is bright and talented, but often conceals her gifts behind layers of suspicion, guilt, and suffering. Above all, she longs to love and be loved.

That is why I wrote this book. I pray you will fall in love with her. This Samaritan outcast lives in every town in this country. She doesn't go to your church, shop at your nearby grocery store, or exercise at the local gym. You probably won't find her at beauty parlors, movie theaters, or book clubs. She works odd hours for minimum wage and rides the bus to work, so you won't see her at many back-to-school nights, soccer games, or making cupcakes for the bake sale. She remains isolated from us, the other women in her village who know that she exists but have never spoken to her.

It may seem an unlikely aspiration to hope that you will learn to love her. I have a persuasive motivation, however, with which I undertake this implausible task. Our Lord loved this woman. He went far out of his way to talk to her and spent his longest conversation with her of any recorded in Scripture. That act in itself lends my hope some credibility. Jesus dragged his wary disciples along with him to meet her, and they ended up converting a whole town of Samaritans. Talk about unlikely expectations.

So I will be totally straight with you about what I hope happens to you as you read this book. Not only do I pray you will fall in love with hurting, lonely Samaritan-like women who at first want nothing to do with you, but I also pray you may end up investing your life with them and, in so doing, be changed forever. I pray the relationships you form will shine light into some of the darkest holes on earth, right in your backyard. That's all I want.

The bar may seem terribly high, but don't worry. My intent is not a guilt-producing appeal, like the wide-eyed, starving Biafran children holding empty bowls asking if someone cares. I cry and feel over-whelmed when I see those children, and I send them money. I am not, however, asking you to send money to these women. I just want you to pray through these pages and watch closely how Jesus loves the Samaritan woman, how he works with her, and how he gently men-tors his disciples in her regard. The rest, my ambition, I leave in his able hands.

Augustine once wrote that the only way to understand something is to love it first—to study it with sympathy, patience, and apprecia-tion. True understanding, he said, requires the courage to surrender ourselves to the subject and let it have its way with us.[1] Our subject is women living in poverty on the streets of the wealthiest nation on earth. The journey takes patience and courage, but just give it a try. Let it have its way.

I certainly didn't set out to get involved with Samaritan women. I just thought I'd try to help someone. I resisted work that brought me into seedy parts of town, dingy apartments, and messy lives. Before I began, no one could have convinced me that I would find deep abiding love and joy like I've never known among the poorest of women. Who knew, when I let the Lord have his way, that it would forever change my life as he called me deeper and deeper into a world unknown to me, but very much in his heart. So I want to thank you in advance for journey-ing with me into that world. If I can woo you into true understanding of the Samaritan woman, we'll leave the loving part up to God.

I begin each chapter with a short vignette of the Samaritan wom-an's story imagined from her own perspective. Though fictional, many of the details come from stories I hear every day. Then, each chapter invites you to study a specific lesson in what biblical commentator Dale Bruner calls Jesus' "School of Discipleship,"[2] a metaphor for the course of study we undertake to become capable disciples to women living in poverty. Each chapter explores a principle Jesus utilized in mentoring the Samaritan woman into life-changing relationships. Specific approaches to implementing Christ's methods of discipleship are illustrated through examples from Christ Kitchen, its employees, staff, director, and volunteers. Interwoven throughout each section are relevant research and statistics on poverty in the United States, expertise from others engaged in the eradication of poverty, and inspirational stories of transformation.

At the back of the book you'll find questions and ideas for further reflection on each chapter. The *Digging Deeper* questions serve as tools to explore additional scriptural references and thought. For those interested in starting a ministry with the poor or a project like Christ Kitchen, suggestions and questions in the *For Those Digging a Well* section are intended to focus thought on relevant issues and offer ideas for ministry development. You'll find additional tools in the *Appendix,* which are intended to help you get started.

I will be praying for you. I trust that the Lord, who thunders with a mighty voice or speaks in gentle whispers, will direct your thoughts and guide this journey.

Blessings to you,

Jan Martinez

Prologue

I awoke with a knife at my neck and the palpable pounding of a rapist's heartbeat on my chest. "You're going to die," he hissed into my ear as he drew his knife all over my body, violating its core. I believed him. "Why are you doing this?" was the only thing I could think to say before frozen terror numbed all volition. Sensing that the knife was small, dying, it seemed, would take a while. It did. Even as that evil disappeared into the night, the slightest confidence of having my life spared was replaced by the certainty that not only my body, but also my heart, mind, and soul had been inextricably wounded. The demise of all I'd held dear soon began. It was a journey I'd never have chosen back on the fourth of July 1980.

Before that night, I would have told you I was a twenty-six-year-old, single, altruistic, idealistic, woman. Equipped with a master's degree in public health, and having been raised with a Navajo woman who lived with my family, I had the illusion of saving the world through work with the Indian Health Service on the reservations in New Mexico. I was applying to medical school, engaged to a wonderful man, and thought I had the world by the tail. After that night, I couldn't have told you who I was. I was terrified to live, to answer the phone, to get out of the shower. Experiencing absolute powerlessness destroyed the illusion that I could control anything. Vengeance began eroding my liberal worldviews and pacifist beliefs, as terror besieged my confidence and depression disguised my helplessness. Having touched the raw edge of what must be sanity, I dared ponder its loss. The putrid smell of evil permeated and consumed me. Nothing took it away, numbed it, or masked it—though, believe me, for months I tried everything. Suicide became terrifyingly attractive.

As a last ditch effort, I tried going to church. Considering that I had been rather hostile to Christianity in the past, it was nothing short of desperation to consider looking for healing in a church. Although I'd attended church obediently with my family as a child, the tepid lessons learned there in boredom, and later rebellion, left me unprotected and unprepared to defend the insular, indulged life I'd led. And so I sat through sermons on predestination and Paul, knelt through elaborate rituals, and walked out of a Sunday morning slide show of aborted fetuses. A dear friend of mine, hearing of this spiritual quest, took me aside one day and asked, "Jan, why do you think God wanted you raped?" I froze. What?! God wanted me raped? I slammed the church door shut, too horrified to knock again.

But her question plagued me. Did God cause rape? How could anyone believe in such a God? Somehow God must be different than that! There must be some kind of hope in this world. If I couldn't find it, I worried I wouldn't want to live much longer. Raw, fragile, and desperate, I finally begged God to prove to me that he was something other than my friend implied. Almost as if we'd struck a deal, I agreed to read through his Bible and search for his truth as long as I never had to talk to another Christian ever again.

And so I found an old Bible and opened it to Genesis chapter one. Little did I know I had embarked on a journey similar to one taken by the Samaritan woman recorded in the fourth chapter of John's gospel. This "woman at the well" as she is often referred to in church circles, encounters Jesus as she fills her water pitcher alone and away from the disapproving eyes of the other women in the village. With my empty water jug and dubious prospects, I made my way alone along a timeworn path. Day by day for a year, I worked my way through the Scriptures, unsuspectingly nearing the well at which Jesus sat waiting.

Patiently, this man, who didn't even look like he had a bucket, offered living water. He showed me his rape laws in Leviticus, his rod of correction and staff of direction in valleys of despair, and his complete compassion for me as a victim as he bound up my broken heart.

Verses like, "The Lord saves those who are crushed in spirit"[1] and "He will cover you with his feathers and under his wing you will find refuge,"[2] soothed my agitation and quieted the despair. I found a merciful Lord who wept over sin and death, but allowed life's consequences to draw his people to him. With his tender guidance, I found biblical characters who endured slimy pits far worse than mine and who were rescued from overwhelming enemies. The Lord's vengeance toward unrepentant offenders assured me of justice and actually helped me trust that this crime would not go unpunished even when the police could find no culprit. Verses like, "God will bring every deed into judgment, including every hidden thing,"[3] allowed my anger and fear to become less and less necessary. By the time I got to 1 Peter 2:24, "By my wounds you are healed," I had fallen in love with the Lord. Now I did not want to live without him. He was my lifeline. The "Peace of God that transcends all understanding,"[4] was mine for the asking. I had found my answer, my Savior.

I returned to my village, the community I now more than ever wanted to serve, with a passion to bring the word of life to a hurting, dark world. With a master's degree in counseling, I became a psychotherapist to "comfort those in trouble with the same comfort I had received."[5]

I studied trauma and its effect on life and development. I found its victims and offenders in psychiatric wards, prisons, and hospitals. I learned about character, relationships, communication, and pathology. For eighteen years, I saw patients in community, mental health, rape recovery, private practice settings, and indigent clinics. More than all other practice settings, I most loved my work at Christ Clinic,[6] a volunteer medical clinic for the working poor, among addicts, prostitutes, the beaten down, and the poor. I understood their trauma, their defensive and erratic behaviors, the idiosyncrasies of addictions, and their desperate need for redemption. I discovered women with adept schemes for avoiding community, whose history of abuse made mine seem miniscule. I understood why they steered clear of the other village women, of churches, and of Christians. I knew if Jesus could save the likes of me, he would welcome them with open arms.

I also realized I understood the village women, those who didn't approve of or even like their promiscuous Samaritan outcast. I'd been raised by them. I'm the great-granddaughter of two turn-of-the-century circuit riders, whose legacies extend generations later. Clad in starched dresses, hats, and white gloves, I grew up following my Methodist grandmother to church every Sunday. Periodically, she conscripted my sisters and me to pass trays of cookies and jelly jars filled with cranberry juice to the women in her Dorcas Circle. She found ample opportunity to fill us with wisdom and warnings like, "Women smoke, ladies don't."

I can also recall lessons learned at my mother's knee on class and race. Her demeanor toward "the help" differed from her manner with friends and neighbors. All lessons—golf, dance, and even curtsy—taught a kind of elitism, success, and prestige, without much emphasis on fairness, impartiality, or equality. Although politeness was demonstrated outside our house, seminars were conducted inside explaining the various strata of society, extolling our position near the top. "Look right, marry well," seemed to be our mission statement.

And so I understand how the village women can exclude their promiscuous sister, gathering together at the well every day rejecting those who don't measure up. I understand how ignorance and bias is passed from generation to generation. I understand how difficult it seems for women raised on radically different streets to transcend such vast divides of race, class, and experience to serve each other.

Women have struggled with these issues for centuries. The story of Sarah and Hagar in Genesis 16 and 21 sadly demonstrates our tendency to pass oppression on to our sisters, rather than rally against the systems that promote it. Thankfully, in a little story in the eighth chapter of Luke,[7] we find perfect role models of servanthood. A small group of women disciples, among them Mary Magdalene and Joanna, are described as women on the road with Jesus, supporting him and the other disciples with their own money. From divergent backgrounds, these women, whose relationships would likely have been considered scandalous in that day, were unique in that they had all been healed by Jesus. Being cured of evil spirits and diseases seemed to distinguish them from the male disciples and made them able to follow Jesus. From a purely cultural point-of-view, it seems unlikely that Joanna, one of the most affluent, connected women of the day, whose husband was the manager of King Herod's household, would be consorting with the likes of Mary, consistently described in commentaries as "probably not a prostitute."

But Jesus models relationships that bridge artificial barriers of class, color, and creed. Their suffering and healing transformed them, created common bonds, and enabled unprecedented unity. Mary and Joanna took to the road as disciples of Christ, as new creations, able and empowered to wash the feet of others. They shared a deep intimacy and passion for their Lord, helping form a healing community within which they could learn, grow, and serve together.

Suffering is a great equalizer, teaching me lessons I am learning in my new village. The Lord's equal-opportunity grace and all-inclusive Word is what every woman, regardless of her place in the village, craves. Every one of us can be "redeemed from the empty way of life handed down from our forefathers,"[8] and all of us fail if we repeat our father's sins without the Lord's saving grace.

My experience of suffering and my compassion for other desperate souls led me to create a village of sorts in which every woman can drink at the well. It's a job-training project called Christ Kitchen birthed on the tough and gritty streets of Spokane, Washington. We hire women living in poverty to make a line of gourmet food mixes. Volunteers from local churches come and help. At Christ Kitchen we simply want to meet the women when they come to the well, point to the Bearer of living water, and create a community of village women who care, understand, and will help draw the water.

My hope for the readers of this book, for every Mary and any Joanna who turn these pages, is that they will be transformed as they gather together at the well. I pray the broken, the brokenhearted, the recovering, and the mended will help each other discover their God-ordained dignity. I pray they will find healing, wholeness, and truth, surrounded by the gifts, talents, and resources of their sisters. I pray together each of us can learn to humbly serve one another simply because we've been healed by our Lord. I pray that our village extends beyond ourselves to other women on the road and that we can serve as a model for others to follow.

CHAPTER ONE

If Only We'll Obey

*S*he didn't recognize the man. She thought she saw movement around the well as she climbed the hill. And now, squinting into the hot sun, she watched him finding a seat on the wall. Shading the sun from her eyes with her hand provided a bit of cover from which to watch him. Although he wasn't looking her way, she was an expert at observing men without appearing to do so. He was a Jew, she could tell that much. He was dressed in similar clothes as the group of men she'd passed on her way to the well. They must all be together, she thought, but why was this one alone, away from his group? This man looked exhausted, she quickly surmised as she steadied the empty jug balanced on her head.

Her shoulders sagged slightly with disappointment. Her trip to the well had been timed so she wouldn't have to interact with anyone. Mid-day heat was the worst time to fill water jugs, which was precisely why she'd chosen this time to fill hers. The other women in the village wouldn't be here for hours. And avoiding them was her intention. This well-timed ritual was her daily escape from the critical eyes of her neighbors. This was the one place in her day where she could breathe unrestricted, where a fleeting sense of peace displaced reality. Here, she was unsupervised; her actions unavailable for scrutiny. Here, she felt momentarily unencumbered by past transgressions. Sometimes, on these hot journeys to the well, she imagined what it might be like to feel joy. But now, seeing this man, her retreat was interrupted.

Disappointment gave way to vigilance. Nearing the well, she felt her breath quicken and her senses sharpen as she braced herself to be *in another's presence and yet ignored. It was a frequent experience among the women in the village, but a poignant one for those considered outcasts. She was well versed in this ritual of practiced inattention, the approved method of men's conduct toward women, particularly a Samaritan woman with a Jewish man. She knew she would likely go about filling her water jug without any interference or engagement from him. But stories of Dinah and Tamar, Jewish foremothers raped without provocation, recounted by every mother to her daughters, were never far from the edges of an unaccompanied woman's awareness. They encouraged caution. One would never guess the depth and perception of her thoughts from the evasive expression that settled on her face as she set about filling her water jug.*

And then he spoke to her. He asked her for a drink.

Over the years, she had become a hard woman. A dense shroud, knit together alternately by sadness and guilt, blanketed her heart. It could readily absorb insults and abuse. Cynicism was her companion, a constant thread. But, when this stranger, this Jew, asked her for water, disbelief overtook her usual reserve. She spat out the obvious with an insolent laugh. "You're a Jew and I'm a Samaritan. How can you ask me for a drink?"

She was not prepared for his response. "If only you knew the free gift of God and who it is that asks you for a drink, you would have asked him and he would have given you living water." A rumble began deep within, beyond her awareness; an earthshaking, rock-splitting tear in the shroud.

Tucked away in the story of the Samaritan woman at the well in the fourth chapter of John's gospel, lies one of the great declarations of our Lord's heart: *If only you knew the free gift of God and who it is that asks you for a drink, you would have asked him and he would have given you living water.*[1] It's the very soul of God exposed, pouring itself out through this lament of his Son. To a woman despised and alienated because of her gender, nationality, and morality, comes

God's revealed plan: the conjoined gift of Holy Spirit and Christ. Like her foremothers, Hagar and Mary, she is the recipient of unsolicited, divine visitation and sacred proclamation. And yet, his gracious present is wrapped in shades of doubt, or perhaps desire. His gift is utterly free, life giving, eternal, and yet, there seems to be a catch—this *if only*. He will give it . . . if only. And therein lies the hint of lament—the condition, and thus the sorrow—the gift must be received.

Oh, how I have pondered this verse, its timing, delivery, and meaning. It comes at such an odd time in my meager estimation of the conversation between Jesus and this unnamed woman. He has just asked her for a drink from the well. With surprising temerity and incredulity she questions being spoken to by a man, particularly a Jew. It is then that he says in effect, "If you knew who I was, you'd ask and I'd give you more than you could imagine." Out of the blue the statement roils like a thundercloud over her head. He is a stranger disrupting centuries of protocol and she is, what, impertinent? He is offering salvation and she is looking for water buckets.

How could she miss his offer? Would I, if I was in her place and the King of the universe showed up at my well? You've got to admit his words are a bit murky. What *is* Jesus talking about? If only she knew exactly what. I search with her among the water jugs for clues to this obscure offer. How did he say it? Was his voice full of longing and pleading, or discouragement and resignation? Did he say it with gentle compassion or reserved insight? Did he emphasize the word *only* like a mother might when her child falls, fails, or flails and she exclaims, "If *only* you'd done what I said!" Or did he stress the word *knew*, lamenting ignorance from her and the Samaritans' years of rebellion away from their Lord?

Though the depth of this verse remains unplumbed, I am reminded of it too often in my work with women living in poverty. Some of them are homeless, some have made disastrous choices, many are victims of unspeakable crimes, all of them are poor. They are in many ways like the Samaritan woman. They know the chains of sin, rejection, and alienation. I hear myself utter similar words longingly to them when they walk through tragedies: *If only you knew how God is going to bring you through this trial.* I whisper them pleadingly to women who haven't yet surrendered their lives: *If only you knew how much he loves you, how he will guide you, comfort you, wipe away every tear.* I scream them in desperation and discouragement when we lose one of our women to the streets or drugs or death: *If only she knew Holy Spirit power and her Christ!* To my shame, I say them at times with resignation to the apostate, as if without protest I've already given up on her: *If only she'd known . . . she wouldn't have done thus and so. Tsk, tsk.* "If onlys" are a common occurrence around my neighborhood.

But if I were to plead as our Lord did to this solitary woman, I would plead to all women of faith who don't live in my neighborhood, who know little of unspeakable crimes and disastrous choices. If only this verse broke their hearts. If only, every time the local news announced another drug bust, a murdered child, a battered woman, a suicide, our hearts would fill with pain so severe that we would scream, "*If only you knew* God's free gift and its Bearer!" If only the pain would not subside until we land on our knees and pray for intervention, pray for miracles. If only we would pray for saints to enter those crack houses, dirty motels, barrooms, and jail cells. If only we would pray for how they might bring living water to such a parched earth.

But this isn't the whole story. Of course our hearts break at tragedy. We women of faith in the United States are not hard-hearted, dull-witted, or tight-fisted. For the most part, we pray for the lost, forgotten, sick, and dying. We help with food drives, clothes banks, mission fairs, and special offerings for the poor. We work hard, respect our husbands, raise our kids in loving homes, and actively pray for our schools and government. We attend Bible studies, support missionaries, recruit friends to come to church, tithe, and delve into the issues of our land. We are good citizens and faithful believers. So what is it about the Samaritan woman that disturbs us? Why doesn't she fill her water jugs at the well when we do? Why does she avoid us?

Why doesn't she attend our church services, friendship coffees, or faith conferences? Why does the Lord spend his longest conversation recorded in the Bible[2] with this woman we know little about? Why do we cheer when Jesus talks with her but have little inclination to do the same? Who is this Samaritan woman anyway?

"Come," our Lord calls, "follow me." Follow me into the back alleys of your town, into ramshackle, subsidized housing, courtrooms, AA meetings, free clinics, and taverns. Leave your safe fishing boats, your secure nets, your known waters. We've been commissioned to Samaria, the land of our enemies, the half-breeds and outcasts, the dispossessed and underserved. His School of Discipleship is open, and he promises Holy Spirit power to make us effective fishers of people. Our towns are full of Samaritan women who need us to feed, clothe, and visit, yes. But mostly, they need us to get to know them, to invest our hearts with theirs, to joyfully, soberly, lovingly live out the ways of the Lord with them as we walk together, to love them and allow their lives to transform ours.

How can we do such a monumental task with women we don't even know? The best way I've found is to watch how the Lord did it. He shows us step by step how he mentors the Samaritan woman and his disciples in her regard. We have a meeting at the well and he is expecting us. Together we will learn to reach our sisters who have never entered a church, never opened a Bible, and rarely felt worthy enough to pray. This unchurched, undiscipled people group lives within a few miles of your home. What if just one lonely woman found living water through friendship with you? Who knows how many more might ultimately stand with us some day and say, "This man really is the Savior of the world."

If only we'll obey.

CHAPTER TWO

Going Where He Leads

*S*he searched his face for understanding. Free gift? Living water? The words lapped on the edge of her consciousness but, finding no foothold, no base from which to proceed, plunged into a murky pool just beyond her awareness. It was clear that some intense, momentous thing was happening, like the first report of an underwater volcanic disruption that is sure to slam tsunami waves against some far off, unsuspecting shore. But fear, her default response to such onslaught, was strangely muted by his sincerity, his honest face, his perceptive eyes. Distant sounds of hope temporarily caught her off guard.

Could it be a gift exists that requires nothing from her, no strings attached, no price to pay? Oh, she'd been offered plenty of gifts in her life, but they were never free. Men offered her affection, security, a place to live, even love, but such gifts were purchased at great cost: her integrity, virtue, and reputation. She was never deceived by what men offered. Well, maybe at first, but not anymore. Was it possible to be given something free of motive, not based on performance, but solely because someone desired to give? Could she ever warrant such unrestricted award, undeserved bounty? Free. The man said he had a free gift. A singular sense of joy, the kind she imagined while walking to the well, flirted with her misgivings.

Her joy was fleeting. Like a sentry standing watch on the parapet of disappointment, she justified her response to him. Doubt reared its head and commenced battle. "You're a Jew" it spat, "and I am a Samaritan woman! How can you ask me for a drink? Jews don't' associate with Samaritans." Incredulously, she reviewed the words she'd said to the man.

Where they came from astounded her, but not more so than the insolence to say them. Certainly, they came from surprise rather than contempt. For centuries, Samaritans were hated by the Jews. They never associated with each other. She'd rarely seen one, let alone spoken to one. So how in the world could she know to whom she was speaking? What did he mean by that? He was a total stranger. How dare he offer ambiguous gifts! The murky water of doubt swept over her head and she sank under its weight.

"I never had no girlfriends before," Lori admitted, as she scooped red lentils into a bag of Blessed Bean Soup. "Guess I never trusted 'em; never wanted any," she shrugged as the other women on the food prep table nodded in agreement. This conversation took place at Christ Kitchen among employees of our job-training ministry in Spokane, Washington. We hire women living in poverty to make a line of gourmet food mixes and catered fare. "And we still don't like ya!" teased another woman down the line and they all broke up laughing as they continued scooping brightly colored beans into clear plastic packages. "I been here for over a year now," Lori went on, smiling slightly at the gentle ribbing, "and now I got friends. This right here is my family. Christ Kitchen is my family."

Lori's love for Christ Kitchen is typical of the women who've graced our doors over the years we've been in business. They are very much like I imagine the Samaritan woman: tough, suspicious, burdened, and so lonely. Most have never had women friends, preferring instead to chase illusive promises of security, love, or rent offered by available men. Sheryl, for example, had lived with eight men in a crack house. She came to Christ Kitchen the week after her man died. "I don't know how to do it by myself," she confessed. "Jimmy always took care of me." After he was diagnosed with terminal cancer, Jimmy made her promise to leave him and get clean. "He said he couldn't protect me no more and my only chance was to leave our old way of life; to go into treatment. He was leaving me high and dry, and I felt totally worthless and incompetent," she said, tears streaming down her face. "I cried out to God, 'Please help me get clean! Show me a new way!'" And he led her to Christ Kitchen.

I remember the first day Sheryl walked into the Kitchen. She bore a striking resemblance to Rod Stewart in her tight jeans and red t-shirt that read "Biker Chick" below a picture of a voluptuous woman riding a Harley Davidson. Her combat boots and leather coat with tassels hanging from the edge left no doubt that she was a tough babe. She had a beautiful face, thick makeup, and ratted hair. I could tell she'd spent time composing her guise. With averted eyes, she nervously toyed with twenty or more silver bracelets that adorned her tattooed arms, her unease incongruous with her appearance.

She had not wanted to come to Christ Kitchen, but her friend Carly, a recovering addict she'd met at Narcotics Anonymous, convinced her to try it out. I welcomed her and asked if she was clean, sober, and able to work. She nodded meekly, receiving the message that we run a business and have no room for active addictions or inappropriate behavior. I studied her face. Light flickered somewhere deep behind those shy, mistrusting eyes.

When women like Lori and Sheryl first come to Christ Kitchen, I know we only have a few seconds to make an impression. They seem to have uncanny radar to detect who is safe and who is not. It's a split second test disguised behind tough facades designed to protect a battered self buried deep inside. I smiled at Sheryl the first day she came and explained what the day involved. I told her I was glad she came. I meant it and prayed she would hear truth behind my words and her walls of defense. She nodded and hesitantly smiled back at me as if surprised at the acknowledgment or kindness. I prayed as she joined the group of women gathering for Bible study. *Lord, let her be surprised at your joy in this place. Let it draw her to your living water.*

To reveal Christ to women trapped in poverty is essentially the goal of our inner city mission. By offering work and job training, we are also able to provide group support, individual discipleship, and fellowship. The work itself is not difficult or technical, we make delicious packages of gourmet mixes with clever names like Disciple (12 Bean) Soup, Chariots of Chile, Corn Bread of Life, Testament Tea, and Benevolent Brownies, which we sell in our shop and ship all over the country. Christian music, laughter, and conversation accompany tasks like mixing ingredients, cutting labels, and tying bows.

It is neither fun nor friendship, however, that draws Sheryl, Lori, and women like them to Christ Kitchen. The incentive to walk in the door is cash—three-and-a-half hours of work at minimum wage, paid at the end of the day. Some women come to earn enough to pay off a bill, make rent money, or buy diapers. Many are on disability or government assistance of some kind and can't make ends meet, particularly when it comes to buying prescription medications. One woman, whose boyfriend broke her back with his foot, came because she could alternate sitting or standing at various jobs throughout the day. We try to find specific jobs that each woman can do despite individual handicaps. Many women echo Lori's sentiment, "I came for the money, but now I stay for the fellowship."

Others, like Sheryl, have found a lifeline in the Bible study and supportive atmosphere as a way out of loneliness and despair. Fractured relationships, a common characteristic among the women, begin to heal as they talk and work together—telling their stories, revealing their hurts, confessing their sins. Our Bible study is relevant and spontaneous, proclaiming Good News to mothers who've left their kids, sisters who've been raped by their father, women escaping violent men, addicts escaping life, grandmothers raising their children's children. When supported, the women learn how to manage the truths of their lives. They learn how to laugh over imperfections, tease each other through transitions, weep with each other over defeats, sigh over misfortune, rejoice and praise at the slightest victory.

And so I smile as women like Sheryl are warmly welcomed into the fellowship of Christ Kitchen. The other women try to lessen the terror they once felt being "the new woman." Each can recall her own first step inside our door, daring to start back to work after raising kids or Cain, after husbands have left, after illness, age, abuse, addiction or injury has destroyed. I often marvel at their ability to accept new women into their fellowship. Such simple friendship creates a caring, open environment for women who are yet unwilling or unable to care for themselves very well. Community is essential to learning how to take care of oneself. Friendship, acceptance, and accountability start the process. The Lord promises to teach each woman what is needed next.

But freedom is a process. Just like the Samaritan woman climbing the hill to the well alone at midday, Christ Kitchen workers have avoided judgment and hidden guilt most of their lives. They don't need to be told the Samaritan woman's reason for drawing water alone at the well out of sight of the other village women. Most have never stepped foot inside a church. Their explanation is familiar. "I don't have the clothes for it," they say, which we all know means, "I don't fit in there," or "I wouldn't be accepted there." With neglect, abuse, and failure so often their life's classroom, and fractured relationships as their teachers, many have escaped into poor health, harmful relationships, and bad decisions. Their resulting assumptions warn that the village women who go together to the well would never understand, could never relate, will only judge. At Christ Kitchen we simply want to meet women like Sheryl and Lori when they come to the well, point to the Bearer of living water, create a community of village women who do understand and will help draw the water.

Finding the Dispossessed

How many women like Sheryl are there in your town and what issues do they struggle with? Of course, there are lonely, isolated women in every town from every walk of life, but if you're serious about enrolling in what biblical commentator, Dale Brunner calls

"Jesus' School of Discipleship"[1] with women living in poverty, you should find out. You'll likely find answers from local missionaries cleverly disguised as teachers, food bank workers, TANF[2] employees, church secretaries, counselors at rescue missions, or second-hand store owners. Your city council will likely have demographic statistics on your town. If we're going to be effective fishers of people, we have to know the people we serve.

When I moved to Spokane, I never could have imagined there were more than 8,000 homeless people living here. Spokane is a quaint, mid-sized community of some 460,000 mostly white, mostly middle-class people. The Spokane City Council advertised it as a "great place to raise a family." It seemed like such a nice community—great public schools, great parks, kind people. My husband and I found it to be a wonderful town, a great place for his medical practice, my counseling practice, and a terrific place to raise our kids. Until I became acquainted with women like Sheryl, I never imagined there were 16,000 families headed by single moms who lived below the poverty line.[3] I had lived in Denver, Boston, and St. Louis, which all had very obvious inner city neighborhoods, but Spokane had a thriving downtown that seemed to have avoided the inner-city blight of larger metropolitan cities. I couldn't imagine the poverty here because I rarely *saw* it. Women like Sheryl didn't go to my church, their kids weren't in school with mine, they didn't shop at my local grocery store. They were off my radar, out of sight, and, quite truly, out of mind.

Considering my own ignorance and naïveté, I'm fairly certain that is why Jesus' first word of instruction to his disciples in his Great Commission is "*go.*" "*Go,*" he commands them in his final lesson before being taken up to heaven, "move out and make disciples of all nations."[4] The Gospel of Mark puts it this way: "*Go* into all the world and preach the good news to all creation."[5] There is no way I could have had the awesome privilege of knowing Sheryl, Lori, and hundreds of women like them if I hadn't moved out from my lovely, sated life in Spokane and gone a few miles from my home. Interestingly, it took a long, circuitous path to teach me this lesson.

If we're serious about signing up for Jesus' School of Discipleship, our first lesson is simply *go*. Now, before you panic—and believe me, I did—listen to what goes with you: Holy Spirit power! To his eleven ragtag, baffled, loyal followers, Jesus promised the resources of heaven would go with them. "God authorized and commanded me to commission you, so go out,"[6] he tells them. Their *going* was amply supplied with all authority on heaven and earth. Nothing—no hardness of others, no ridicule, no hostility or ruling power, no snakes, demons, or poison! — could limit the power of the gospel. Nothing will prevail against us when we obey Christ's command.[7] Our going out is commanded, empowered, and protected.

Going happens before the other responsibilities of the Great Commission. We *go* or *move out* before the three main charges of the commission—discipling, baptizing, and teaching—can occur. These three responsibilities are "slow, corporate, and earthy ways of carefully working with people, taking time to bring them along gently."[8] In Jesus' School of Discipleship, *going* is assumed when making disciples. It could be translated, "as you are going, make disciples."

To disciple means *to mentor* or *to apprentice*. It is a slower, less obvious verb than *preach, convert,* or *win,* and it reflects the Lord's desire that our obedience *to go* and make disciples will result in intimate communities where people live in good fellowship with each other[9] Perhaps that has been your experience of church fellowship groups—warm intimate relationships. For women like Sheryl and Lori, it was not.

Commissioned to Disciple

Commissioning to discipleship calls the church to ministry with others, not merely to an experience of personal salvation, a prayer room or sinner's bench, but to school, an extension course of continuing studies.[10]

The intent of Jesus' discipleship lessons is to connect people to him, which births ministry with others, and ongoing relationships within communities of faith. Clearly, the first lesson we must learn in order to become disciples is to go out from where we are and what we know.

But Jesus doesn't send us off unattended, ill equipped, or without a plan. We are not only promised the resources of heaven, but Jesus himself pledges to be with us always, to the very end of the age.[11] He promises to equip us with everything good for doing his will.[12] At the disciples' last meeting, Mark tells us Jesus confirmed all he promised with signs and wonders.[13] Luke goes on to say that Jesus *clothed* them with the Holy Spirit. Their instructions were to witness in Jerusalem, Judea, Samaria, and to the ends of the earth.[14] When Jesus says *"Go,"* he gives us everything we need to witness to those nearest and dearest to us (Jerusalem), our towns and nation (Judea), our enemies (Samaria), and everyone else all over the world.

This *going*-lesson is not new. It comes from the heart of the Old Testament when Abraham is told by God to "move out" from his country so that through him *all families* of the earth will be blessed. The disciple's commissioning finalizes the promise made to Abraham.[15] The circle is complete; the end connects with the beginning. Continuing in Abraham's blessing, the disciples are given an all-world, all-families vision to go, make, baptize, and teach. It's the same vision each one of us receives when we earnestly aspire to become disciples.

Just where did Jesus *go* to disciple and mentor in his earthly ministry? Well, we can be sure he didn't stay home. Remember, he said he didn't even have a place to lay down his head. Consistently throughout the Gospels we read that Jesus went to the lost, the injured, the unsightly, the sinners. Oh, he spoke with church leaders—the serious, the sophisticated,[16] the movers-and-shakers—but they always came to him. Quite intentionally, he went to the most unlikely people, like demoniacs, prostitutes, tax collectors, and Samaritans.

The story of the Samaritan woman is a case in point. Jesus went to enemy territory, to Samaritan turf, to meet with a Samaritan woman.

He didn't send for her or request her pleasure at a banquet. He walked to her village. She was a member of a mixed race, part Jew and part Gentile, who was hated by the Jews. Her people grew out of the Assyrian captivity of the ten northern Israelite tribes in 727 BC. After the Israelites departed, other nations with foreign gods were brought in by the king of Assyria to intermarry and occupy their land. A mongrel-religion developed in which the God of Israel was worshiped along with other gods. The Jews, therefore, viewed the racially mixed Samaritans as an inferior sect. Their radically different view of the sanctity of Jerusalem, legal traditions, and worship of other gods caused great strife between the two, resulting in the common Jewish practice of avoiding Samaria on pilgrimages to Jerusalem.[17] Even though Sychar, the Samaritan woman's village, was situated on the shortest route between Judea and Galilee, the Jews of the day preferred instead to take the longer eastern route through Perea, east of the Jordan River.[18]

But Jesus did not. The text says Jesus *had* to go through Samaria. He had an appointment with a despised, alienated outcast: a Samaritan woman who, according to Rabbinic law, was considered habitually unclean.[19] He was on a direct path to a disenfranchised woman and her community that would ultimately bridge hundreds of years of strife.

It's ironic that Jesus, himself accused by the Pharisees of being a Samaritan and demon-possessed,[20] used stories of Samaritans to exemplify gratitude and compassion. Only the Samaritan leper, one out of ten lepers Jesus healed, returned to thank Jesus.[21] Only the Good Samaritan had mercy on the victim of robbery and paid for his enemy's health care.[22] Only to our Samaritan woman, a three-time loser in Jewish estimation—a woman, a Samaritan, and one with an irregular past[23]—did Jesus first disclose he is the Messiah.[24] His stories make incontestable the fact that God's grace is a free gift, completely independent of merit, gender, nationality, or past history.

This is the free gift that our Samaritan woman must have found so baffling. No wonder she is suspicious of Jesus, confuses his gift, and sinks under its weighty offer of grace. The disciples didn't even get it. They'd just followed Jesus directly into enemy territory. Can you imagine their murmuring at the crossroads when Jesus goes straight toward Sychar instead of turning right to Perea? Can you just picture Peter, MapQuest in hand, insisting they're going the wrong way? Had they been sleeping though the lecture on the Samaritan leper? Did they flunk the Good Samaritan segment on their final exam? Everyone, it seems, is startled by the path Jesus chose.

Startling as it may be, the first class in Jesus' School of Discipleship is to *go*. If we believe him, we will obey. If we trust him, if we want to be true disciples, if we want to mentor in the manner he did, we will go where he leads. Jesus had to go to Samaria. We do, too.

CHAPTER THREE

Discovering Where to Go

*T*he sun beat down with a vengeance on the Samaritan woman and Jewish man as they conversed on the knoll where Jacob's well was situated in the parched spot of land in the middle of Palestine. The sun penetrated every cell, every crevice with agonizing heat. Nothing was left unscathed whether in shade or not. Her linen tunics protected her skin from the unremitting rays, but nothing prevented the temperature from smothering her like woolen garments in a sauna bath. Perspiration drenched her small frame, forming into drops around her hairline, splashing onto her cheeks like tears.

Quickly she returned to the task of filling her water jug. Uncertainty altered the simplicity of this perfunctory chore. Brow furrowed, she concentrated on the firmness of the thick rough rope that lowered the bucket down the deep shaft of the well's limestone walls. From deep subterranean waters cool air wafted up and skirted off her face as she leaned in close to the edge. Its crispness restored some sense of composure, but could not dispel the impression that something considerable was at hand. She could feel the attraction to this stranger as tangibly as the pull from the water's weight in the bucket. But this attraction wasn't familiar. It was like being drawn to a mirror, to an image she'd forgotten. "He's just a man," some broken part of her argued. But comparing him to other men seemed wrong, almost shameful.

Being commissioned and equipped to go into "all the world" is truly the essence of discipleship and the first lesson in disciple school. Obedient hearts say, "Yes, Lord!" They are stirred as they repeat

Isaiah's cry, "Here I am. Send me!"[1] The question remains, however, *where* will we go? We've established that Jesus went to the lost traveling avoided roads to ignored people. His route to Samaria took him into foreign territory, places unknown and unfamiliar to his disciples.

Modern-Day Samaria

So where is our modern-day Samaria here in the United States? Do we have to travel far to find today's equivalent of the Samaritan women? Do we really have to sell the house, quit our jobs, bundle up the kids and head off to Africa? Is that what Jesus means when he says "*go*"?

Let me tell you a story about how I ended up in the Samaritan-side of Spokane, Washington. There is a small bit about Africa in the story, but believe me, it was not what I had in mind when I dedicated my life to the Lord, telling him I would do whatever and go wherever he led. Honestly, I had absolutely no intention of leaving my home.

My plan, which I thought was a very good one, was to work part-time as a psychotherapist until my kids reached school age and then get my PhD in psychology with an emphasis in Christian family development. Clearly, that implied I was following Jesus, didn't it? Really, I believed *my* plans were *his* plans, so I couldn't imagine what else I could do. Oh, me of little faith.

My plans began to unravel, which all uninspired schemes tend to do, when my chosen graduate program turned out to be a huge disappointment. I had envisioned a faculty supportive of my goals to study faith development within family systems, but found they didn't understand the concept and were resistant to the idea. In addition, I'd become very sick during the interview at the school and had to leave in the middle of it. Tearfully, through the haze of a 104-degree temperature in the Seattle airport, I laid my future down at the Lord's feet, honestly and earnestly telling him I would do whatever he wanted. "Take my life, Lord." I pleaded. "Do with it what you please. If it's not psychology then lead me to the path you desire." And before the words were out of my heart, my raging influenza disappeared. Yep, total miracle—no cough, no sniffles, no aches, right back to 98.6 normal. Now, I don't know what you make of this, but I was a bit shocked and *totally* convinced that the PhD route was history.

For the next few weeks, I was giddy with excitement. I couldn't wait to hear what the new plan would be, fully expecting God to let me know and soon! "Let's go, God, let's get out there!" But nothing happened. For months I heard not a word. You should have heard my prayers. "Hellooooo, God, I'm yours." "Just give me the sign, I'll do it." "Any time now, I'm ready." Devotions with Oswald Chambers steadied me, particularly the day I read, "When God gives you a vision and darkness follows, wait. God will bring the vision he has given you to reality in your life if you will wait on his timing. Never try to help him fulfill his Word."[2] It was hard to wait. I was obviously all about helping God do his thing. It was irritating to not fill in the time with plans of my own. I liked having a goal. For goodness sake, I'm a White Anglo-Saxon Protestant, born and raised to make things happen. What was I waiting for? I didn't even know.

Clearly, understanding how independent and ignorant I am was part of God's plan. It would have helped to find a little note on my pillow that said, "Cool your jets. I'm in charge. Signed God." But no, I had to suffer my impatience and face my impertinence the hard way—one grueling disobedience at a time. It finally got to the point that I wasn't sure there even was a plan. Maybe I'd made that up. Maybe I was just supposed to simply live obediently each day. What a concept! Yet, when I recalled that total, miraculous airport healing, I couldn't shake the thought that something was brewing. Somewhere I read that while we wait for God, he is at work engineering circumstances that will glorify him, sometimes on the other side of the world. That's just what happened.

Months later, I took a phone message for my husband from a friend wondering if he might serve short term in a missionary hospital in Kenya. That was it! I knew this was where God was leading me. There was certainty in my soul and the phone call wasn't even for me! "Yes, yes, we'll go!" I told our friend, who thought it might be wise if he first spoke to my husband. After hanging up the phone, it occurred to me I knew nothing about missions. *Missions? Seriously, God? You want me to go into missions?* I had worked with the Indian Health Service and at the time was volunteering as a counselor at an indigent clinic, Christ Clinic, but the idea of missions felt totally foreign. I had never left the United States. Was this what Sarah felt when God told her husband, Abraham, to "Leave your country, your people and your father's household and go to the land I will show you?"[3] I had no frame of reference, no map, no idea what I was getting into in the first place.

Right about now, if I were you, I'd be smugly thinking, *Well of course this is how God works. He wants us to be absolutely dependent on Him.* OK, I was not there yet. I'd just spent months wrangling with him over control issues. I was just taking one step at a time.

So yes, when the Lord said, "*Go,*" we did bundle the kids up and head off to Africa for a short time. Little did I know, in a far off village on the other side of the world, I'd have my first encounter with the Samaritan woman. Our meeting started rather awkwardly, as many relationships do, but developed into a life long bond with her. That seems to be the way the Lord works. We take a small step of obedience, and he blesses us with more than we can imagine.

Our short-term mission assignment was at the Kijabe Medical Centre in a small village an hour north of Nairobi, Kenya. My husband worked as a pathologist, filling in for a missionary on furlough, and I homeschooled our five-year-old and eight-year-old. (Now, *that* was an adventure.) When the hospital's chief of staff learned that I was a Christian therapist, he asked me to start an AIDS counseling program for the nurses at the hospital. Of course, I said no. I declined not only because I was a tiny white lady who practiced psychotherapy in the United States with mainly white, middle class, fairly normal, fairly healthy people none of whom were HIV positive or had AIDS, and not only because I didn't know the first thing about HIV/AIDS except what I'd read in the newspaper. Mostly I said no because the nurses at Kijabe Medical Centre worked with dying AIDS patients all day long and had years more experience than I did. What could I possibly teach them? They were experts in the field and I knew nothing. I said no to the chief of staff in the sweetest way possible admitting that I was unfit, unqualified, and had no doubts about my ineptitude. "Oh, you'll do fine," he said waving me off as if I was the only silly dolt in the room. "The three hour seminar is next Tuesday."

The word panic just doesn't adequately describe my state of mind. I could go on and on about how incompetent I was, and that's just what I did to a poor unsuspecting missionary lady that night at dinner. I'll never forget her; she reminded me of Barbara Bush, minus the pearls. She listened to my tirade for a bit, grabbed my hand from across the table, stared me down hard, and said, "Christ reaches people, you don't." OK, that stopped my ranting, but I am ashamed to say that my first thought, which, if heard in high, squeaky, panicky tones went something like, "What does this have to do with Christ? This is me we're talking about." Knowing better than to say anything, I just stared at her. Satisfied that she had made her point, she sat back, waved me off (just like, I might add, the chief of staff did, as if it was some secret missionary handshake) and said, "Just use the story of the Samaritan woman at the well. It's perfect." I had no idea what she was talking about.

But she was right. She was my Nathan, my Gabriel, my angel of the Lord bringing good news of great joy to the lowliest, most terrified shepherd. While I was reading about the Samaritan woman in the fourth chapter of John over and over that weekend, the Lord showed me that the story is all about Jesus welcoming total strangers, talking to societal outcasts, addressing weaknesses, offering living water, and loving the most unlovely into the Kingdom. What I didn't know was the Kijabe nurses were critical of their patients with AIDS and treated them like outcasts. When presented to them, the story of the Samaritan woman cut to the quick of their judgment, role-modeled

appropriate intervention, and taught them how to relate to the lepers of their community. Jesus used me, a semi-neurotic white lady
from America to bring a needed Word to his soldiers on the front line
of a horrific battle in Kenya. This first encounter with the Samaritan woman taught me that Jesus bridges gaps between cultures, races,
continents, experiences, and competences. Jesus taught me to trust
his Word and showed me his total provision. I really did learn to cool
my jets and trust his lead.

Our missionary work would lead us in later years to Nepal and
Viet Nam. The experiences were intense and life changing for this
little terrified woman who'd never been out of the country. Who'd
have thought such experiences would fan my desire to serve a hurting
world into a full-blown passion to bring his Word into dark places?
The Samaritan woman initiated my education. I learned additional
lessons in devastating poverty, overwhelming disease, inhumane living conditions, degrading abuse, religious oppression, and political
tyranny. Evil, I learned, had many more potent, extensive, destructive
faces than I dreamed possible. My own suffering at the hand of a rapist seemed miniscule compared to this misery. Just as the Lord had
shown me that he was capable of redeeming my desolate life, I also
found, amid the destruction in these foreign lands, community and
hope. I'd never felt more worshipful than when I was singing praises
in five-part harmony with my Kenyan sisters, more joyful than praying with Nepali lepers, more hopeful than seeing freedom dawn in
the heart of an aging prisoner of war in Denang. I had the awesome
privilege of observing missionaries work, pray, pastor, struggle, laugh,
and love the people they'd been called to serve. I saw Christ at work.
His dedicated, dynamic, devoted followers formed communities all
over the world, living on the edge, living to spread his gospel.

In the darkest corners of the earth, I'd found the work I wanted
to do and felt suited for, and the people with whom I wanted to learn,
live, and serve. I'd found mentors and kindred spirits living to tell
the world about Christ. I had tasted life on the edge, mission in the

extreme. I'd felt alive, stimulated, and challenged. I'd even been offered a perfect job with United Missions of Nepal. There was just one little problem. I kept returning to my little bed in Spokane.

Returning from these mountaintop experiences to my lovely, comfy life in Spokane might have been disastrous had it not been for Jane, a saint God placed at Christ Clinic. As reentry shocked my former lifestyle and I retaliated by raging against American afflu-ence and greed, the Clinic's nurse practitioner, a former missionary to Papua New Guinea, calmly pointed out the vast mission field in America and the difficulty of evangelism here. As I decried the com-placency of nominal American Christians, she insisted on their need for redemption. As I elevated the simplicity and wonder of other cul-tures, she challenged me to love the poor in our city. As I bemoaned my husband's desire to work in this country, she quoted Oswald Chambers' view on drudgery, as "one of the finest tests to determine the genuineness of our character."[4] She even dared warn me that if I became obsessed with exceptional moments, God would fade out of my life until I was obedient to the work he'd placed closest to me. So the question became, when God said *"Go,"* did that mean only to the foreign field that I'd learned to love or was I a humble, faithful, dependent servant of Jesus Christ, who desired nothing but to follow him wherever he led?

Determined to be the latter, I looked at the work he'd placed clos-est to me. Disease, pain, and poverty, though on a different scale then the third world, devastated my patients at Christ Clinic as surely as those in Kenyan villages. The working poor of Spokane lacked skills, access, and education that limited their advancement beyond mini-mum wage jobs. The work history of women living in poverty was often inconsistent and intermittent reflecting their priority of rela-tionships; a value found throughout the world. Women in low-income areas of Spokane told tales of rape and battering no different than women in the hills outside Katmandu. Drugs, alcohol, promiscuous-ness, poor-decisions, missed opportunities, errant parenting, and lethargy seemed far worse in my patients at Christ Clinic than I'd seen anywhere in the world.

So I started listening more carefully to my patients in therapy at Christ Clinic. I heard tales of mothers who'd abandoned their kids, sisters raped by fathers, women escaping violent men, addicts escaping life, and grandmothers raising their children's children, and my heart would ache. Their tortured childhoods left them suspicious, hurting, and isolated. Most of the women I talked with confessed they'd never had a girlfriend, preferring instead the tenuous, chaotic attention of a man offering love or at least a place to stay. They made disastrous choices with devastating consequences. I knew they were hungry for God; they loved Bible stories relevant to their situations. But all efforts to draw them to a Bible study failed. They just didn't show up.

"Let's pay them to come," I finally suggested to Jane, my nurse friend at Christ Clinic, knowing that money was also a significant need. The old missionary in her kicked in and she soundly vetoed the idea, thankfully without letting me see her roll her eyes. "OK then," I said, not about to give up, "let's pay them for something else and do a Bible study when they get here."

Finding some form of income-generating work took some thought. Knowing the women, I knew the work could not be technical, physically strenuous, or stressful. It had to be something I could do well and train others to do. It also had to produce a marketable product to generate revenue. Gourmet food mixes met all three categories. We began packaging my family recipes for dried soups, salads, cookies, drinks and breads. In time, we developed a line of thirty-five different products and, eventually, added on a commercial kitchen to cook our products for deli, catering, and restaurant sales. To this day, we meet together for Bible study on Thursday mornings and never begin a day without prayer.

The endeavor was simply a desire to offer the Word in relevant, meaningful ways to my un-discipled patients at Christ Clinic which eventually led to the development of this job-training, discipleship project we call Christ Kitchen. The concept is simple; we offer wages to draw low-income women to work together, to study the Bible, and to support and fellowship. Christ Kitchen is a place where isolated, lonely, poor women gather to hear the Word, make some money, and find some friends. Discipleship occurs on every level of the organization from the simplest task to long-range planning. Our little business of selling beans provides the atmosphere for God to do his big business of saving lives.

By conscious obedience to Jesus, we are blessed to witness the radical transformation of abused, disenfranchised, poverty-stricken women into vibrant, passionate, disciples of Christ. At the same time, we mentor volunteers from local churches in their desire to become compassionate companions and advocates of the poor. Quite frankly, one beneficial side effect to this coupling of multi-layers of mentors and mentoring is that the volunteers grow as much as those they serve. The Lord has inspired the development of a community of women at Christ Kitchen —those from the street and from local churches— who are transcending barriers of class, race, and opportunity to form meaningful, faithful relationships which aid mutual maturity.

As I reflect on these experiences, it seems so odd that when God said, *"Go,"* and I went to the ends of the earth, he was actually preparing me to serve in my own backyard. He patiently made clear to me that anyone who was without Christ, particularly the poor, lacked the power to live free no matter what their situation or where they called home. He kept impressing on me that the "harvest is plentiful"[5] and my job was to "preach the Word. . . with great patience and careful instruction."[6] It took all that to teach me that the mission field is simply between my two feet. Samaria, I learned, is right down the street.

CHAPTER FOUR

Following Into the Unknown

Keeping her back to the man, the Samaritan woman's mind searched for relief as if she was engaged in battle, and a losing one at that. She was off balance and didn't like how vulnerable it suddenly made her feel. She had exchanged weakness for callousness years ago. Unassailable pride was her default reaction at times like this. It yielded confidence, whether valid or not, that shielded a rickety scaffolding of self, buried deep within. Now this. The rules of engagement were shifting, insufficient with this gentle stranger. She searched for an advantage, a foothold on the slippery slope.

Always the pragmatist, she thought about his words. Living water, the very idea! Who'd ever heard of such a thing? Why, he doesn't even have a bucket. How exactly did he think he could draw such water? Ah, finally, her foot found purchase. Without drinking utensils, how could he offer water, even this living water? Ridiculous! And yet, it was the word "living" that caused the framework to shudder; that threatened an ill-defined danger. What did this stranger have?

Curiosity got the best of her. Fiddling with her own jug and feigning disinterest, she casually replied, "Sir, you have nothing to draw with and the well is deep. Where can you get this living water?" Turning, she covered her face with disingenuous attentiveness; that look she gave many men when sparring for a prize. But when her eyes met his, shock rocked the scaffolds. He was looking at her with such tender acuity, like he'd known her game all along, all her life. Her breath caught at the raw certainty that she was known.

It took many miles and many years to discover a poverty stricken mission field a few miles from my house. Why had I missed it? Why had I not even considered it a mission field? "Felony Flats," the idiomatic name given to Spokane's West Central neighborhood, was literally seven miles away from my home and I had never considered the poor who lived in that blighted neighborhood worthy of my attention. What was that about? Was I blind, ignorant, narrowminded? Gosh, I had prided myself (OK, first mistake) on my caring outlook toward the poor and oppressed. Why hadn't the poor and oppressed a few miles from my house even made the radar of my obviously lacking open-mindedness? I had served as a missionary in far-away third world countries and hadn't even noticed the need so close to home. I'd read, studied, and prayed more for the poor in foreign lands than in my own. Did I assume the poor of the third world more worthy than the American poor? When I reached down deep inside, I found a disturbing notion that I didn't even know anything about the American poor. Worse, I found a loathsome reality that I might not like them if I did. In the next chapter we'll take a short course on the history of inner-city deterioration in the United States to understand how I (and maybe you) acquired this view of American poverty.

Following Jesus to Samaria

Following Jesus into Samaritan land is always a personal crossroads, a defining moment. The journey is ripe with minefields. Discovering judgmental opinions like mine, uncomfortable truths, and prejudice is part of the journey. It's like opening a suitcase you've packed for a trip and finding someone else's clothing. "Hey," you say incredulously, "where are my things, my comfortable shoes, my makeup? I can't wear these clothes. Take, for example, this pathetic little ensemble named bias or this pitiful get-up called hypocrisy. No, no, no. They're way too small. I can't fit into them. I agree with the disciples. Let's not take the direct route through Samaria; lets turn and go far around this minefield. I packed for a different trip and I certainly didn't bring any bomb-proof outfits."

"Oh, Little Faith," you might hear Christ whisper into your ear. "Like your sister Martha, you are worried and upset about many things. Choose your sister Mary's way. Sit at my feet and listen to me.[1] Come to me and learn from me.[2] Don't you know that my Father desires truth in the inner most place?[3] Hold to my teaching and then you will know the truth and the truth will set you free.[4] Remember, you are to *follow me* and you will be equipped with everything you need."

The first lesson in Jesus' School of Discipleship established in the last chapter was to *"go"* and now we find the second one is to *follow*. Jesus never avoided bad neighborhoods, questionable people, or narrow-minded intolerance. If we're going to follow him, he just might lead us to parts of town and parts of ourselves we've purposefully avoided: places off our map, outside our awareness, and out of our comfort zone. He may bring us face to face with despised people who often have dismal attitudes and questionable motivations, wanting little of what we have to offer. These people may have an uncanny resemblance to the image in the mirror. The deck is stacked. Our myths have instructed avoidance of certain parts of town and self. We believe we have little, if anything, in common with modern-day Samaritans. Despite all this, the question remains, will we follow him wherever he leads?

The call to discipleship is a call to leave nets, boats, and family in order to minister to others. *"Follow* me," Jesus tells Peter and Andrew in Matthew 4:19, "and I will make you fishers of men." Disciples are made with a word. Jesus says, *"Follow,"* and they immediately drop their nets and follow. The power that makes disciples is not human potential, but the spiritual potency of the Word."[5]

Oswald Chambers describes the difficulty and progression of obedience to follow. He writes that the first time Jesus told Peter to "Follow me," Peter did so without hesitation. "There was nothing mysterious in this type of external following," Chambers writes, "but three years later, when Peter was called to follow once again after denying Jesus with oaths and curses, internal sacrifice and yielding was required."[6] My own impatient anticipation for God to reveal his plans for my life did not include God-therapy on my Peter-like headstrong independence. I can't count the number of times I've needed to cool my jets, get on my knees, and place my plots, plans, and thoughts on the altar. "Your way, your timing, your cup," I pleaded with him. "Break me, make me live only to glorify You." The tough part about following Jesus clearly has less to do with where or to whom he leads than with the despicable characters we find within. I am certain this is what "burn-out" is all about, but more about that later.

Thankfully, the supplies always accompany the orders. Following Jesus comes with a promise to be effective fishers of people. It also involves a leaving: disconnecting with known, sure dependencies. The disciples left family, work, habit, and property for the promise of effective mission. Dietrich Bonhoeffer, a German pastor and author murdered by the Nazis, describes this leaving as a "first step." He says, "Those called to discipleship must get out of their situations, in which they cannot believe, into a situation in which faith can begin."[7]

Just as Peter had to get out of the boat into the waves, just as Levi had to leave his tax collection booth, those who want to minister to the poor in their cities, must leave familiar neighborhoods, nice homes, and comfortable church fellowships to discover the realities of poverty and godly, realistic compassion for the poor. Likewise, those living impoverished lives must leave abusers, crack pipes, or destructive lifestyles and find safe places in which faith can begin. Following Jesus involves an inner transformation.

Discipleship projects like Christ Kitchen provide a safe place, a mentored path, which enables transformation. "Do not conform to the pattern of this world," Paul advised the Romans, "but be transformed by the renewing of your mind."[8] Finding missionaries among the American poor who've been learning new patterns of ministry certainly aids the process. You'll read about several of them throughout these chapters and will find mentors in your own town. Soaking in Scriptures that describe God's heart for the poor renews our thoughts, challenges inaccurate beliefs and creates a safe environment to change. Walking alongside those who live the reality of poverty every day renovates our hearts. Christ Kitchen is a community of women from every walk of life—some of the most wealthy and lots of the poorest— working together day by day, studying Scripture, holding each other up, holding each other accountable, mentoring each other, learning to serve with joy and presenting ourselves to our Lord for renewal.

Paul describes this transformation in his letter to the church at Ephesus. He reminds new, Gentile believers (former pagans who did not grown up in the church) and newly converted Jews (those with long church traditions) that, because of Christ's teaching, the old self must be put off. *The Message* writes it this way: "The old way of life has to go. Get rid of it! It's rotten through and through. And then take on an entirely new way of life—a God-fashioned life!"[9] The purpose of this transformation, Paul tells us, is so that we will "no longer be tossed and blown about by every wind of teaching and by the cunning and craftiness of men in their deceitful scheming."[10] We become stable, in other words, safe to ourselves and to others. The result is that we grow up into Christ, no longer outsiders, foreigners or aliens, but fellow citizens with God's people and members of his household.[11] Dale Bruner describes this process succinctly: "Disciples who hear Jesus' Word will find the power to leave what they should and follow what they ought."[12] The safe shelter of Christ Kitchen encourages faithful, compassionate transformation among God's people—those from the established church and those right off the street—and creates a community of God-fashioned women.

Hazards of Being Unprepared

If we aren't following Jesus, voyaging into the bad neighborhoods in our cities might be unwise. A Christ Kitchen volunteer, who had lived in Spokane all her life but had never driven to our location in the West Central neighborhood, said her father warned her not to go. "You have no business going to Felony Flats," he said, "it's just not safe." Fear is clearly part of the reason people from community churches haven't ventured into unknown neighborhoods. Christ Kitchen is a refuge in the midst of devastation. It provides a safe place and exposure to things our fathers feared would hurt us.

Physical safety is just one of the fears on the Samaritan road. When asked to describe the emotional anxiety of working with the poor, one thoughtful volunteer wrote the following:

> *I was worried I'd have a difficult time relating to the women (or them relating to me) because of our different life experiences. I haven't had any personal encounters with women in poverty. How can I be of use if I cannot connect with these women? I am afraid that I don't have enough love and compassion for them. You know, the kind that God extends to us, accepting us just the way we are, no matter what we have done. I didn't know how I would react to them and their life stories. Would I extend grace or would I have a critical spirit?*

Discovering critical thoughts is another peril exposed on Samaritan turf. Just like the disciples' surprise when they found Jesus talking with a woman, Christ Kitchen volunteers sometimes find uncomfortable truths and biases when they return to the well.

"I just have such a hard time with entitlement," admitted Judy, a volunteer struggling to reconcile her political theories with Scripture. Karen, another volunteer, confessed she felt critical talking with the Christ Kitchen employees, wondering if the women were lying to her. She surmised she'd been raised in a "protected and critical upbringing," one in which she had no experience with poor people, nor an understanding of how to be helpful. She said, "Coming to Christ Kitchen made me think about what a disadvantage it is to be raised with a prejudice. We should have been in God's Word and learned to love all of God's creation. He tells us that there will always be poor among us and he wants to use us."

Several volunteers say they were slow to follow the clear Holy Spirit summons to go to Christ Kitchen because they couldn't imagine how they could be useful. Others felt uncomfortable going into an unknown situation where they didn't know the ropes. One woman said she didn't feel like her skills would be put to good use merely working alongside Kitchen employees. She preferred accounting or managerial work. A woman at my church, upon hearing that I'd given up my therapy practice to start Christ Kitchen, coaxed me into explaining this career change by the off-handed remark that she couldn't believe I would give up a profession to "simply volunteer to put beans in a bag."

Achieving a goal, feeling useful, having a profession, knowing the ropes are all successful orientations of the middle class. People raised in middle class homes in America are taught to value achievement, self-governance, and self-sufficiency.[13] Such qualities, which promote success in education, careers, and culture, can sometimes hinder the call to "follow." Timothy Keller observes that the Bible "does not say, blessed are the middle-class in spirit. We must come to Jesus with nothing."[14] We have a motto at Christ Kitchen that reminds us to value each person. It says, "At the foot of the cross, the ground is level."[15] By it, we mean we commit to seeing each other as God sees us, equal in his sight, no one better than, higher than, more significant than someone else. This is particularly important to women who've felt less-than all their lives. It evens the odds and is a radical departure from cultural norms. It takes intentional prayer and thought. We want to create an atmosphere in which we all offer different gifts and skills and are working on our various sins. We are learning to, "use the gifts we've received to serve others, faithfully administering God's grace in its various forms."[16] Deciding to follow Christ makes us so very dependent on God's grace.

Here's an example of how one volunteer used her gifts to help. Marilyn, a long time volunteer was incensed when she learned that a local bank was charging Christ Kitchen employees five dollars to cash each paycheck. She investigated the policy, prayed diligently for direction, and felt called to confront the problem, even if it entailed withdrawing her family's sizeable business account from the bank. Members of her church were also prepared to withdraw their accounts in support of her action. After discussing the issue with the bank president, he made an exception to the policy for all Christ Kitchen employees. This village woman put her reputation on the line for her Samaritan sisters and ended up correcting an injustice. The key to becoming a credible advocate was through her exposure to Christ Kitchen employees and the realities of poverty she had learned from them.

Following Christ doesn't always end so pleasantly. When you hang out in the back alleys of Samaria, you discover deep pain and pathology. For example, our manager, Sheryl, after being healthy, clean and sober for nine years, died a painful death from cirrhosis. Another woman, Terry, who gave her life to the Lord, got clean and sober, and reunited with her husband, was then convicted on past offenses and sent to prison for six years. Cory decided to stop having sex with her boyfriend and ended up alone and pregnant. Ilene cleaned up her life and reunited with her children after serving time in prison only to have them taken away by her Mormon father. Elise, who had worked her way into management, got entangled with an old boyfriend and ended up using and selling drugs and getting fired. Clearly, finding and following Christ doesn't eliminate consequences, suffering, or persecution. Following, despite the consequences, requires internal sacrifice and yielding.

Ministering Wherever You Are

The second lesson in our metaphorical School of Discipleship, *following* Jesus, is not just applicable to our individual lives and ministry, but also to other business and personal settings as well. Whether one is a business owner with few employees, a director of multiple enterprises, a busy mother, or simply an employee, we are called to connect people to Jesus, to minister with others, and to develop relationships within which faith blossoms. The setting in which relationships develop are as varied and unique as individual believers. Providing a job for an employee creates an opportunity for relationship within which faith mentoring can occur. Helping a fellow student with homework provides an opportunity to get to know another's needs. Befriending a neighbor opens up the possibility of compassionate interaction. Volunteering at a local food pantry begins contact with missionaries who love the poor and an acquaintance with new paradigms. Simple actions in response to God's commands to follow him begin a transformation that changes the world one person at a time.

Following Jesus into the Samaritan-side of our towns might be easier if we had role models who had been there before us, who could take us by the hand and show us the ropes. We need role models who could explain what we are seeing and teach us how to minister in that setting. This is essentially what Christ Kitchen does for the community and Church in Spokane, but our ministry is not a new idea. Did you know there were hundreds of thousands of missionary women throughout the centuries who cared for the poor and oppressed? I'll introduce you to a few of them and look briefly at biblical and Christian traditions that were specifically designed to care for the poor. We'll take a look at how and why the contemporary church veered from those traditions in order to understand the current demise of inner-city missions.

CHAPTER FIVE

Preparing to Serve

*H*er hand touched her face, a light sweeping motion over her cheek. She caught herself doing this sometimes when deep emotion loomed. Her middle finger brushed gently under her eye, a gesture so familiar its origin was forgotten. But this time, rather than mindless repetition of habit, she found a tear. She froze. The wet drop on her fingertip signaled alarm, sending waves of fright streaming through her, communicating some unknown sign of dread. She groaned while she felt for the wall to steady herself.

The memory surfaced unbidden of her small head, maybe three or four years old, resting on her mother's soft, warm arm, occasionally turning to wipe her eyes on the damp blanket that held them both. Her mother's groans, belly wreathing upward, brought other women to them; helpers, midwives, neighbors, and some she recognized as mothers of the other children she played with. One of them kept trying to shoo her away, but she would not be moved. Her life depended on staying right there next to her Uma.

So intent was this memory, she could not will it away. Women with hushed voices rushed in and out of the room. They moved her mother's legs and touched her belly, uttering sighs when they did. "Go away, go away, go away," she chanted to herself, creating a little trance-like song. She'd been singing it for a long time, she thought, ever since her mother cried out and her skirt became wet with blood and she'd fallen onto the pallet. Uma never cried or lay down or neglected her daughter's cries. Something was terribly wrong.

"Now, now," her mother should have been saying to her. "None of this crying. You're a big girl and must be strong to help me take of your *new brother and your Baba." But no such reassurances came from her Uma, and so not knowing what to do without her mother's calm command, she'd just curled up next to her body on the dirt floor. It was a long time until her Baba found them, her small body still clinging to her mother's. He'd bellowed great threats to all who didn't come quickly and take care of things. He thundered and cajoled Allah to intervene. It only made her burrow even deeper into her mother's panting, wet body.*

"Uma?" she said, waiting for her mother's reassuring pat on her back confirming that they were ok, that everything was fine. No pat this time. Her mother's hot, sweaty hand dropped wearily onto the floor. "Uma!" she cried out louder, staring into her exhausted face, willing her words, her voice to shake her mother up and away from the mat, now red with blood. And that's when her mother stroked her cheek, brushing her tears away with gentle fingers and smiling, sad eyes before they closed forever. That same motion was what she'd just repeated on her own face.

There'd never been tears found there since that day so many years ago, since they'd held her screaming little form trying to follow her mother's body as it was dragged out of their room. She hadn't cried when her Baba staggered around her after that, swearing and swinging at her, cursing her for not being a boy and thus killing her mother. No tears when he disappeared completely and she was sent to live with her aunt who had ten children of her own and was too overwhelmed to utter, "Now, now," or pat her on the back.

Dry eyed and stoic, she been given to a husband at age twelve right after she'd found blood on her own skirt and was certain she too would die. If only she had. If only she'd died before his huge bulk carelessly tore into her innocence leaving her shattered, eviscerated. No tears were shed the night he screamed in pain, clutching his chest when his heart stopped and they dragged his fat, clammy body away, leaving her a widow at thirteen.

No, tears had no place in her sullen, hardened reality. She was proud they no longer confused things and wasn't even sure if her eyes

were still capable of them. But now this—this man, a stranger, a Jew—
and her tears fell as effortlessly as a cherished child.

When missionaries prepare to serve in foreign lands, they spend
months, if not years, learning about that particular country and its
language, culture, history, current problems, and assets. Planning to
serve the poor in your town, whether you live in Sychar or Spokane,
deserves the same preparation. Thus, our third principle in Jesus'
School of Discipleship is *preparing to serve.* It requires intentional
study to understand and appreciate the people you will find on your
journey. Prior to making grand plans, it is essential to learn pertinent historical and factual information about the people to whom you
are called to serve. Our disciple training with low-income, American
women continues with a brief review of contemporary and historical
understandings of poverty.

Poverty

Because the phrase "women living in poverty" is used throughout
these pages, let's begin with a discussion of the word *poverty.* Then,
because our purpose is to equip the church in the United States to
reach out to women living in poverty, we'll discuss Christian traditions that, in the past, attended to the needs of the poor and the
unconverted. The brief overview of discipleship, hospitality, and
women in missions will help us understand the importance, decline,
and potential restoration of these traditions.

A word of warning: poverty is a dangerous subject. Just try bringing it up at a dinner party. Half the table will flee, the other half will
bristle, and, if there's any alcohol involved, you could end up losing a
friend or two. I've studied this phenomenon for quite a while now and
I trust my husband's raised eyebrows across the table that warn "not
a good time or crowd" to broach the topic. Discussion of poverty is
perilous, if not taboo, for a couple of reasons. One is that many Americans have made it into a political issue forming opinions based on

information from the media or party platforms, rather than personal experience or reliable research. Few people at your typical dinner parties really know the poor and reflect a quote by Mother Teresa, "There are many who think about the poor, few talk with them."[1]

Another reason discussions about poverty get heated is that many Americans have a limited worldview or understanding of poverty. A worldview is the framework of ideas and beliefs through which we interpret the world and interact with it.[2] "These beliefs cannot be proven in a logical sense," argue Christian philosophers Hill and Rauser, "because they are convictions accepted as true and are typically argued *from* rather than argued *for*."[3] Sigmund Freud described worldview as "an intellectual construction, which solves all the problems of our existence uniformly on the basis of one overriding hypothesis, which, accordingly, leaves no question unanswered and in which everything that interests us finds its fixed place."[4] Those dinner party conversations can become fractious if closely held beliefs and perspectives are challenged.

Paul insists in his letter to the Romans that we resist cultural mandates and traditions. "Do not conform any longer to the pattern of this world," he says, "but be transformed by the renewing of your mind."[5] In *The Message*, Eugene Peterson clarifies the meaning of this verse. "Don't become so well-adjusted to your culture," he writes, "that you fit into it without even thinking."[6] In an effort to renew our minds and worldview, let's look at some contemporary definitions of poverty and then observe how Scripture defines the poor.

Definitions of Poverty

All definitions of poverty involve a lack of resources. The most common understanding of the word *poverty* recognizes a lack of monetary resources. Webster's dictionary, for example, defines poverty as "the state or condition of having little or no money, goods, or means of support."[7] That definition has cultural and societal connotations depending on where you live. For example, I often tell the women at Christ Kitchen they would feel wealthy compared to poor women in the Sudan or Somalia. So the definition of poverty would be more accurate if it was understood to mean "a lack of those goods and services commonly taken for granted by members of the mainstream society."[8] According to the United States Census Bureau, those goods and services are defined as "food, shelter, and clothing needed to preserve health."[9] A family of four in the US is considered to be living in poverty if their total income is less than a threshold amount set by the Health and Human Services Poverty Guidelines. In 2012, that amount was $23,050.[10]

If the definition of poverty is merely the absence of "things," it follows that the solution would be to provide that which is lacking. "That approach," says Bryant Myers, "leads to a perception that the provider is the development "Santa Claus," and the poor are passive recipients who are somehow defective and incomplete."[11] Americans bristle at these concepts. Thoughtful people require additional information to adequately define poverty.

Several authors broaden the definition. Educator Ruby Payne describes poverty as "the extent to which an individual does without emotional, mental, spiritual, and physical resources, or support systems, relationships, role models, and coping strategies."[12] Lewis coined the term *generational poverty* in the 1960s to describe poverty that has persisted for two or more generations in a family.[13] That term is contrasted with *situational poverty,* a transitory experience of poverty caused often by uncontrollable financial circumstances such as divorce, death, job loss, or healthcare cost crisis.

Community organizer Robert Linthicum defines poverty from a systems perspective, stating that poverty is not so much an absence of goods as an absence of power—the capability of being able to change one's situation.[14] Similarly, John Friedman describes poverty within the context of powerlessness, stating that poverty is the lack of access to social power.[15] Robert Chambers defines poverty as entanglement, describing the poor as "living in a cluster of disadvantage."[16] World

Vision developer, Jayakumar Christian, describes the poor as "trapped inside a system of disempowerment made up of interacting systems."[17]

Political scientists and economists describe and study non-economic assessments of poverty under the term "social capital." In his book, *Bowling Alone: The Collapse and Revival of American Community*, Robert Putnam explains that people in poverty in the inner city are less likely to trust their neighbors, which minimizes reciprocation, neighborhood networking, and trust in community systems. Consequently, community improvement projects meant to address poverty are often unsuccessful. The lower the social capital in a community the less the poor participate in a variety of civic arenas: politics, churches, labor unions, parent-teacher organizations, fraternal organizations. Putnam claims that as civic participation in these arenas declines, so too, do the connections between people that foster cooperation and trust.[18] The poor become isolated, disengaged, and uncooperative, even in measures or events that might help them.

Tex Sample, a pastor and sociologist who studies the church and society, divides the poor in the United States into three distinct segments: respectables, hard-living, and desperate.[19] He refers to the great bulk of the lower middle class as "respectables"; blue-collar people devoted to family, faith, and flag who focus on making ends meet and struggle to be loyal to standards of respectability—their measure of success. Conservative socially and politically, the "respectables" are the most contented of the three groups.

When I talk with people about poverty, some tell me that they were raised poor. They say something like, "We didn't have any money when I was growing up, but my folks worked hard." or "We might not have had much, but we loved each other." Or "We were poor as church mice, but we got by." They often say this in an effort to suggest that they "made it" even though they weren't raised with money. What is usually left unsaid is their assumption that all poor people should do the same. These folks are by and large white and would be considered "respectables" in Sample's estimation. Their pull-yourself-up-by-your-bootstraps mentality made them what they are today and enabled them to be secure enough to take advantage of advancement opportunities in the United States.

People of color who I talk with never imply that others are inferior if they don't move out of poverty. They say something like, "I was lucky," or "The chips fell my way," or "My grandmother would not let any of us fall through the cracks." Their understanding of the hardships of racism and realities of poverty temper their judgment of others. These folks undergird their opinions with compassion.

The "hard-living poor," according to Sample are tough, politically alienated, rootless people who are deeply committed to an individualism that prizes independence and self-reliance. Often unemployed or working part-time at semi- or unskilled labor jobs, they are distrustful, angry, rebellious, and anxious. They are understandably dissatisfied with their occupations and financial conditions and tend to drink heavily, drug habitually, and experience high rates of chaotic relationships. They deeply mistrust systems, politicians, and corporations and reject the organized church.[20] The majority of women at Christ Kitchen, their parents and families, would identify with this group.

Sample's third category, the "desperate poor," is made up of the poorest of the poor, who are often old, ill, and poorly educated. They are either trapped in intergenerational poverty or have slipped there due to misfortune. A high percentage of them are ethnic minorities living in city ghettos or isolated rural communities. Despairing, withdrawn, and mistrustful, they struggle to survive and avoid utter loss.[21]

None of Christ Kitchen's current employees fits the description of desperate poor, although some, who can no longer work, have fallen into that category after facing major health crises.[22] Dorothy is a case in point. She was 66-years-old when she started coming to the Kitchen. She was respectful, kind, clean, and well kept. She never mentioned family and lived alone in a one-room apartment in a low-income housing unit downtown. Although reticent to share, she alluded to years of alcohol abuse and resulting devastation. She was a very proud woman and lived on the $32.50 per week she made at Christ Kitchen. Raised Catholic, she'd never opened a Bible before coming to Christ Kitchen. She was a voracious reader and borrowed many of my Christian books. Slowly, we watched her fall in love with Jesus as light dawned in her beautiful eyes.

One day Dorothy felt sick at work had to leave early. She didn't show up the next few weeks and didn't call. Even though she didn't have a phone, she had always called from her apartment manager's office to let us know if she'd be late or absent. We worried about her, so emissaries from the Kitchen knocked on her door and searched for her at the bus plaza, but she'd disappeared. Finally, we convinced her apartment manager to tell us what happened. He'd found her severely dehydrated and starving in her bed after several weeks of influenza. She revived at the hospital after a long stay and, due to her weakened state, was sent to a nursing home to live. She was the poorest of the poor, but you never would have known it. We had become the only family she had, but didn't know she needed help. She slipped from Sample's category of "respectable" to "desperate" in just a few weeks. Thankfully, our health care system filled in the gap.

American sociologist, Elijah Anderson, approaches poverty from a structural and cultural perspective. He uses the terms "decent," and "street" to describe the poor in terms of their degree of alienation from mainstream society. Decent families are those that can accept mainstream values, ally themselves with outside institutions, respect authority, and sacrifice for their children.[23] Street families, on the other hand, are disorganized, show a lack of consideration for others, and have a superficial sense of family and community. They show limited understanding of priorities, have a high degree of frustration, and demonstrate self-destructive behavior.[24]

James Gilligan, a psychiatrist and director of the Center for the Study of Violence at Harvard Medical School, describes poverty through the lens of violence. He believes that structural violence is at the core of American poverty. "Violence is deeply rooted in our society and has become woven into the fabric of the American lifestyle. You cannot work for one day among the violent people who fill American prisons and mental hospitals for the criminally insane without being forcibly and constantly reminded of the extreme poverty and discrimination that characterize their lives. Hearing about their lives. . . you are forced to recognize the truth in Gandhi's observation that the deadliest form of violence is poverty."[25]

Gilligan's insight into the relationship between poverty and violence helps us understand the differences often cited between the poor in the United States and the poor in other countries. People returning from mission trips or vacations abroad compare (often with some derision) the poor in the United States to those they encountered abroad, noting the extraordinary familial love, joy, and kindness found among the poor in other countries. This difference is also noted when comparing new immigrants to the United States with those born here. Recent immigrants, having survived tragedies like war and famine, often arrive with their historical patterns of life, family, community, identity, and work ethic intact and are able to take advantage of available resources.[26] The American poor born into despair and pathology, however, do not generally have such historic patterns or resources in place, in part because violence in the United States inherently breaks down family and community. This dynamic—the breakdown of family and community—may not be as significant a part of poverty in other countries. Clearly, it is necessary, as Gilligan points out, to understand underlying structures when defining and clarifying poverty.

Also critical to developing a working definition of poverty is understanding the term *relative deprivation*; the gap or disparity between the wealth and income of those at the top and those at the bottom of the social hierarchy. Several authors contend that this gap is a much more powerful contributor to feelings of inferiority and shame than is absolute poverty. "It is not poverty itself that humiliates people," states Gilligan. "It is not the fact that one lives in a hovel, but rather, that one lives in a hovel next to a palace, that causes shame."[27] Karl Marx capitalized on this fact, noting that shame is the emotion of revolution.[28] Poet and author Maya Angelou captures this disparity beautifully when she writes:

> It is hateful to be young, bright, ambitious and poor. The added insult is to be aware of one's poverty. Before television brought pictures of luxurious living rooms and glistening kitchens into the view of the impoverished, they could pretend, tell themselves that only the few, the lucky, maybe just their employers, lived lives of refined comfort. But today, when every soap opera is rife with characters whose great wealth is only equaled by their moral neediness, paupers watching in shacks on every street are forced to admit that they are indeed poverty-stricken. With that knowledge and acknowledgement, there comes inevitably a lingering despair and a puzzling wretchedness. Why them and not me? Those questions are followed by a sense of worthlessness—a remorseful regret at being alive. Then comes full-blown anger, resentment, a rankling bitterness that, if directed outward, can foment riots, revolution and social chaos. Most often, however, the convulsions of anger are directed inward. Thus the poor, the needy, the misfits of society implode. After the debris settles, they appear to the onlookers as dry husks of hopelessness.[29]

This brief review of poverty from the perspective of philosophers, educators, sociologists, economists, political scientists, psychiatrists, and community developers is helpful in broadening our worldview. Let's turn now to Scripture and observe how poverty is defined there.

Biblical Understanding of Poverty

Interestingly, Scripture's definition of poverty encompasses many of the above explanations. A poor person in Scripture is described as a laborer, "one who works for daily bread."[30] The word *poverty* in Hebrew means *destitution*. In the New Testament, the primary word for the poor is *ptōchos* from which we get the verb *to beg.* It means "one who crouches, cowers, or hides in fear."[31] It is the Greek equivalent of *ani,* which denotes one who is wrongfully impoverished or dispossessed and *dal,* which connotes a thin, weakly person such as an impoverished, deprived peasant.[32]

Poverty, or the state of being poor, is mentioned in three ways in Scripture. In a limited sense, poverty is encountered as the consequence of moral lassitude, especially laziness.[33] Verses like, "He who ignores discipline comes to poverty and shame,"[34] and "Do not love sleep or you will grow poor,"[35] warn against indolence and idleness. In a few places, Scripture speaks of voluntary poverty for the sake of the kingdom. In the primary sense, however, when the poor are encountered in the Bible, their situation is understood, not as a consequence of personal failings, but as a result of social factors, particularly injustice.[36]

The most common biblical connotation of the poor relates to those who are economically impoverished due to calamity or exploitation.[37] "A poor man's field may produce abundant food but injustice sweeps it away."[38] "Leviticus defines the poor as those who are lowly because their 'power wavers' (25:35) or is insufficient (14:21). They do not have the capacity to provide for themselves the essentials of life. Their deficiency in life-supporting power is understood to exist in relation to the rest of the community, that is, their crisis is based in the network of power relationships that form society."[39]

It should be noted that God is not partial. He has the same loving concern for each person he has created. In contrast, however, to the way the comfortable and powerful in every age and society normally act toward the poor, God seems to have an overwhelming bias in favor of the poor. Ron Sider says, "He is biased only in contrast with our sinful unconcern. It is only when we take our sinful preoccupation with the successful and wealthy as natural and normative that God's equal concern for all looks like a bias for the poor."[40]

Thus, the biblical understanding of poverty takes into consideration contemporary definitions. It addresses the poor as needy, without power, and abused by those with greater power. It includes a lack of resources to meet basic needs, a lack of power to alter one's situation, and, to a limited degree, a lack of diligence.

Considering what we learned, let's get back to that dinner party scenario. It's clear why conversations about poverty get so fractious. If one's worldview of poverty is defined by the narrow biblical explanation of the word as the "consequence of moral lassitude, especially laziness," you might expect poor people to be depraved, idle, or lazy and consider their economic or social condition a result of personal failings. That worldview interprets poverty as an individual problem, absolves others of responsibility for its cause or solution, and suggests no need for resolution or involvement. Disdain becomes the refuge of the unaware. The question remains, how do we transform our current view of poverty to conform to the biblical perspective of injustice without falling into the trap of personal judgments or political ideologies? Let me tell you the story of Ida as a means of answering this complex question.

I heard a knock at my door early one morning while I was reading my morning devotional. It was only five a.m., so I was pretty sure I'd heard the wind rattling or a sleepy child bumping around in bed upstairs. But the hard, persistent knocking continued at my back door that faces the Spokane River. Rarely, my husband will come to that door if he's locked out, but he was very soundly asleep in the other room. Alarmed, I opened the door and found a little girl standing there, crying, asking to use my phone. Her face was bruised and swollen and she was soaking wet. "They're trying to kill me," she said, looking over her shoulder at the river.

"Who's trying to kill you?" I gasped, sharing her concern. Behind her, in the predawn light, the river rolled on—no killers in sight.

"Gang bangers," she said, shivering from cold and fear. "They punched me all over and then tried to drown me. I have to call the police."

Stunned, I went to get my phone and handed it to her. She clearly knew what to do and I was just catching on. I grabbed a blanket from the bedroom, waking my husband. "There's a little girl on our porch," I told him incredulously.

She was speaking to someone on the phone when I returned and I covered her shaking, little grass-stained body with the blanket. Her matted, wet hair dripped onto my porch. I tucked the blanket around her as she told the 911 operator that her name was Ida, "Ida Marie Bella . . . " something. I missed the last name because I gasped when she said her age. This little wet urchin on my porch was only thirteen-years-old.

I noticed her eyes, tired and bloodshot, as she mechanically told the operator about a bonfire gone bad, drunken revelers, the assault with fists and boots, the attempt to silence her by drowning, and her escape down the river: Down the river and to my back door! "Am I bleeding?" she asked me at one point as she dutifully responded to one of the operator's questions. I examined what I could see around her t-shirt and shorts, found massive bruising, welts and scrapes, but no blood. The bruises seemed to grow larger and bluer in the emerging light. I felt sick to my stomach. She asked for my address and said the EMTs were coming as she hung up the phone.

My husband gave her a pair of his flannel pajamas and I led her to the bathroom to get out of her filthy wet clothes. I made peppermint tea for her and grabbed a banana and crackers by the time she padded out of the bathroom in clothes that were way too big for her. She was such a little thing swallowed up in those big clothes. She began to cry when she saw the food and said, "I haven't eaten in five days."

"Were you at People's Park?" I asked, figuring she must have been a few miles up river at the hellhole notorious for drug crimes and gang activity. It's the only place near the river where a bonfire could occur and a gang of thugs could attack a little thirteen year-old without notice. I'd heard they'd increased patrols there during the day, but obviously not at night. She nodded her head.

"You stay away from there!" I admonished her in my firmest mother-voice. "Don't ever go there again," I said, as if that could cure all her problems, like the "just say no to drugs" campaign really worked. "Honey, somebody's worried about you," I meekly added, finishing my mother-rant.

"Somebody's worried about me?" she asked, genuinely surprised, like I knew something she didn't.

"Your mother . . . or someone . . . somewhere, has to be worried if you've been gone for five days," I said, unconvincingly like I had any idea.

"Oh," she said, finally grasping my naiveté. She huffed slightly and added sarcastically, "Yeah right, my mother's worried about me." Her words pierced my heart like daggers. This little girl had no one who worried about her, no one who even cared that she'd almost been killed. Then, in an almost professorial tone, like she was speaking to her slowest student, she added, "There are some problems at home."

"Come sit down," I said, leading her into my study next to windows that faced the street so we could see the EMTs when they got there. "I was sitting right here reading my Bible when you knocked on my door."

"I'm sorry I woke you," she said gobbling the banana. This intelligent little girl, whose life was just threatened, was apologizing to me.

"I'm not. I'm glad you came to my door. When you're better, I want you to come back and see me. I'll wash your clothes for you in the mean time." Everything inside me wanted to save this little waif.

A hook-and-ladder truck, two ambulances, and various emergency vehicles arrived within minutes, spilling EMTs with medical bags and firefighters in gigantic boots onto my lawn. I moved out of the way as eight huge men congregated in my small study around the big, brown chair that held Ida. She was tiny in the sea of big men, but she held her own with them, answering questions confidently, calmly, as if she was a pro at this kind of thing. Obviously, she didn't have the luxury of hysterical carrying on that would elicit sympathy or response. Unattended children never do. Their cries go unheard so often, they stop crying. A mother somewhere should be proud of her.

Never had there been so much activity in my study. One man said something about foster care for runaways. Several walked in and out of my house speaking quietly into walkie-talkies. Another said she lived with one of the attackers. My husband offered them chairs. He and I looked at each other with shared concern as we viewed the bizarre scene. Ida looked dazed but attended to each question carefully. At times she would sigh and look away as they examined her, exhaustion settling in her bones.

I knew that look. It reminded me of being in the ER after I was raped. People were rushing around taking care of me, but I sat very still, as if slow motion would calm the storm raging inside. I still remember every detail of what happened in that hospital room even though I probably looked just as inattentive as Ida. The most poignant memory was of a nurse who gave me an injection of antibiotics. Before she left the room, she hugged me and whispered in my ear, "You're going to be OK." That tiny gesture, those few words sustained me, offering something I didn't quite understand at the time. It sparked the frayed feeling that became the only thing I held on to for weeks: hope.

I maneuvered my way through the thick crowd of firefighters to sit down on the stool beside Ida. I stroked her hair, praying it would inspire the same hope in her. "You're going to be OK," I smiled with as much reassurance as I could force. It was the kind of look I'd learned to put on my face when my children were sick or hurt; I was scared, but didn't want to show it.

I was scared for Ida. Foster care? Seriously? This little thing just spent five days in a park with her family of gang bangers and they think foster care would be able to hold her? She needs a real family who loves her, worries about her, holds her close, and teaches her to pray to survive this big, bad world. Pressing my business card into her hand I told her to find her way to Christ Kitchen and we would figure out how to keep her safe.

They all left as suddenly as they came. Ida padded down the front walk draped in my husband's clothes, dutifully following the EMTs to the ambulance. She looked back at us without expression. We smiled and waved, like when the school bus took our children off to school or camp. Deep sorrow hid behind our smiles. Nothing good was going to happen at her destination. Two police cars showed up just as she was leaving. They asked a few questions hiding little disdain, as if we'd all interrupted their breakfast. I doubted any gang-bangers around a cold fire pit would be arrested this morning. Just another Native American assault case, their bored expressions implied. Just another dumb runaway.

I burst into tears when they all were gone. "She doesn't have a chance!" I mourned to my husband whose eyes were also filled with tears of despair. "What's going to happen to her?"

"God brought her to our door for a purpose," he said. In the desolate silence of the early morning dawn, we couldn't imagine what that might be. We prayed for Ida, prayed she would follow that spark of hope, that she would make her way to Christ Kitchen or that the Lord would bring saints into her life. Would the Christ on my card sustain her? We have a big God, I kept reminding myself. He loves her more than anyone possibly can.

How does Ida's story expand our understanding of poverty? Well, what do you think is going to happen to her? What do you see for her future? Without intervention, can you see her getting excited about math class, preparing for debate club, studying for the SATs? Can you see her explaining all of this to the school counselor? Let's see. Where to begin in today's session? Shall we discuss drunk mothers, missing fathers, or how about the time I was nearly drowned by gang bangers? How about those bootstraps? Can you see her just pulling herself up by them? Do you see a prosperous future for her? No, I don't either. Unfortunately, I can see her staring off into space during social studies, apathetic about her English grade, smoking in the alley during study hall. I can see her slow acceptance of the policeman's contempt; her resigned repetition of whatever started her family's problems. It breaks my heart to think that someday she might be so overwhelmed or numb that she might not know where her own daughter is.

Let's apply the biblical perspective of poverty to Ida. Clearly, her poverty is a result of social factors. She lacks the life-supporting relationships which make loved and cared for children thrive. Obviously, her economic and social condition is not due to personal failings. Her lethargy is not due to laziness. Her crisis is unjust and based in the complex system of neglectful relationships, overwhelmed social service systems, indifferent law enforcement, and an absent church. Without intervention, the sins of the parents will very likely revisit this child.[41]

What should happen to Ida? Here's what God says. "Do not be hard-hearted or tightfisted toward your poor brother or sister. Rather, be open-handed and freely lend her whatever she needs. Give generously to her and do so without a grudging heart. There should be no poor among you in the land the Lord your God is giving you."[42] Ida does not need money. If you read these Scriptures, with eyes conformed to this world, you might fear God is telling you to give all your money to Ida. What would little thirteen-year-old Ida need with money? For that matter, what good would money do for her mother, father, or attackers? They don't need money; they need you. "Give till the need is gone," instructs the writer of Deuteronomy. "Defend the cause of the weak and fatherless; maintain the rights of the poor and oppressed."[43] Giving yourself, your love, your faith to Ida is what will rectify the power imbalance that envelops her. Getting involved in her life now will prevent disastrous consequences later on that, wrongly, will be labeled as laziness. When we are transformed by the renewing of our minds, as it says in Romans, grace will revolutionize our relationship to possessions, power, injustice, and Ida—maybe even to those gang-bangers. For goodness sake, who is praying for them? And there's a bonus! "He will richly bless you if only you fully obey the Lord your God and are careful to follow all these commands."[44] It's a win, win, win, win. *You* are what should happen to Ida.

Christian History and Traditions

Having established the contemporary understanding of poverty through expert's opinions and practical example, let's turn our attention to institutions in our Christian heritage and past traditions in Christianity that attended to the poor. By reviewing discipleship, hospitality, and women in missions, we'll discover a rich history of mentors who cared for people like Ida, people who were needy, dispossessed, unconverted—those whom Jesus referred to as "the least [significant] of these brothers and sisters of mine."[45] We'll expand our current worldview by looking at the past.

Discipleship

I love Eugene Peterson's description of a disciple as someone who spends [her] life apprenticed to our master, Jesus Christ, in a growing-learning relationship.[46] He presents discipleship as a relationship of personalized education in faith and commitment among Christ-followers. This is the model advanced by Christ and the early church, but is one that, according to authors Dennis McCallum and Jessica Lowery, has been lacking in practice today in the church in the United States.[47] A brief look at the history of discipleship explains why.

The New Testament notion of discipleship involved a complete shaping of followers after their teacher. In the rabbinic tradition of Jesus' day, transmission of biblical knowledge took place within close, trusting relationships.[48] Expanding on this model, Jesus lived among his disciples, communicating to them both biblical knowledge and his character, insights, values, and wisdom.[49] Fully modeling his Father, Jesus served his disciples, loved them, and showed them the full extent of God's love.

In the New Testament church, leaders were developed by a similar process of personal discipleship.[50] Paul was committed to helping each Christian reach a significant level of maturity through personal mentoring, admonition, and teaching.[51] A good example for our purposes is Paul's encouragement to Titus to teach older women to be reverent and teach what is good, so that they can train younger women.[52] The process of discipleship facilitated growth of the church during the first centuries through house churches, church planting, and leadership development.

Although evident throughout the ages in stories of the saints, the concept of personal discipleship as a church discipline gradually declined during subsequent centuries. A church hierarchy developed that became burdened by clergy-laity distinctions and replaced the early church's more intimate, personal relationships.[53]

Little is written about discipleship until it reappeared in the nineteenth and twentieth centuries, more widely among mission's circles than in the Western church, with the help of para-church organizations, such as the Navigators and Campus Crusade for Christ.[54] The idea became somewhat discredited in the United States during the late seventies and eighties by the so-called "shepherding or discipleship movement" that encouraged obedience to a human authority. Unfortunately, the word *discipleship* became tainted or at least had grown out of use. Some church leaders today still harbor lingering suspicion when the word is used.[55]

Many Americans distrust the word "discipleship" because the word itself is mistrusted or out of use. Additionally, if biblical knowledge is being transmitted solely in mega churches or from pulpits and not in close personal relationships, we won't learn how to disciple others outside our immediate families. If women are not training up younger women, if Christians are not being shaped after their teacher (learning to duplicate Christ's model of personal discipleship with each other through mentoring, admonishing, and training), if discipleship is not occurring among friends and people with whom one is comfortable, it surely won't occur among the poor or those with whom one feels uncomfortable.

Hospitality

For most of us, the word *hospitality* conjures what Henry Nouwen observes as "tea parties, bland conversation and a general atmosphere of coziness."[56] But, according to Christine Pohl, the practice of hospitality is the Christian tradition in which the most vulnerable people in a society are cared for. For most Church history, hospitality was understood to encompass the physical, social, and spiritual dimensions of human existence and relationships. Hospitality was the key means by which the church responded to the physical needs of strangers for food, shelter, and protection. Hospitality recognized the worth and common humanity of every person.[57]

In almost every case, it involved shared meals. Table fellowship was an important way of recognizing a person's equal value and dignity. The distinctive Christian contribution to hospitality was the emphasis on including the poorest and neediest into one's home, life, and fellowship: including the ones who could never return the favor.[58] The gospel spread throughout the world as national and ethnic distinctions in the church were transcended because of the commitment of the early church to hospitality that was expressed in their care for strangers, pilgrims, and the sick. Hospitality provides a theological framework connecting theology with daily life and concerns.[59]

But a question remains: If hospitality was such an important part of the Christian faith and life, how did it virtually disappear and get supplanted by images of the Holiday Inn? Many of the answers will sound familiar to our modern ears. Concerns about needy strangers gave rise to hospitals, hospices, and hostels, more anonymous, distanced ways of responding to strangers. Generous, gracious welcome became reserved for people of equal or higher rank. Highly insulated, individualized, smaller households replaced those with extended family. State and social welfare institutions supplanted the church's care for the poor.[60]

With the decline in hospitality, Pohl says we've lost an understanding of how generations of Christians struggled with issues of recognition and dignity, transcended social differences, built community, distributed limited resources, and negotiated tensions with strangers. Without these stories and understandings, the American church struggles to find ways to respond to people in need, questions diversity, and searches for personal bonds and meaning. Pohl writes, "Among Christians in the United States today, discussions about poverty, welfare, inclusion, diversity, scarcity and distribution are conducted without the benefit of a coherent theological framework."[61] The result, she believes, is that the stands we take on complex social and public policy issues are little affected by our deepest Christian values and commitments.[62]

Although the tradition of hospitality is now much more obscure, Scripture concerning the subject is not. God's guest list includes the undeserving, the poor, and the broken. God provides manna in the wilderness to ungrateful people, shelter in a hot, dry land to the discouraged, and streams of living water to the disgruntled. Israel was both dependent on God for provision and answerable to God for its treatment of aliens. Jesus welcomed children, prostitutes, tax collectors, and sinners into his presence, while he himself experienced the vulnerability of being a homeless refugee and prisoner. Paul challenged believers to "pursue" hospitality. Hospitality was a qualification for leadership in the early church and offered the possibility of entertaining angels. Pohl suggests that Christians are to regard hospitality to strangers as a fundamental expression of the gospel.[63]

No wonder there's a disconnect today between the church and women living in poverty. We've lost the theological framework of caring for the most vulnerable. Our discomfort with disability, disease, and difference; our intolerance of weakness, our fear of helplessness, our contempt for powerlessness, our practiced disregard for strangers, our disdain for the lowly all testify to this loss and to our shame. Without traditions that practice gracious welcome, without rituals that teach nurture, without routines of generosity, expectations of liberality and examples to follow, we fail.

There were, however, Christ-followers throughout the centuries who loved the Lord and his poor. For our purposes, I've limited the review of missions specifically to women noted on the pages of Christian history with a concern for proclamation of the gospel to the poor. Although most were not taught Christian traditions in the church, you'll see that they discipled each other and practiced hospitality out of their great love for God. We turn now to women in missions who cared for the most vulnerable to find mentor saints from the past.

Women in Missions

I long to have known Dorcas. We meet Dorcas in Acts 9:36 where she is described as "always doing good and helping the poor." Also known as Tabitha, she is the only woman in Scripture to be called a disciple; the word used for her is *mathetria*, the only feminine form of *disciple* found in the New Testament.[64] Dorcas cared for widows in the town of Joppa, northwest of Jerusalem. Likely a widow herself, she used her own resources to help widows in the most practical ways— she sewed clothing for them.[65] She made tunics and coats, that served not only for warmth but also as mats for the homeless poor to sleep on at night. Having a tunic was a means of survival to many widows in that day and was commanded in Hebrew law to be protected.[66]

Dorcas' home was a center for mercy and hope, a forerunner of the early order of widows who dedicated themselves to the service of the church.[67] When she died, Peter raised her from the dead, making her the only person recorded to have been brought back to life by a disciple of Jesus.[68]

Dorcas is the first woman I found in Scripture who dedicated her life to taking care of the poor. Reading about her in the ninth chapter of Acts began my quest for foremothers, women throughout history who read the Word or heard the Holy Spirit's call, who risked their lives and reputations, and even gave up family ties, inheritances, or marriage to serve the Lord, his poor, and each other. When I found Dorcas, I was in great need of role models at the time to inspire my work at Christ Kitchen. I was growing weary, stunned actually, by the mother-stories told by our women. Many of them didn't really know their mothers; some wish they hadn't. Many say it was their own mother who introduced them to drugs or alcohol. "She felt guilty, Jan," Sherrie offered in explanation of this deadly parenting technique. "She was smoking crack in front of me anyway. Why not just include me in the drill so she didn't have to feel ashamed?"

Maternal neglect or at least disinterest seems to have been a common occurrence for many of our women. Almost in passing, I hear one say, "I guess I just raised myself. My mom wasn't around." or "I remember my mom sleeping all the time, like she was sick or something, but I don't think she was." Isabel, one of our oldest employees, told me she was in seventeen foster homes before the age of eighteen. Her mother would intermittently find her and take her back to some semblance of a home, but it would always fall apart when a new boyfriend moved in. "I felt like a little lost bird," Isabel sighed, "kicked out of the nest and never knowing where I'd fall. To this day, I am always getting lost. I have the hardest time with maps. I just never know where I am." It is staggering to learn how much of their trauma started at home.

So you see, I was in big need of role models—examples of women who understood this suffering, who'd tread these tortuous paths before me, who could show the way, light the path, ease the load. But I didn't know any. There were wonderful older women at my church on the mission committee who held a sale every year supporting third-world crafts. And there were the namesake Dorcas Circle ladies: blue-haired, buxom, Methodist ladies who gathered at my grandmother's house when I was a child, singing together in high-pitched, squeaky tones with sewing projects in their laps. I remember my sisters and I, with hair neatly combed and petticoats adjusted, were sent out from my Nana's kitchen like little soldiers carrying silver trays of open-faced sandwiches to offer sustenance to these church ladies on the front lines stitching baby blankets for poor orphans in India. As fond as I am of memories of this sweet little sewing group and missions committee-women, they didn't prepare me for the misery I encountered.

But Dorcas changed that. This radical servant who dedicated her life to the poor proved there were women on the pages of history who put their lives on the line to serve Christ in service to the poor. Dorcas became a patron saint for the work I'd begun at Christ Kitchen. She encouraged me to find other mentors in Christian history to ground my work in a legacy of missionary women. Although few and far between, I found enough to encourage me to walk the path well tread by the quiet, usually unobtrusive feet of our foremothers.

A whirlwind tour of missional women serving the poor spans the life of Christianity. From widows like Dorcas in the New Testament to Mother Teresa in recent years, I found women throughout the centuries who had extraordinary devotion to God and his poor. They were not typical believers in any century. Many, particularly those in earlier epochs, were from wealthy, aristocratic families, who voluntarily gave away their riches choosing instead lives of poverty. The women I found were deeply spiritual, bold, confident, devoted, and idealistic. As a group, they renounced traditional roles for women in their day and thus challenged the traditions of their church and culture. To ascribe feminist motivations to their actions, says historian Susan Smith, would be wrong.[69] They sincerely sought to follow Jesus, plainly, wholly, radically. This is why they are my heroines, why I introduce them to you.

First Through Third Centuries

In the first and second centuries, we are not told the names of the women who took the needy into their homes, but learn that evangelism took place in kitchens, shops, and markets among the "rabble" for whom widows were caring.[70] These women and others typified the early Christian community with their radical generosity, welcoming outsiders regardless of background, thus overcoming the obvious divisions of gender, ethnicity, and class that characterized the Roman world. As the apologist Tatian noted, the early church seemed to include everyone, making no "distinctions in rank and outward appearance, or wealth and education, or age and sex."[71]

Interestingly, in the years after the death of Christ, we learn more about these women through those opposed to Christianity. Their hostility to this new religion was deeply rooted in class prejudice. Celsus, during the reign of Marcus Aurelius (161-180) described Christianity as a "lowbrow" religion that attracted the underclass.[72] He wrote, "By the fact that they themselves admit that [the underclass] are worthy of their God, they show that they are able to convince only the foolish, dishonorable and stupid, and only slaves, women and little children." He noted with some derision that Christians won converts not through public debate among elites but through quiet witness in their homes and places of work, which he found disconcerting, though there was little he could do about it.[73] He writes, "In some private homes we find people who work with wool and rags, and cobblers, that is, the least cultured and most ignorant kind. If you really wish to know the truth . . . go with the women and the children to the women's quarters, or go to the cobbler's shops, or to the tannery, and there you will learn the perfect life. It is thus that these Christians find those who will believe them."[74]

It is obvious that the cultured and sophisticated in Roman society could not conceive of the possibility that Christians knew a truth hidden to them, that women caring for the sick and poor held secret knowledge. They argued that worship of this Christian God destroyed the very fiber of society because Christ's followers abstained from most social activities and fell outside traditional structures that embraced traditional patriarchal households and conventional gender roles.[75]

I am in awe of these brave, faithful women, these first and second century "lowbrow" mentors, whose names we'll never know. Their silent witness to keep the gospel alive in its purest and most radical form humbles me. I wonder if they were extraordinarily courageous to buck the status quo or if their lives and ministries just flowed faithfully, invisibly far below the clamor of society. They clearly embody the verse in Romans that warns, "Do not conform any longer to the pattern of this world,"[76] but I wish I knew if they were terrified while they did it; when they stood in opposition to the very fibers that seem to hold a culture together.

Their courage reminds me of Kari, our office manager, on the day a man came to Christ Kitchen to change our outdoor sign. The man was angry, argumentative and so mean to several of the women attempting to help him that I decided to ask him to leave. "Oh my gosh! that man needs prayer," Kari said intently, interrupting my plans to remedy the situation. With that, I watched her march out the door headed straight for the man who'd just spurned our women like Goliath defied the ranks of Israel. To my great shame, my immediate thought was, "You can't go pray with that man! He's mean!"

Like the disgrace David's brothers must have felt while their little brother pelted Goliath with rocks, I watched her put her hand on his shoulder and say, "It must be a terrible day. Can I pray for you?" She grabbed his big, puffy, calloused hand and held her other one out to me, like I had any right to join this sweet miracle taking place before my eyes. I don't remember what she prayed but his tears are seared in my mind. Turns out, that morning he'd found his mother laying on the floor of her apartment where she'd been immobilized by a stroke for two days. The grumpy sign man was in dire need of prayer and care and I was going to fire him. I don't think Kari had any sense she was participating in the centuries old traditions of her unworldly foremothers by breaching some absurd protocol that insists you pray only under certain conditions, only with sympathetic fellow believers or likely converts, and only when absolutely necessary like during church, before meals, or last rites. She stood faithfully by a man in a world of hurt. I stood condemned in a world of nonsense.

It's not that I don't understand my reluctance to rush right out and pray with a total stranger. In the world of middle class professionals and wealthy patrons, I encounter suspicious eyes when I tell them I run a ministry. Their threatened expressions warn against religious tirades or political rants, as they protect their throats from inevitable stuffing. Decorum, I've found, is the province of the wealthy and restraint the domain of the wise. But I am brought up short when I read that God is delighted by the foolishness of preaching to save those who believe, that he chose the foolish, weak and lowly things of the world to shame the wise and strong.[77]

So it is not that I don't understand my hesitation; I am ashamed of it. I want to be sensitive and appropriate, not brash and pushy, but mostly I want to be fearless and winsome in my love for my Lord. Interestingly, those with suspicious eyes, those well-off, very educated, independent, even hostile sorts seem to tolerate stories of homeless women changing their lives. They actually love hearing tales of transformation and hard-fought stability.

A Buddhist politician from our district, for example, came into the Kitchen one day simply on a routine visit to a constituent. His bored, dull eyes sized us up like he might any other church-y group. But when he heard about the radical renovations happening within our employees, a light went on. "It's a community!" he said with enthusiasm, "You're helping women get back on their feet. Government can never do what you all are doing here!" He got it. Unlike Celsus, his Roman counterpart, he appreciated the value in quiet witness at work as opposed to grander public forum. I pray that someday he'll get much more.

Fourth Century

The importance of widows' ministries and house churches diminished upon the arrival of Christianity as the official, imperial religion under emperor Constantine in the fourth century.[78] Ironically, as the church grew legitimate in the eyes of the state, its enemy became privilege not persecution. A worldly church caused many Christ-followers to flee into monastic-type communities in the desert to protest this compromise. According to Gerald Sittser, women were among the "desert saints" of the era, who fled to the desert where they came under the influence of a mentor or Amma. These Ammas introduced their apprentices to the rigors of discipleship and instructed them in Christian doctrine.[79]

Many of those who fled to the desert, devoting their lives to prayer, study, and good works, were wealthy women from aristocratic families who voluntarily gave away their riches to the poor, choosing instead lives of poverty. Women like Syncletica, Paula, Fabiola, and Olympias combined servanthood with influence. They cared for the dying, founded hospitals for the sick and hostels for the stranger, supported churches, monasteries, convents, beggars, prisoners, and exiles. They lived in poverty, humility, simple dress, and intensity of faith,[80] but also provided close connections with church leaders and their authority and power.[81] They created an alternative to the ordinary household[82] and embraced new ways of Christian discipleship. Their servanthood marked an era in women's story of mission in the Western church.

I rejoiced when I found these women. They didn't just donate money, they distributed all their substantial wealth in service to their Lord. They didn't just tithe money, they lived in abject poverty along side the poor. It is said that Jerome, a fourth century historian and writer, was deeply affected by the contrast between Fabiola's former status as a Roman matron and her present ascetic and charitable life. Although he and other leaders of the time denied the significance of social status, its voluntary rejection was very compelling.[83] Timothy Keller states, "Christians' unreasonable generosity was the engine of success that converted pagan society. It gave them power to change the world."[84]

Not growing up in a Christ-based family, I didn't learn how to tithe, let alone distribute money to the needy. "We work hard for our money," said my father during long debates about politics, privilege, and power. We didn't seem to like people who asked for money; even missionaries were seen as beggars. "Never a borrower or lender be," left absolutely no endorsement for *giving* away money. Shakespeare, the author of the quote, had more influence than Scripture at this point in my family's development. This "proper stinginess" never sat right with me. I quoted scripture to my mother when I was twelve about how God clothes the lilies so we, therefore, shouldn't worry about what to wear. Likely that was more my closing argument in favor of wearing blue jeans and tennis shoes to a party than support of the poor, but I was becoming attuned to class differences at a young age.

I wish I could have known about the Ammas back then—about Paula caring for the dying and bedridden and Olympias offering her great wealth to support the poor of Constantinople. It might have saved years of adolescent acting out. It does, however, make me pause to wonder how my life might have been different had I mentors like Syncletica, who gave large sums of money to the poor in hopes of "putting an end to the deceit of a frivolous life."[85] I can imagine how the teenager in me would have tortured my poor mother with examples of these mentors.

What I know to be true is that "In all things God works for the good of those who love him."[86] I am so thankful that grace is revolutionizing my attitude toward money. I figure, if the Lord's radical love could bring me back from the brink of death like no amount of money or prestige ever could have, he can have my stuff. I know this still isn't a popular notion, but these fourth century women are my heroes.

Middle Ages and Reformation

In the Middle Ages and Reformation years, women emerge as lights in the church as the church came to grips with the reality of urbanization and revolution. Great abbesses (mother superior types) with wonderful names like Hilda, Leoba, and Walburga and mendicants (those who lived by begging) responded to these new challenges by serving the poor, sick, and outcasts who fled to newly established cities. The Poor Clares and Beguines, for example, established communities of mission-focused life that later became orders of Catholic nuns. European women, known as the Ursulines and Visitandines, in the 1600's, exercised public roles in education, nursing, and care of the poor. Vincent de Paul, who founded The Daughters of Charity in 1633 with Louise de Marillac in the slums of Paris is said to have commissioned Louise with the following: "Your convent will be the house of the sick; your cell, a hired room; your chapel, the parish church; your cloister, the streets of the city and the wards of the hospital; your enclosure, obedience; your grating, the fear of God; your veil, holy modesty."[87]

The religious women of this era came together for the first time in organized communities. They forged new missionary identities for themselves in ways that a more stable and settled era would never have tolerated. In community, they struggled against efforts by the church to limit their activities and did works of mercy during great cultural and political shifts.[88]

Similarly, community of this sort is a critical element in restoration at Christ Kitchen. Working within a supportive atmosphere of women struggling together to improve their lives, provides a first step, a way out of loneliness and despair. Fractured relationships are the most common characteristic among our women. Healing begins as women talk and work together, telling their stories, revealing their hurts, confessing their sins, holding each other accountable. When supported, women can learn how to manage the truths of their lives. They learn how to laugh over imperfections, tease each other through transitions, weep with each other over defeats, sigh over misfortune, rejoice and praise at the slightest victory.

Charles Duhigg, who studied the power of habits, believes that we can change habits only if we learn how to believe in ourselves from others. Community, in other words, is a key to changing and maintaining new habits. He sites Alcoholics Anonymous as an example of the power of community. People in Alcoholics Anonymous understand that new habits only last until the next crisis. By offering new habits reinforced within a group setting, members begin to really believe change is possible by hearing the testimony of others and being in relationships that demand accountable.[89] Duhigg's research supports our experience at Christ Kitchen and helps us understand the necessity of missionary women fashioning new identities within groups.

Seventeenth Through Nineteenth Centuries

The seventeenth and eighteenth centuries saw significant changes in religious life. Stories of women creating active roles in ministry in the New World abound. Women such as Anne Hutchinson, Mary

Dyer, Susanna Wesley and Sarah Crosby, to name just a few, made significant inroads into women's ministry, but had to also endure the scorn of respectable society and defy male leadership in the institutionalized churches.[90]

It was during the last part of the eighteenth century and the early decades of the nineteenth century, when the Second Great Awakening was making a permanent impact on society, that women's missionary work began to flourish.[91] Women of any economic background today might best relate to the women in this era who desired to carry their religious influence beyond the realm of family to make a difference in society.[92]

Because the scale of poverty was increasing dramatically in both Europe and the United States due to industrialization, urbanization and immigration, and because governments of the time did not see care of the poor through social welfare structures as part of their responsibility,[93] benevolent societies of laywomen developed to improve conditions in domestic slums and foreign fields. One author, describing the arrival of these organizations as a societal craze this way:

> There were societies for putting down gin-mills, closing cook-shops on Sundays, and educating infants and orphans. There were societies for the deaf and dumb, the insane, the blind, the ruptured, the club-footed, the penitent syphilitic, illegitimate children, chimneysweepers, and juvenile prostitutes. There were societies for distressed respectable widows, poor females in maritime districts, for distressed foreigners, small debtors, and sick people in hospitals, out of hospitals, and simple ordinary sick strangers.[94]

Missionary societies drew millions of women into their sphere and offered women meaningful ministries in preaching, translating, evangelizing, planting churches, training nationals, establishing schools, and serving the poor.[95] They sponsored thousands of women to go to the ends of the earth as teachers, doctors, evangelists, and relief workers. Throughout the third world, women had significant influence improving social and legal injustices. They were influential in discussions on missionary boards, denominationalism, single women on the field, specialization, salaries vs. faith-mission strategies, and missiology. Examples of these mentor saints include: Mary Slessor in Africa, Gladys Alyward in China and Lottie Moon and Amy Carmichael in India.

Women's missionary societies appeared in the US in unprecedented numbers on such a broad scale as had never before existed.[96] Women administered community centers in inner cities established by Protestant churches struggling to adjust their ministries to the new industrialism and spread of urban poverty.[97] They became very active in ministries to the sick, poor, orphans, prostitutes and prisoners.[98]

Although most remain nameless and unknown to history, we know the names of some. Sarah and Angelina Grimke struggled against slavery. Dorothea Dix worked for better treatment of the mentally ill, and Jane Adams did social work in inner cities.[99] One of the most renowned Catholic women of the century was Elizabeth Seton, who founded the American Sisters of Charity, an order that established orphanages, schools, and hospitals.[100] Catherine Booth, well known for co-founding of the Salvation Army in England with her husband, chose seven women to inaugurate their work in America. Their success prompted William Booth to say, "My best men are women."[101]

Twentieth Century

No list of influential missionaries of the twentieth century would be complete without mentioning Dorothy Day, founder of the Catholic Worker Movement and Mother Teresa, who served the poorest of the poor in Calcutta. Both women were born at the turn of the century and were undeterred from their compassion toward the poor.

Let's pause here a moment and put this brief survey of missionary women in the early twentieth century into perspective. In 1915 there were more than three million women on the membership rolls of some forty denominational female missionary societies in the United States.[102] *Three million women* were working with the poor not forty years before I was born, but, in 1998, I couldn't even find *one* to mentor me! What happened to them? Where did they go? Why aren't millions more responding to the much larger numbers of poor in our world today?

Oh, how Satan prowls like a lion and masquerades as an angel of light. He can take our best intentions and twist them. As Syncletica said in the fourth century, "When the devil does not use the goads of poverty to tempt, he uses wealth for the purpose. When he cannot win by scorn and mockery, he tries praise and flattery."[103] Her insight lends understanding to the drastic change that occurred in women's missions in the last century.

Four factors, in the early 1900's, contributed to the decline in women's ministry focused on the poor. First was the natural progression from social work on behalf of others to personal liberation. Women's missionary societies slowly evolved from ministry to the needy into large organizations that dealt with massive societal issues, including the abolition of slavery, the war against alcohol, and women's right to vote. Well-known temperance leaders like Frances Willard, Antoinette Brown and Carrie Nation were churchwomen or pastor's wives who became advocates for women's rights.

This evolution occurred among women in foreign missions, as well. When women in Europe and the US, who were forbidden leadership roles at home, heard news of successful women missionaries leading organizations overseas, they demanded the opportunity to do the same.[104] Historian Mark Noll sees a prominent religious motivation in the progression from intense female involvement in the areas of liberation from the bondage of drink and slavery to women's growing concern for liberation from their own social bondage.[105]

As revivals instigated temperance and abolition movements, which in turn initiated women's rights and suffrage movements, another phenomenon was taking place among religious women: they began to receive recognition for preaching. Phoebe Palmer, Hannah Whitehall Smith, Amanda Smith, and Antoinette Brown, to name a few, preached across denominational and social barriers, even commenting at times on their reservations toward entering the heretofore male domain. Each, however, testified to the special call from God to exercise their gift of preaching.[106] Obviously, this created great opposition and controversy throughout denominations directing women's attention away from the needs of the poor.

A third phenomenon was worldwide revolt against colonialism.[107] As the post-modern world attempted to survive two world wars, revolutions, and economic upheavals, an enlightened Christian worldview could no longer support the alleviation of poverty for millions. In fact, the civilization that believed it was the "white man's burden" to share with the less fortunate had also spread death and destruction throughout the world. A direct consequence of all this was the death of an optimistic view of the future so prevalent in the nineteenth century.[108] Similarly, in the United States, minorities and women revolted against a leadership that welcomed their help during the great wars but insisted on their inferior status upon returning home. Both the civil rights and feminist movements paralleled the dismantling of colonial powers overseas.

A fourth phenomenon was taking place in the United States. The post-war years were a period of unprecedented prosperity for the economy and the church. Millions flocked to the suburbs, abandoning the inner cities, which became populated by the poor and racial minorities. Anderson traces the development of inner-city deterioration to this period in the late 1960s. Deindustrialization and growth of a global economy led to a steady loss of unskilled and semi-skilled manufacturing jobs that traditionally had sustained the urban working class. The move from a manufacturing-based economy to a service and high-tech economy subordinated those with low skills and little education to the business bottom line.

The profound societal changes brought on by this change had enormous implications for the ability of poorer populations to function in accordance with mainstream norms. Widespread joblessness, alienation, stressed families, and distressed communities led to further problems including teen pregnancy, welfare dependency, and the growth of an underground economy which brought with it cottage industries of drugs, prostitution, welfare scams, and rackets.[109]

Meanwhile, churches in the suburbs grew rapidly. An inner-peace and happiness religiosity grew in suburbia that was, according to historian Sydney Ahlstorm, "well suited for the times, for it provided peace in the midst of a confusing world, said little about social responsibility, and did not risk conflict with...political opinion."[110] The modern church's understanding of, and ministry with, the poor declined along with our inner cities.

Like the decline in missions as a whole, women's ministry took on a new focus. Christian historian Mark Noll explains that the opening of American society after World War II made a great deal of difference for the practice of Christianity by women. Unlike the voluntary associations of women early in the twentieth century that focused on service, during the 1960s and '70s, many evangelical women's ministries focused on self-help groups with an emphasis on health, exercise, marriage enrichment, and political action.[111] Though women became more visible in parachurch and independent ministries, Tucker and Liefeld believe that "respectability" no longer permitted middle-class evangelical women to be "called" to preach. They assert that this reaction appears to have developed largely as a reaction to the feminist movement.[112]

The result of these societal changes for Christian women today is that we are without contemporary role models of missional women. Women of faith and their daughters have no bridge to see or understand deprivation and want. We need current role models to serve as a lens through which we can see devastation in order to focus on its causes and solutions. We need to hear about women working in missions with the poor in order for their light to shine on a path for us to follow and join the work.

I enrolled in a doctoral program in ministry to find contemporary role models. I was being called upon to teach and preach about Christ Kitchen, but I longed for friends and colleagues who were doing similar work. During my course of study, I found a few modern-day saints humbly working with the poor in some of the most abysmal settings in the world. The stories they told offered thoughtful experience, deep understanding, and realistic hope that encouraged my soul. My favorite was Jember Teffera.

On my first day at Bakke Graduate University, I was introduced to Jember, fondly known as Sister Jember, the "slum saint" of Addis Abba, Ethiopia. Her first words enlisted her as a mentor for life. She said, "I work for the poor and the weak. They are powerless and voiceless. They live for today and not for tomorrow. If you ask a poor woman what she wants, she will tell you to leave her alone, because, you see, reinstating dignity takes a long time. It takes time and energy because they see themselves as the lowest class. They laugh when we say we are equal. They are powerless and have physical deficiencies and dismal attitudes. They are suspicious. It takes wisdom and patience, love and compassion to help them think they matter."[113]

I had never heard anyone say something like this. Jember had been a political prisoner during political turmoil in Ethiopia in the 1970s. In a prison cell, dispossessed of familial position, money, and power, with four hundred women and one toilet, she humbly learned to rely solely on God's power. She learned to listen to the poor and understand Jesus' model of rehabilitation. As a nurse in the prison, she established an accredited health training school that trained more than eighty-five health assistants among the prisoners and guards, a program that continued even after she was released from prison. She is now the founder and director of the Integrated Holistic Approach Urban Development Project in Addis Abba, an organization that rebuilds slums, builds houses, and administers more than fifty-two programs that improve job training, health care, schooling, and sanitation programs, and assists the elderly and the disabled.

I am inspired and encouraged by Jember and other mentor saints discovered in this historical survey of women in missions. I want to find Ammas for the employees and volunteers at Christ Kitchen who will introduce them to the Lord's wisdom and rigorous discipleship. When I consider the number of Christian women in my town and across the country today who know nothing of their sisters living in crack houses, taverns, and neglected housing without the Lord, I am challenged by Syncletica to fearlessly confront traditional notions of how Christian women should function in society. Fabiola and Paula convict me that I have yet to give up all on behalf of the poor. I have never experienced disapproval and condemnation like the Beguines or forced enclosure, control, and censorship like so many of my Catholic sisters. My courageous missionary sisters of the eighteenth century test my resolve and make me question if I could leave home, family, and treasures and set off for distant lands not knowing if any of my efforts would be successful. Could I endure scorn as they did to struggle for a place in ministry, or be content to be overlooked and marginalized?

It is my nineteenth century Ammas that truly challenge me. I yearn to see a societal craze of countless organizations of Christian women working on every distressing issue of our time, seeking to make a difference in society. When I look at myself and my contemporaries, longing for satisfaction from careers, education, and self-growth, I wonder if we could find lasting satisfaction as the deaconesses did, when they gave up luxuries, left society and friends, and condescended to unselfish ministry. I wonder if currently my sisters and I have taken the liberation hard won from our suffragette great grandmothers to a selfish extreme? I wonder if the historic progression from social work to personal liberation and equality has been over-extended, if we've now created our own hierarchical organizations that mimic the power-based structures we once fought to join.

Nevertheless, I am encouraged that so many young women today in universities and Christian colleges across the land are considering foreign and urban missions like our twentieth century mentors. From the dedication I've seen when I teach at Whitworth University, I dare say some will be the Dorothy Day and Mother Teresa of our times. I pray their fresh, optimistic spirits will breathe new life into the world of their grandparents, still reeling from the drastic changes brought on by war and economic upheaval, and the world of their parents, still navigating prosperity.

Women Christ-followers of the twenty-first century need vigilance to live up to the examples of our foremothers. No doubt, we will be ordained and preach without limitations fairly soon. We likely will run mega-churches and Christian organizations. Our challenge will be to maintain a servant's heart like Fabiola and Mother Teresa, carry our-selves with selfless deportment like Jember Teffera, fervently pray like our desert Ammas, stand firm like Dorothy Day, work indefatigably like Catherine Booth, behave humbly like the Beguines, and care deeply for God's poor like all the women we've learned about here. Future mis-sionaries, our daughters, our sons, our men, our world depend on it.

These missional women are my heroes: stars shining in the uni-verse holding out the Word of life to a crooked and depraved genera-tion.[114] Their willingness to follow the commands of God in relation to the poor and oppressed stand in contrast to the various entities within the church whose commitment lessened as they struggled for legitimacy within mainstream culture. We've seen through this brief examination of scripture and Christian traditions that the more inward we turn and the more defensive we become to ensure our own rights, the less we recognize the needs of the disenfranchised. As significant as our accomplishments are, we suffer in comparison to the radical generosity, lowliness, and selflessness of the first century church. If you feel inspired to reclaim some of the practices of Chris-tian traditions with your Bible study or church group, I've listed a few practical suggestions in the Appendix that might get you started.

No wonder it's frightening to follow Jesus to the Samaritan side of town. We drive over or around deteriorated neighborhoods on thoroughfares specifically designed to avoid and circumvent them. We've grown up learning to not *see* whole communities, let alone the individuals living there. We understand the disciple's reluctance to walk with Jesus straight through Samaria. Most everyone we know has always taken the well-traveled, indirect route around deteriorating communities to avoid those we've been told are less than or unworthy. Thus, the history of care for the poor encourages us to not be lulled by cultural indifference.

CHAPTER SIX

Mentoring is Key

*B*rushing the tears quickly away and gathering herself, she busied her hands brushing dust off her skirt and straightening her hair. She looked away from the man, hoping he hadn't seen her emotion. Tears were an unacceptable sign of weakness; they only brought more pain. She had promised herself that no man would ever see her vulnerable like that again.

She'd learned that from her first husband's brother, Korah. A sneer crossed her face as she recalled how he'd bullied his way into his brother's house the day after his funeral, saying it was now his, insisting on his right to take his brother's wife as his own. She had been such a fool back then, so weak and confused and gullible. What did she know of marital law or traditions at such a young age?

She discovered it was her helplessness that seemed to enrage him. If she cried out when he struck her—for getting in his way, for not preparing the meal right, for being outside when he wanted her, for being inside when he did not—he'd only do it more viciously. He wore his meanness like a badge of honor. She learned to get out of the way of his foul moods and scoff at his attempts to dominate. Korah actually laughed when she mimicked his calloused ways, like he finally respected her for mastering his nastiness.

But it finally got the better of him. He'd been accused of stealing their neighbor's sickle and they used it to chop off his hand. An infection developed that spread quickly through his body, as if there was nothing good inside of him to stop it, and he died a wicked, miserable death.

He was the last one, the only one, to strike her. At sixteen, she learned a cold, stoic pride that always sought the upper hand with men. Not so with women. For a while, she attempted to connect with the other girls her age, suspecting they had a lot in common. There were moments when she yearned for girlfriends to chatter with as they went about their endless chores. Being available once again to wed coupled with her emerging beauty, threatened them. They turned away when they saw her and derided her as she passed by them. In their eyes, she became the reason for their husbands' disaffection and was accused of infidelity with most of them. Her very presence presumed to cause miscarriages, warts, and fevers. It was ridiculous, of course, but she excused them their superstitions, because she guessed how miserable they were. It was the ones who knew her mother—the ones she caught occasionally looking at her with pity, who infuriated her. Their refusal to help or to care about her circumstances was bad enough, but their acquiescence to others' scorn was unforgiveable. Indifference became the face she bore for all.

In the last chapter, we looked at cultural and historical reasons the church moved away from ministry in the inner city. We discovered inadequate definitions of poverty and few role models practicing faithful traditions caring for the poor contributed to the demise of missions to the poor in the United States. If, however, those were the only reasons to explain our negligence of the poor, then education and awareness would resolve it. There is a more insidious side to our neglect. Our inattentiveness, lack of role models, and inadequate teaching explains why we don't *know* our poor neighbors, not why we don't *care* about them. Ah, now . . . following Jesus into Samaria gets personal. As we broach subjects like individual accountability for poverty, personal responsibility in societal sin, and a scapegoat mentality, our discipleship training becomes uncomfortable. This could cause us to drop out of disciple school altogether, to shut our ears and avert our eyes once again.

But wait! Let me assure you that you really will feel better after a full examination of these issues. Jesus has taught me, educated and schooled me (I mean this in the scrappy, basketball, smack-talk kind of way) about these matters for years. At least we're in good company. Even though the disciples were committed to following Jesus to Samaria, they couldn't have told Jesus *why* they didn't like the Samaritans. They didn't even know any. He loved them anyway, so there's hope for us.

Jesus explained to his disciples, "If you hold to my teaching, you are really my disciples. Then you will know the truth, and the truth will set you free."[1] Obtaining a clear understanding of God's perspective on the poor will lead to truth. Truth will set you free from prior bias, ignorance, and favoritism. It will lead to a deeper understand of God's heart and mercy, not just for the poor, but also for you! If willing, the Lord will simply not leave us alone in our ignorance or failure to care for his people. He mentors us so we can mentor others. Thus, *mentoring* is our fourth lesson in disciple school.

God's Heart for the Poor

I think the topic of poverty disturbs our conscience because we just can't get away from Scriptures that make us compare God's heart for the poor to our own. "*You* feed them,"[2] Jesus told his not-so-polite disciples when they counseled him to send 5000 hungry people away. *How can I possibly feed 5000 people?* "When you give a dinner, don't invite your friends. . . " Jesus instructs a prominent Pharisee, " . . . invite the poor, the maimed, the lame, the blind, and you will be blessed, because they cannot repay you."[3] *What? I don't know these people. How can I invite them to my house?* "Who loves me more?"[4] he asked the sanctimonious Pharisee comparing his debt to that of the humble woman who washed his feet with her hair. *Hey, she's a sinner and lived a terrible life. . . I haven't.* Paul asks, "How does God's love abide in anyone who has the world's goods and sees a brother or sister in need and yet refuses help?"[5] *So what? You want me to help everybody*? And here's the kicker: Jesus refers to those who do not feed the hungry, clothe the naked, and visit the prisoners as cursed and tells the disciples they will end up in the eternal fire prepared for the devil and his angels.[6] There are more than 2000 verses about poverty and injustice in the Bible.[7] It's disturbing.

"Religion that God our Father accepts as pure and faultless is this . . . . " we read in James 1:27, "To look after orphans and widows in their distress and to keep oneself from being polluted by the world." We like part B; we can do that. Remaining unpolluted is a focus in churches today; we learn about it from the pulpit and Sunday school. But the first part, reaching out to the homeless and loveless in their plight, seems optional. It's a department in the church, a committee. Clearly, Jesus' heart for the poor in these verses is meant as personal instruction. When neglected en masse, it becomes a massive social problem. We'll explore our personal connection to community neglect of the poor first and then look at successful Christian response to community need.

Personal Responsibility

Many thoughtful authors have considered why we deny our personal responsibility in societal sin. "Individual sin has been the major object of attention of evangelical Christians," states theologian Millard Erickson. "Scripture, however, makes frequent reference to group or collective sin."[8] He cites Isaiah 1:17 as an example of a verse that holds us responsible for oppressive conditions in our world. It says, "Stop doing wrong, learn to do right! Seek justice, encourage the oppressed. Defend the cause of the fatherless, plead the case of the widow." Erickson believes we have difficulty recognizing social sin and may not identify personal culpability for it for a number of reasons. The first one was clearly outlined in the last chapter: The further removed we are from evil, the less real it seems and the less likely we are to see ourselves as responsible.[9]

Another reason is that our perception of reality is often conditioned by group membership.[10] Jeremiah Goulka writes eloquently about his change in perception after working in New Orleans after Hurricane Katrina and later in Iraq. He discovered through these experiences that what he believed to be the full spectrum of reality was just a small slice of it. He writes, "Pulling yourself up by your bootstraps makes perfect sense if you assume, as I did, that people who hadn't risen into my world simply hadn't worked hard enough, or wanted it badly enough, or had simply failed. But I had assumed that bootstrapping required about as much as it took to get yourself promoted from junior varsity to varsity. It turns out that it's more like pulling yourself up from tee-ball to the World Series. Sure, some people do it, but they're the exceptions, the outliers, the Olympians."[11]

If you were raised in a middle class family, for example, you might assume that achievement and self-sufficiency are driving forces among all Americans. You'd be surprised, then, by Ruby Payne's research that those within the poverty class place primary importance on relationships not accomplishment.[12] If you were raised in poverty, you might not understand why advanced education and careers are highly valued. Payne believes the poor must be taught to understand the hidden rules of the middle class in order to successfully navigate this middle class world.[13] Understanding our conditioning as middle class Americans can help us establish relevant relationships with the poor.

An encounter between a Christ Kitchen manager and a wealthy donor helps to illustrate the conditioning of group membership. A benefactor of Whitworth University received a Christ Kitchen gift basket from the college for Christmas and asked if he could talk with one of our employees when he visited the area. Sheryl, one of our managers, agreed to talk to David but asked me to accompany her. At one point in their conversation, David said, "Sheryl, tell me how you've moved on."

Sheryl thought and thought. I could tell that she didn't quite understand the question, but after a bit, she shrugged and said, "Well, I'm not eating out of garbage cans anymore." David's question implied an economic perspective of the phrase "moving on." Like other middle or upper-class Americans might, he expected to hear how she'd gotten a better job, how her finances had improved or perhaps how she was now attending college to better herself. In other words, he expected to hear evidence of achievement. Sheryl's answer implied a more personal, practical perspective that brought David to tears.

I am frequently asked if the women at Christ Kitchen ever "move on." In response, I tell the story of Sheryl and David to illustrate how one's perception of reality (in this case, just exactly what "moving on" means) is conditioned by group membership. I also tell the story of Pam, a sixty-five-year-old grandmother with multiple sclerosis, who said, "I screwed up my kids, but I am not going to screw up my grandkids. They come over to my house every day after school and I give them healthy snacks, help them with their homework and read them Bible stories." Pam lives on disability benefits; sadly, her health is failing rapidly. She has become less self-sufficient each day but she has most definitely "moved on." Recognizing one's own perception of reality is a first step in accommodating that of another.

Another reason Erickson cites that we are considerably less aware of collective sin is that we don't readily assume responsibility for matters in which we do not make active choices.[14] A current example is mortgage bankers who were accused of selling subprime loans to unsuspecting or unsophisticated consumers, many of whom were poor, during the financial crisis of 2008. They admit they were simply selling products from reputable brokers. Because the brokers did not require income or job verification, the bankers didn't comply with long-standing industry standards.[15] Not making the decision themselves to require verification, they didn't feel responsible for contributing to the worst financial crisis since the Great Depression.

James Alison offers another reason for individual abdication of social responsibility. He observes collective sin through the concept of the scapegoat. Alison contends that the only means humans have to control their immensely violent nature is to search for collective unanimity against a chosen victim; a scapegoat. "Fallen human nature," he writes, "rushes to produce a false peace by the expulsion of someone held to be responsible for our conflicts. The reason for this whole murderous system, fabricated on a lie, is to maintain security and order."[16]

Nazi Germany's extermination of Jews is a horrendous example of this concept. It's terrifying how closely the Nazi's final solution resembles the chief priests and Pharisees who plotted to kill Jesus to save their temple and nation from the Romans. The high priest, Caiaphas, advocated Christ as the scapegoat. "It is better for you that one man die for the people than that the whole nation perish."[17] How little he knew the consequences of his words.

For our purposes, we could view the Samaritan woman as the scapegoat for her village. As an outcast she goes to the well alone at noon away from the judgment and scrutiny of the other women in the village. Ostracized and marked off as immoral, she doesn't fight for reputation or status but accepts expulsion and isolation and prefers to fill her water pitchers alone. Rather than reach out to her, the village women of Sychar shun her and are satisfied that their own sinful desires and actions are nullified.

Examples of how the poor are seen as scapegoats sometimes visit us at Christ Kitchen. Setting up our sales display at a local church a few years ago, an older woman came rushing up to me horrified that one of our employees was smoking outside. "You will ruin the reputation of your business if you let them do that, Jan. How can you let them waste their money like that?" she accused. Another time, at a sale in between church services, a shopper said, "Well finally, someone is getting those women off of welfare. They have got to work. We just can't afford them anymore." The two employees sitting beside me looked away as I took the woman aside and told her about our mission. That next week we studied how to deal with insults in our Bible study.[18]

Alison concludes that the resurrection of Christ destroyed and annulled this fatal scapegoat system while, at the same time, made possible a new understanding of God's mercy. "The resurrection unleashed . . . a change in perception of who God is: God is not the author of violence or judgment but rather a loving God who, through the death of His son, was planning a way to get us out of our violent and sinful life."[19] When God writes his law in our minds and on our hearts[20] we become responsible for our own actions and are thus judged according to our own deeds, not necessarily those of our group. The blood of Christ cleanses our individual conscience[21] and we can approach the throne of grace with confidence.[22] By his undeserved mercy, we grow more merciful. We learn to comfort those in trouble with the comfort we received from God.[23]

Similarly, Gilligan explains social class exclusion. He writes, "The rulers of a society lull the middle class into accepting its subordination and exploitation by creating a poverty class . . . over whom they feel superior, thus distracting the middle class from resentments it might feel and express toward the upper class." He cites the example of middle class voters in towns across America who get angrier at welfare recipients than at members of the Forbes 400, whom they admire and want to emulate.[24]

James explains this same thing to believers who show special attention to the rich but insult the poor. He writes, "Isn't it the rich who are exploiting you, who use the courts to rob you? Are they not the ones who scorn the noble name of him to whom you belong?"[25] Gilligan writes, "The inferior classes are more likely to fight against each other than against the ruling class, making them easier to control." His opinion seems to concur with James when he states that favoritism to the rich causes discrimination in the church body and creates judges with evil thoughts. "Has not God chosen those who are poor in the eyes of the world to be rich in faith and to inherit the kingdom he promised those who love him?"[26] James concludes. Ah, the heart of God amid the trauma of culture.

The Cure

There is a cure for our lack of concern for the poor. "Moral problems are only solved by obedience," says Oswald Chambers[27] and Scripture is replete with verses to help us. "Remove from me scorn and contempt," pleads the Psalmist, "for I keep your statutes. Though princes sit together and slander me, your servant will meditate on your decrees."[28] We read in Proverbs, "With his mouth the godless destroys his neighbor, but through knowledge the righteous escape."[29] Clearly, we are capable of rejecting the sin of our class or group but it takes intentional prayer, confession, concentrated effort and bathing in Scripture. It also helps to learn what others are doing to model successful work with the poor.

Just as individual repentance and regeneration follow individual confession, the same process is available for collective sin. My father, who never had much interest in social justice, began supporting a tutoring program for inner-city kids in Denver. How he got involved is a good example of how societal sins can be recognized, confessed, repented, and rehabilitated through prayer, submission, personal integrity, and group effort. My dad's transformation began one day when a young man named Brad came to his Bible study and told the men a story that changed their lives. These serious, faithful men were mostly business owners and professionals who'd been meeting together with the senior pastor of their large, suburban church for years.

The story Brad told was of his eight-year-old son, Charlie, and his best friend, Tyrone. Charlie had been very concerned about Tyrone's recent absences from school. One morning, he begged his dad to go by Tyrone's house and pick him up because, according to Charlie, Tyrone didn't have any way to get to school. Brad didn't understand why with school buses and public transportation, Tyrone had been absent for weeks. His son was so worried and so adamant that Brad agreed, just this once, to go pick him up.

He noted his son's visible relief as he hopped into Brad's silver Mercedes like he did every other school day morning, curious about his child's connection to his new friend. Tyrone's address, printed carefully on a small scrape of wrinkled paper, led them to Five Points, a neighborhood in downtown Denver that, in 1981, was a dangerous place for a Mercedes to go.

Charlie jumped out of the car when they found the address and started to run up to the door of the ramshackle house. Brad had never been to this part of town before and sensing what he later described as divine intervention, climbed out of the car and followed after him. Charlie's excitement to meet up with his friend waned as his knocks went unanswered. He called out Tyrone's name, as a concern well beyond his years, descended over the little boy. Finally, they heard a faint scratching like someone was working the lock and Tyrone poked his head out a small slit in the doorway. He couldn't reach the chain that prevented the door from opening all the way, so Brad reached his hand in and unhooked it.

As the door fell open, Brad entered a world he never dreamed existed. Lying haphazardly on the floor of the unfurnished house were several men of various ages and one woman crumpled in the corner as if she'd been thrown there. All were passed out among beer cans, fast food containers, half-eaten pizza and trash. The smell was nauseating but not as upsetting as Tyrone's unemotional response to seeing them at his door. "I didn't know if you was cops or not 'till I heard your voice." Looking at the room with eyes immune to the carnage, he simply said, "My mom can't take me to school."

Charlie's joy at seeing his friend masked Brad's horror at seeing the squalor in his home. His disgust was tempered by his son's disarming ability to see Tyrone and not his circumstances. "Get dressed, Tyrone. I'll take you to school," Brad said, chastened by his son's integrity.

Within minutes, they'd fled the scene. The boys hopped out of the car at school chatting about Teenage Ninja Mutant Turtles like they'd carpooled together for years. Charlie turned back to his dad with a big smile saying, "Thanks, Dad," as if rescuing his friend from desolation was a common father/son event.

At dinner that evening, Brad asked a lot of questions about Tyrone. Charlie didn't know many details except that he'd been getting in trouble lately for not doing his homework. "I suppose we can swing by and pick him up tomorrow," Brad offered, not knowing the consequences of his proposal.

Brad showed up at Bible study the next day still shaken. The worry over Tyrone's living conditions and concern for his welfare spread through the men in my dad's Bible study. They committed to pray for Tyrone and his family. Brad decided to help him with his homework. Over the next few weeks, as he learned about Tyrone's life, Brad recounted the horrors to the men at Bible study. Their committed prayer and concern over what they learned eventually led the men to begin a tutoring program for Tyrone and other little boys in Five Points. The entire men's group got involved in the boys' lives, started a Bible study for them and several became surrogate father figures. One man financed college education for several of the boys.

These men took God's command in Isaiah 1:17 seriously. They had to stop doing wrong (by continuing to live in ignorance of Tyrone's living conditions) and learn to do right (by figuring out what could actually help). The closer they came to know oppression, the more they sought justice for these little boys. Their love for these fatherless boys began relationships that ultimately defended them against the evil that prowled the Five Points neighborhood. My dad admits that, at first, none of them felt personally responsible for conditions they observed in the boys' lives. The more they got involved, however, the more they understood how their lack of knowledge about such living conditions only perpetuated them. They began to feel responsible to correct the injustice that entered their awareness the day Brad and Charlie knocked on Tyrone's door. The personal relationship forged by two little boys and a dad developed into accountability for a much wider group.

Solutions to Poverty

This idea of meaningful, personal relationships as the key to solutions of poverty is found throughout faith-based literature. Shelton, for example, says that to become a credible advocate, we must engage ourselves with struggling people. He notes that to "be effective at overcoming poverty, we must listen and interact, learn and empathize, and allow our lives to be shaped by our less fortunate neighbors."[30] This is exactly what happened with my dad's Bible study.

Others agree that before people of faith can commit to helping the "least of these" they must *be with* those for whom they speak. Pastors at Willow Creek describe this essential factor as the "Be-With" factor, noting Mark 3:14, the passage in which Jesus spends a night in prayer and then selects a few men and women to "be with him." They add that at the heart of any ministry seeking to emulate Jesus, leaders must commit to walking with others in the daily aspects of living.[31] People of faith are called to engage in authentic relationships with people needing help.

According to the Christian Community Development Association (CCDA), solutions to poverty come from people who see themselves as agents for Jesus here on earth in their own neighborhood.[32] "Jesus relocated," says CCDA Board member Wayne Gordon, "He became one of us. He didn't commute back and forth to heaven. Jesus knew his people's experiences because he walked and talked with them, knew their struggles and personally connected with those who were down and out."[33] Horace Pratt, a pastor working with single mothers, advises "Relationships are the keys to changing lives. Regardless of his or her plight, everyone wants to be in relationship with someone whom he or she can respect and trust. Poor people, especially single, poor, black mothers, are no exception."[34]

Faith literature offers other reasons for engagement with the needy. Solidarity with the poor is seen as a crucial component of faithful discipleship that develops stronger, deeper, more discerning faith.[35] Gerald West, a South African biblical scholar, joined a Bible study of rural, poor, black, South African women during the apartheid struggle. He found that critical, contextual reading of Scripture together with and from the perspective of the poor is an avenue for social transformation. He states, "To understand the experience of oppression of the poor and marginalized and, thus, construct a theology adequate to address liberation, we must not only seek solidarity with the poor, but also be 'converted from below.'" He coined the phrase "converted from below" to describe his transformation from a "white, middle-class male groomed for greatness" to a willing servant waiting to "be made use of."[36]

This type of conversion is also described by Murphy Davis, co-founder of the Open Door Community in Atlanta, as "de-schooling": the considerable and on-going process by which she, a white, privileged North American, trained as an academic theologian and historian, is learning to enter the world of the poor.[37]

The literature is clear that solutions to poverty involve committed people engaging with the poor, being with them in relationships, seeking solidarity with them, and even finding personal transformation in the process. Barbara Reid describes the depth necessary to join Christ in his love-commitment to others. "Those who accept Jesus' offer of friendship enter into this relationship with freedom, autonomy, mutuality, responsibility, and joy. They form an ever-widening community of friends who are willing to go to calamity's depths for one another, living in and giving to others hope in God's ultimate triumph over suffering and death. From this, friends learn to stand with those who are victimized, support their journeys to safety and healing, and break cycles of violence by refusing to replicate or cooperate with them."[38]

Dorothy Day, quoting Fyodor Dostoevsky in *The Brothers Karamazov*, captures this costly, self-sacrificing love. "Love in action is a harsh and dreadful thing compared with love in dreams. Love in dreams is greedy for immediate action, rapidly performed and in the sight of all. Men will even give their lives if only the ordeal does not last long but is soon over, with all looking on and applauding as though on the stage. But active love requires labor and fortitude . . ." [39]

The only way to accomplish such love in action, says Bargeron, is to "abide in the love of Jesus. And the only way to do that is to face the awful limitations of our own love, our own sin, our own brokenness."[40] Clearly, transformative work on solutions to poverty requires open, intentional surrender to an intense, life-changing process. Those engaged in work with the poor attest to the power of relationships to accomplish their mission.

In addition to being in relationship with the poor, the literature is also clear that the intention and quality of relationships are critical. "Disciples aren't made in classrooms," state authors McCallum and Lowery, "They're shaped through a relational transfer of knowledge, experience, and the work of the Holy Spirit. Attitudes and values are mostly transmitted through modeling."[41]

Mentoring

Mentoring is a concept often reported as the means by which relationships between the church and the poor are formed and transformation takes place. The word *mentor* commonly means a trusted counselor or guide. Though the term doesn't appear in Scripture, the Greek term *meno,* meaning *enduring relationship*, does.[42] Carruthers suggests that mentoring finds its source in *meno,* which occurs 118 times in the New Testament and describes the type of relationship Jesus desires with his disciples.[43]

Cultural anthropologists report that almost every society across history and around the globe has clearly recognized adult mentors or role-models. Often referred to as elders, tribal chieftains, village head-men, clan leaders or family patriarchs, these generally older, more experienced, stronger members of the group guide younger members and are looked to for identity. Until recently, this role has been conspicuously absent from modern American culture, at least in formal social structures.[44] It has been popularized more recently by Erik Erikson,[45] and has been referred to in current literature as a viable means to counteract adversity, increase resiliency, extend familial-type relationships, transcend cultural barriers, deepen discipleship and positively affect employment.

Several authors contend that mentoring counteracts adversity. Elana Dorfman works with women leaving domestic violence. "Because women living in poverty face intense adversity in their homes and communities, when they start new lives outside the cycle of domestic violence, mentoring improves their rehabilitation and stops the generational cycle of violence."[46] Joel Brown agrees that, "being emotionally connected with adults and people in communities is a significant part of what allows nearly seventy percent of the participants in our program to thrive despite adversity."[47] Resiliency expert, Waln Brown, draws on his own experiences of surmounting adversity, and finds that a common thread in his and others' success is the power of mentors.[48]

Mentoring is also a way of creating extended family. Mary Cagney reports that many of the women she works with in impoverished communities lack family support and finds that mentoring is a way of creating much needed extended family. "Because of the increasing breakdown of the family and the lack of contact between generations," she writes, "women no longer have the luxury of being raised by an extended family, which, therefore, increases their need for mentoring relationships.[49]

Mentoring is also cited in the literature as a means of discipleship. "Spiritual mentors are extremely important in one's spiritual development," writes Lynn Anderson.[50] Esther Burroughs believes that women seek relationships with other women to find their own way as Christians.[51] According to Keith Anderson and Randy Reese, having a relationship with a spiritual mentor is one of the best ways to progress in the lifelong work of spiritual formation. Spiritual formation is nurtured most profoundly when people are "apprenticed" to a spiritual mentor who will partner with God's Holy Spirit toward spiritual development.[52]

Co-authors Payne, DeVol, and Smith believe an individual's ability to move from poverty into the middle class, crossing barriers of ethnic and socioeconomic culture, is learned through adequate support systems and mentoring relationships.[53] They describe a mentor as someone willing to give time and energy to help someone else succeed.[54] Because relationships are key to moving individuals out of poverty, the authors contend that it is practical to use mentoring to increase achievement outcomes.[55] Their book, *Bridges Out of Poverty*, offers helpful insights for mentors not raised in poverty to understand those that are, particularly in terms of hidden rules among classes.[56]

There is also evidence that mentoring has a profound effect on successful job training, securing a job, and staying employed. Ready-4Work, a re-entry initiative mentoring ex-prisoners, found that job-training participants who met with a mentor remained in the program longer, were twice as likely to obtain a job, and were more likely to stay employed than participants who did not meet with a mentor.[57]

It's clear from faith-based literature and examples that *mentoring* is key to solutions of poverty. It involves committed, authentic, faithful people, who are becoming personally accountable while developing a deep love for, and commitment to, the people they serve. As a result, *mentoring* relationships develop between credible advocates and struggling people. Being grounded in Scripture, obedience and mercy is critical, because personal relationships are messy, as we discover in this next go-round between our Lord and our Samaritan.

CHAPTER SEVEN

Learning Directly from Jesus

*D*o something, she admonished herself, distract him. He was still looking at her, although only seconds must have passed since she questioned his ability to draw this living water from her well. It was time to gain the upper hand, to stop this nonsense. Who did this Jew think he was anyway? This was her land, her people, her water.

"Sir," she said turning around, taking the offensive, "You don't think that you are greater than our father Jacob, do you," she hazarded, "who gave us the well and drank from it himself, along with his children and flocks?" She might as well put this upstart in his place. She knew how to venture close to insult without going too far.

And she knew her theology. She'd grown up learning about their great patriarch Jacob and knew both their religions honored him. He had bought the very plot of land they were standing on from the sons of Hamor, the father of Shechem, for one hundred pieces of silver. His well supplied abundant, fresh, flowing, spring water fed by subterranean streams from the adjacent mountain slopes. Her fellow villagers prided themselves on its fine, pure quality, which enabled Jacob to settle there. Every Samaritan knew the history and this man might as well know the quality of her water if he was going to drink from it. She would show him how knowledgeable she was. She commenced battle in defense of her self or her people or maybe their water; she wasn't sure which one. She was getting confused. Perhaps it didn't matter.

Being mentored to care for the poor leads us directly to the heart of God, to personal relationships and responsibility that expand our understanding of his mercy and transform our hearts. We discover God's mercy is available for our collective sin as surely as it is for individual sin. We find his remedy for the poor to be the same as his remedy for our lack of concern for the poor: personal relationships—with him, with each other, with the suffering. People of faith, who've been working in the field for a long time, agree that mentoring is the key to solutions to poverty and the means of developing personal relationships with the poor. How do you get started? Where do you begin work with the poor? In this chapter, we'll embark on the fifth lesson in our School of Discipleship: *learning directly from Jesus.* We'll discover how Jesus engaged the Samaritan woman, why he chooses a well to talk with her and observe his unique mentoring approach.

"Learn from me," Jesus clearly states in Matthew 11:29, as he calls all the weary and burdened to come to him. *The Message* puts it this way: "Walk with me and work with me—watch how I do it. Learn the unforced rhythms of grace. I won't lay anything heavy or ill fitting on you. Keep company with me and you'll learn to live freely and lightly."[1] According to this verse, it seems the only prerequisite to a mentorship program with Jesus is to be thoroughly exhausted or burdened. Once that is understood, we are invited to come to him and to take on his yoke. Jesus offers what we might think tired workers need least. "They need a mattress or a vacation, not a yoke," says theologian Dale Bruner. "But Jesus realizes that the most restful gift he can give the tired is a new way to carry life, a fresh way to bear responsibilities. Instead of escape, Jesus offers equipment."[2] Obedience to the Sermon on the Mount (the yoke) will develop a balanced way of carrying life's burdens. Modeling Jesus comes from being with him, allowing him, as Chrysostom commented, to "set you in all quietness,"[3] and then to equip you.

Let's observe how Jesus works with the Samaritan woman. In the first place, he goes to her—her well, her place of business. He doesn't expect her to find him. She's not a seeker; she doesn't know him and frankly, doesn't even seem to want to know him. Going out of his way to meet one estranged woman with whom he has his longest conversation recorded in the Gospels is a unique mission strategy. It's a bit different than that of the seeker-friendly, purpose driven, explosion of churches, which critic Don Koenig calls the largest Christian movement of the 21st century. According to Koenig, large seeker-friendly churches attempt to make their churches so appealing that [others] will want to be a part of it.[4] Jesus is the seeker in his mission approach with the Samaritan woman, and, knowing her lack of interest, engages her on her own home turf where she feels comfortable.

The time and place Jesus chooses to initiate contact with the woman is also important. In the semi-arid climate of ancient Israel, the availability of water was a constant concern. Wells were the source of the most precious commodity and served the needs of animals as well as people. They were located in various settings, in the wilderness, fields, courtyards, and near towns. Town wells, like the one in Sychar, were usually located outside the city wall and often served as meeting places for women with the task of drawing water. The digging of a well could be a time for celebration for townsfolk, but wells were also fought over as rivals tried to control the precious resource.[5] Throughout Scripture, momentous meetings happened around a well: Abraham's servant found Rebekah, Jacob met Rachel and Moses met Zipporah. Hagar, an Egyptian slave, was found at a well and comforted there by the Lord.

Jesus chooses a common gathering place for our story but an uncommon time. He didn't go at a time in the cooler part of the day when women would usually gather to fill their water pots, but rather at noon, the hottest hour; the time he knew our Samaritan woman would be able to hear him.

Elijah Anderson would call Jacob's well the *staging area* of this story. Staging areas in the inner city are hangouts where a wide mix of people gather for various reasons, most important of which is waging campaigns for respect.[6] Like the well for women of Sychar, the mall, bus plaza, or basketball court are staging areas for people in poor neighborhoods. It is in these public arenas, Anderson suggests, that kids in urban ghettos learn the "code of the street," a set of informal rules of behavior that govern social relations.[7] Developed out of the hard reality of street life and a profound sense of alienation, the code of the street is the cultural adaptation to an extreme lack of faith in the police, judicial system, and others thought to champion personal safety.[8] The code revolves around the presentation of self: a public, unmistakable announcement that the successful can take care of themselves, to the point of violence if necessary.[9] It conveys a message of victory to others on the street. At the heart of the code is the issue of respect, being treated right with the deference a successful code bearer deserves.[10] And so it is at the staging area of the well that Jesus begins his campaign for the Samaritan woman's respect, her heart, and her life.

Next, we notice that Jesus engages the woman with a question. He asks her for a drink. Filling water cups is something she's familiar with, something she can readily do and something she is already good at. He doesn't ask her to attend his synagogue, command her to give him a drink nor begin the conversation by pointing out that she is a sinner. His question teaches volumes about evangelism. "Questions are not only the best way to begin conversations; they are the very lifeblood of conversations," says Bruner. "An asker, as we know from human experience, momentarily places oneself beneath the asked one in social power. So Jesus goes down low in his initial relation to the woman."[11] "The way to call anyone into fellowship with us," William Temple suggested in 1945, "is not to offer them service, which is liable to arouse the resistance of their pride, but to ask service from them."[12]

This is basically the same principle used in contemporary Christian development work called Asset-Based Community Development (ABCD). It is a large and growing movement that considers local assets as the primary building blocks of sustainable community development. Building on the skills of local residents, the power of local associations, and the supportive functions of local institutions, asset-based community development draws upon existing community strengths to build stronger, more sustainable communities for the future.[13]

A fourth way Jesus initiates personal relationships is by gift giving. He offers the Samaritan woman a free gift. She is suspicious at first and doesn't understand what he's offering, but that isn't the point. We, the readers, understand the gift is the Holy Spirit, a promise of new life and faith in Christ. It is offered with no strings attached. The gift is not earned, has no conditions, and cannot be paid for by works.

I still have a tiny, green Gideon's Bible that was handed to me by a soapbox preacher at the University of Colorado Student Union Center in 1972. I was many tears, beers and years away from ever opening it, but I kept it. That free little gift traveled with me through multiple moves, jobs, and relationships, until I finally read it and received its offering nine years later. Gifts are not always opened or understood when given.

I am reminded of the inventive way gifts were offered by American missionaries to the remote Huaorani tribe of eastern Ecuador as a way of initiating contact. Because of the difficulty and risk of meeting the Huaorani, known for their extreme violence, the missionaries chose to drop gifts to them by fixed-wing aircraft. Their drop technique involved flying around the drop location in tight circles while lowering the gift from the plane on a rope. The first drop released a small kettle containing buttons and rock salt. Subsequent gifts offered machetes, ribbons, clothing, pots, and trinkets.[14]

Offering free gifts is not only a missions approach but also a popular marketing concept. "How can you entice people to your website, spike interest in your product?" affiliate marketers exclaim. "The answer is simpler than it may seem. You need to offer them a free gift." The more "clicks" on your site, the better the bottom line.

Our fifth disciple-lesson teaches us to *learning directly from Jesus.* We saw how he met the Samaritan woman in a comfortable setting at a time they could talk feely and engaged her with questions and gifts. Directly observing Jesus' mentoring approach doesn't mean we can't learn from others. He's *the* master at building personal relationships that shape the Kingdom, but there are other faithful saints from whom we have much to learn.

Faith-Based Projects

As part of my doctoral dissertation research, I set out to find others in faith-based projects like Christ Kitchen that mentor and disciple low-income women in order to learn how they help women break the cycle of poverty. In 2007, I could find nothing written in the literature about any such program. (This was before websites and Google were common forms of disseminating information.) I suspected there were programs attending to the needs of low-income women, but guessed that the people running them were so incredibly busy, they had little time to write about what they were doing.

My research plan was to interview directors of projects helping low-income women and compile a "best practices"[15] anthology of effective ministry strategies. I hoped it could honor and empower those in the trenches while educating and encouraging others to minister to women in poverty. Frankly, I was hungry for mentors in the field and longed to be inspired by their expertise.

I could only find eighteen programs in the United States that fit the criteria as being both faith-based and serving a population of low-income women.[16] Questionnaires asking for information concerning mission, poverty and scope of services were sent to program directors. One administrator of several Job Core sites sent on the questions to all of her directors.

All but one of the respondents cited mentoring as the most effective strategy aiding the women they work with in breaking the cycle of poverty. Ten directors said mentoring was most effective when offered within structured activities that address obvious needs in the lives of poor women. Structured activities include the following: Bible study, educational classes, job training, language classes, housing, and recovery programs. One director said, "We teach life skills classes along with Bible study and provide weekly contact with a mentor. This creates a nurturing, loving environment that enables a woman to learn and discover her beautiful value. We offer her a taste of stability—sometimes her very first taste."[17] Another director said a goal of their GED class is to help women become self-sufficient.[18] "Mentoring is essential," she said, "because self-sufficiency takes practice and needs to be modeled."

Like Jesus seeking out the Samaritan woman, these projects are located in areas of need. A project in El Paso Texas, for example, that teaches English as a second language, is located near the border. A mission to the homeless in Waco takes place under a freeway bridge. A job-training project in Baltimore takes place in the local Catholic Charities shelter. Classes, meals and programs to help the poor, become staging areas for evangelism and mentoring. All are given free of charge, providing participants needed skills while offering the potential for new life in Christ.

When asked about the hardest part of their work, project directors noted the constant chaos and ugliness of poverty, the constant setbacks that happen in low-income women's lives and the need to deal with the repeated unhealthy decisions the women make. One director of a Job Corp project in North Carolina wrote, "What breaks my heart in many pieces is to see women with so much potential give up or not even try." Another director wrote that the hardest thing for her is, "When things beyond their control come against them, just when they seem to be making progress."

As questionnaire respondents attest in their own words, the way they stay buoyed amidst the chaos is by being faithful to God's plan, being in his path, resting in him, reading his Word, seeing miracles happen, and seeing women change their lives. Clearly, the directors and their staff follow Jesus despite the cost through the minefields of their women's lives. "His suffering left us an example to follow," one woman said. "It's what makes discipleship among the suffering possible." These saints allow us an opportunity to see transformation happen.

Discipleship projects around the country offer the poor fresh ways to bear burdens through classes, provision, mentoring and care. They mentor their clients under Jesus' tutelage in order to develop life-long disciples. They exemplify the fifth principle in discipleship training as they learn directly from Jesus and model that for others.

Teaching The Way

At Christ Kitchen, we've found that to learn from Christ, his Word and way has to be studied, proclaimed and integrated into all aspects of the program. Organized Bible study is one way employees and volunteers learn from Christ. Weekly studies consist of question/answer dialogue based on a passage of Scripture. We often use *LifeGuide Bible Studies* from Intervarsity Press[19] and *Fisherman Bible Studyguides* from Shaw Books[20] because of their clarity, simplicity, and relevance to lives of low-income women.[21] The women love to talk, so questions directing discussion about the passage and its application to their individual lives are helpful. Everyone feels included because prior biblical knowledge, doctrine or commentary is not required. We allow ample time for personal reflection, humor, and honesty, creating an atmosphere for growth and inquiry.

Visitors and volunteers who attend Christ Kitchen Bible studies often comment how refreshing and unusual it is to hear such honesty and openness. One volunteer observed that the women's reliance on Scripture was so basic and real that it often left her feeling ashamed of her own petty concerns and trite prayers. She said, "Their dependence on God reveals profound, sincere trust. Prayer is not just wishful thinking for them, but a real cry for help. Many of them don't have a place to live, money to pay the utility bill, rent money, a reliable car, or a full-time job. If God doesn't provide for them, they have nowhere else to turn. They rely on Scripture as if their lives depend on it. Every time I leave Christ Kitchen I feel reoriented toward what is important. I am reminded "with food and covering to be content" (1 Timothy 6:8.)

It is through teaching that former ways of life, the "old self," as Paul puts it in Ephesians[22] can be shed in favor of a new, God-fashioned, true and holy self. Women coming off the streets are well aware of their separation from Christ and exclusion from citizenship in the Kingdom and membership in the church world. With blunt candor, they condemn their guilt, failures, and addictions. Most have very clear "before and after" stories in which the Lord's peace and reconciliation destroyed barriers and divisions, addiction, and self-destruction. When they accept the Lord, most do so without hesitation, understanding implicitly Paul's admonition to put on a new self. Having little to lose, they come to him fully and passionately. Recovery programs reinforce the transformation message, treatment centers emphasize new mind attitudes and mentors and friends are depended upon to walk new righteous paths. Shedding the skin of failure is difficult, but falling off the wagon, going back out, becoming homeless again, portends death. Finding the will to begin again, leads to a new life. Accountability to the new way, to doing what is healthy, is expected and welcomed. Day by day we watch women move out of destitution and poverty.

Another means of learning from Christ is found in the routine of gathering for short devotional readings at the beginning of each workday. The women themselves instituted this ritual after I gave them a daily devotional for Christmas. Praying together over the content of a passage helps employees focus. One of the managers commented that the reading helps her "put God in front of me for the day."

Applying the motto, "Think Scripturally" to daily decisions is another key learning method at Christ Kitchen. Sometimes referred to by the women as the "do-as-Jesus-did method," it sets the tone for finding guidance in Scripture for policies, interpersonal relations, employment issues, and long-term growth strategies. For example, the verse "Pay a laborer his wages each day before sunset, because he is poor and is counting on it,"[23] encouraged the policy of weekly pay, rather than the common business practice of bi-weekly or monthly paychecks. Resolution of conflict is guided by multiple verses dealing with quarrels, confrontations, and personal integrity. "If your [sister] sins against you, go confront [her] privately,"[24] is used frequently to discuss confrontations, affronts, reconciliation, timely interactions, and courage.

Multiple verses encouraging personal integrity within work relations are referred to casually during the workday. Verses like "Make every effort to do what leads to peace and mutual edification";[25] "Warn them before God about quarreling about words. . . it ruins those who listen";[26] and "Do nothing out of selfish ambition or vain conceit, but in humility consider others better than yourselves"[28] are helpful to begin conversations about how to deal with difficult people and situations. "Unless the Lord builds the house, its builders labor in vain,"[29] and "Seek first his kingdom and all these things will be given to you as well,"[29] have been instrumental in developing a strategy for growth based on guidance, patience, and prayer.

Christ Kitchen encourages *studying* and *discussing* Scripture in its context to understand its meaning and to prevent proof texting.[30] Scripture is used to anchor our thoughts and decisions in godly wisdom and to encourage integrity on pertinent issues. We guard against misuse of Scripture. Interestingly, volunteers from local churches seem much more prone to insensitive proof texting than employees, who seem to simply and joyfully, perhaps even naively, extract fundamental value from helpful verses. One first-time volunteer, for example, repeatedly insisted that an employee not allow her sister and boyfriend to visit without initial agreement that they wouldn't sleep together, citing verses on fornication as justification. Baffled, the employee simply responded she was looking forward to reconciling with her sister after five years and that her sister didn't "know no religion anyways." The employee was actually closer in her estimation of Paul's exhortation to purity *for believers* than the volunteer. The incident did help me work with the volunteer's unresolved guilt over a prior abortion in subsequent conversations. Describing Scripture as God's guidelines, an employee said, "I need 'em to help me stay accountable. If I'm gonna walk the righteous path, I need to stay connected with these women and pray and read my Bible."

Creating Places to Learn

There are all kinds of staging areas in your town within which to seek those who will likely never set foot in a church. Christ Kitchen has become a thriving business that attracts women off the street with wages and employment, but we started with just two women and a bag of beans. Three different ministries developed out of the Christ Kitchen model, but have unique business plans. Cross Roads Kitchen in Casper, Wyoming hires women to make hand made stationery and gifts.[31] Bountiful Baskets in Baltimore, Maryland trains women in a homeless shelter to put together gift baskets, and a woman in Panama City sews silk pillowcases with needy women in her neighborhood.

The basic idea is to woo people, just like the Samaritan woman, with something practical that addresses a need. Childcare is an ever-present need for women in poverty, particularly if they're going back to work. Taking care of one child or organizing a larger venture provides opportunity to invest in a precious part of the child's and parent's lives. Food programs certainly attract low-income people, but it's helpful to also think of ways to cultivate long-term relationships. A church in Spokane hands out invitations to their church service while providing breakfast to a homeless camp and sends cars to pick them up Sunday morning. Providing a washing machine and dryer is a great way to spend a couple of hours getting to know a new friend.

Government Programs

As encouraging as it is to find saints working with the poor in our country, the need far exceeds their efforts. Before we move on, we'll briefly address government programs that provide services for the poor. This can be a contentious topic but if you're interested in working with the poor, it's helpful to understand basic facts.

On a national level, the United States federal government has policies in place addressing income inequality and assisting poor households. They include progressive income tax, public assistance programs, economic development programs, and managing the economy.[32] When politicians and the public speak of welfare, they are usually not referring to all government programs (Medicaid, Food Stamps, Supplemental Security Income, and Housing and Urban Development programs) that provide benefits to impoverished Americans. They generally are referring to the TANF (Temporary Assistance to Needy Families) program, a relatively small part of the overall assistance scheme.

This common understanding of welfare was first established in 1935 during the Great Depression as a federal program known as Aid to Dependent Children. It was a relatively modest program focused on widows, orphans and divorced or deserted mothers and their children. Renamed Aid to Families with Dependent Children (AFDC) in the 1960s, it grew to provide assistance to nearly fourteen million people at its peak in 1994. As part of his promise to "end welfare as we know it," President Clinton enacted the TANF program, which eliminated entitlement, established work requirements, and established a sixty-month lifetime limit on assistance. Also during the Clinton administration in 1998, Congress initiated The Workforce Investment Act to consolidate, coordinate and improve employment, training, literacy and vocational rehabilitation programs in the United States. In response, state and local governments designed programs to help low-income families prepare for and go to work.

Success in these programs is indicated by work-related outcome indicators and is greater in populations with higher education and successful previous job experiences.[33] To use Tex Sample's descriptors, it could be said that government job-training and employment programs are most successful and effective among "respectables" and those experiencing job loss due to company layoffs or economic downturn. A friend of mine quipped, "Rehabilitation programs assume there was 'habilitation' somewhere along the way in the first place."

Government solutions to poverty for the hard-living poor, the homeless, and the desperate poor, those who fall under the radar of economic programs, concentrate on basic needs of the very poor—shelter, food, and clothing. They are intended to care for the permanently disabled or are designed as temporary stopgap measures rather than permanent solutions to poverty.

Poverty reduction programs and provision of basic needs by government entities have an essential place. Many of the women at Christ Kitchen utilized these services before turning their lives around. "It got me off the street," said one woman, "kept me fed and safe 'till I found the power of Jesus could do it better." Another said, "I couldn't have gone to work without help with daycare." "I was killing myself with alcohol," admitted another, "and needed the county hospital rehab program to save my life until I was willing to do that myself."

The disadvantage of these programs, according to Manhattan Institute senior fellow Heather MacDonald, is that the "government cannot create personal responsibility and drive in individuals."[34] Similarly, James Towey, Director of the White House Office of Faith-Based & Community Initiatives from 2002–2006, said, "There are certain things the government can't do. The government can't love; it's not capable of developing that kind of relationship with the poor. People in faith-based organizations can develop that compassionate relationship better than other providers. Government . . . is always going to be a Band-Aid. It's never going to lead to lasting effects in the lives of the poor."[35] Obviously, politicians understand the limitations of governmental solutions to poverty.

The saints in America need to work on developing relationships with the poor that ensure lasting effects, responsibility and drive. Regardless of our political affiliation, whether we work one-on-one, in small groups, or in larger programs, we can create safe, loving, effective spaces where low-income people will gather, feel respected, and change their lives. Like Jesus demonstrated at the Samaritan well, relationships begin with willing workers finding godly ways to engage the disinterested and disheartened.

CHAPTER EIGHT

Serving Humbly

He didn't engage in her battle. Her challenge to fight went unheeded. He simply responded by offering more. "Everyone who drinks this water will be thirsty again," he said almost casually, "But whoever drinks the water that I give will never thirst again. In fact, the water I give will become in that person a fountain of water gushing up into deep, lasting life."

More? First he tempts her with so-called living water, declares it will quench her thirst for life, and now he offers eternal springs? He's way too calm and composed to be mad, she considered. She'd heard stories of kings gone mad, insane rulers eating grass like cattle, evil engulfing the hearts of man. But none of those things fit this man. He exuded gentleness and kindness like no other she'd known.

Hesitantly, she let his words wash over her. Sweet words—never thirst, deep lasting life—hovered for just a moment in her imagination. When had she ever known deep peace, lasting love? Longing was too painful to consider, too foreign. She never let herself go there. Stop the words!

Struggle and strife were all she'd ever known. They had invaded her life and kept her prisoner. She never remembered being without her twin tyrants. Their oppression began the day her mother died and had never ceased. They accompanied her into that horrid marriage she'd agreed to with the jailer, Jakum. He was just taking advantage of a young widow, but she hadn't cared about that. She just needed food and a roof over her head. Such a strange man Jakum was with his stooped back bent at an odd angle, forcing him to constantly look at the ground.

She hated living in the tight quarters the jail provided for him, but he didn't require much of her, just fixing meals.

She'd wondered why he never touched her, until she found him with the little girl, Tirzah, from next door doing unspeakable things to her. Her rage when she found him exceeded any she'd ever felt, surprising even herself as she fell on him with murderous frenzy. Tirzah fled, and Jakum cowered, but she still seethed that he had only suffered a broken nose and arm from her assault. She never went back to the jail after that, couldn't bear looking at the man for fear she'd literally kill him. It caused her to forfeit her few possessions but she didn't have much anyway.

Later, she thought it was, perhaps, the noblest thing she'd ever done—rescuing that little girl. Occasionally, she caught sight of Tirzah; without words they exchanged brief smiles, neither wanting to remember further. Sometimes she imagined comforting her, teaching her how to be strong and cunning, teaching her how to stay safe. Now, she knew the meaning of her mother's sad smile right before she died.

That brought her back to this man standing at the well. How dare he! How could he have known? How could he touch her deepest desire? Never thirsting sounded like a luxury of a sweetened life, but how could he offer fountains brimming over with what she longed for most—to be of help, to make a difference in the lives of little Tirzahs, to have a purpose. Excruciating pain accompanied the newfound awareness of this secret longing. Once named, it would forever torment her. Oh, it was better to live without dreams.

"Go away. Go away," the little lost child inside of her began humming, impervious to danger, willing all evil away. It consoled her, helped her think rationally. This man could never deliver on his offer. Shrewdness took its place at the helm of her heart, usurping dreams and desire. There is always a catch; nothing is ever free, only a fool would believe otherwise. For heaven's sake, stop the dribbling. Get to work, it screamed.

"OK mister," she thought to herself, "put your money where your mouth is. Give me some. Go ahead, I dare you." Was this curiosity or was some part of her yearning for truth? What she said out loud was,

"Sir, give me this water so I won't get thirsty and have to keep coming to this well to draw water."

Just as the Lord engaged the woman at the well with the offer of living water, men and women involved in discipleship projects around the United States attract the uninterested and unbelieving with needed services, develop relationships with the poor, and ultimately point the way to the Lord. In the story of the Samaritan woman, we see how Jesus is willing to give her something she cannot earn—living water, eternal life, but she misinterprets his metaphoric language. Was her response, "Give me this water so I don't have to keep coming to the well," practical, or was it shallow? Learning the language, intentions, and even misinterpretations of the poor are critical to developing meaningful relationships and aiding change. In this chapter we'll analyze the lottery-life of the poor and the poor in spirit: wanting what we do not have, wanting life to be easier. The sixth lesson in Jesus' School of Discipleship, *serving humbly*, is offered to equip us to see through the distorted, often tragic presentation of the poor.

We rejoice only briefly when we read that the Samaritan woman finally asks Jesus for his offered water. Our joy is fleeting because we quickly learn that her faith is weak and her ask misdirected; it has an alternative motive. She doesn't want to have to keep drawing water. She misunderstands holy, living water to be some phenomenal faucet, some heavenly hydrant. She has, as of yet, no understanding of grace and like those who are initially blind to Christ and his gift, she is more interested in the affairs of everyday life than the things of eternity.[1] Jesus is speaking of humanity's greatest thirst for a right relationship with God and she is thinking only of physical thirst and fewer chores. It was inconceivable to her how Jesus could get living water from Jacob's well. Little did she know, she is talking to the only person in the universe who could fill her common ordinary water pitcher of life with new meaning, spiritual cleansing, and refreshment.[2]

Misunderstandings

For this misunderstanding, the woman is ridiculed by commentators. Walvoord and Zuck write that because of her sin and materialism, the Samaritan woman could not grasp this dark saying.[3] Wiersbe calls it a shallow emotional response.[4] Calvin is perhaps the most venomous. "There is no doubt the woman knows perfectly well that Christ is speaking of spiritual water," he writes, "but because she despises him, she cares nothing for his promises."[5] My goodness, such malice from those who likely never experienced the drudgery of back-breaking day labor.

Should we not look at the Samaritan woman's lack of understanding as evidence that the veil covering her heart is not yet taken away and thus she can't understand spiritual water? Other, more charitable commentators, see hope. "From this limited perspective," states Lincoln, "the woman has made a little progress. Whatever it is she thinks Jesus is offering, she is at least open to receiving it."[6] She does ask, and that is all Jesus asked of her. Clearly, her faith is far from perfect or even correct, but Jesus didn't ask her for great faith; he just asked her to ask.[7]

Misunderstandings and misinterpretations are typical at Christ Kitchen. They range from humorous to horrendous. On the lighter side, for example, a manager told me she thought our new lentil salad was "snooty." I'm always anxious to understand class-tainted opinions like this, so I asked her what was snooty about red lentils? "Oh, it's not the lentils," she opined, "It's the capers and red wine vinegar in the recipe. Who has capers in their cupboard?" she accused. I conceded that point and agreed most shoppers would drive to the store to make our recipe. "Hey, Alice," she went on, searching for reinforcement, "Do you have red wine vinegar in your cupboard at home?" Alice, a recovering alcoholic, said adamantly, "No! I don't have no alcohol in my whole house!"

Another time, when Christ Kitchen was catering a dinner at a large Presbyterian church, we decided to put the desserts on a cart and let people pick them up as they went through the buffet line. A new employee thought that was a very bad idea because surely the first few people through the line would take them all. When I explained that each person would know to only take one, she shook her head and said, "Gee, we're not in Kansas anymore, are we?"

Sometimes, I can't even guess what they don't know. Once, I saw a woman about to add five tablespoons of powdered garlic to a pot of chile. "Stop!" I yelled from across the kitchen and told her that the recipe called for fresh garlic. She showed me the recipe that read, "5 tablespoons garlic," and wondered how I knew to add fresh garlic. I never thought to write "fresh garlic" on the card.

Another time, we had a luncheon for some older PEO ladies who were a bit apprehensive about our ability to provide a nice lunch. So I went over to chat with them after they were seated and saw that their silverware was placed every which way, with the spoons on the left and the forks and knives scattered around. Now, you might not think this was a big deal, but these octogenarians did. We've found that some people worry about the cleanliness of low-income women, so we try to maintain the highest standards even in little details. Rather than waiting for dessert to describe the ministry of Christ Kitchen, I started right off explaining how many of our employees never had loving mothers or grandmothers who taught them little things like silverware placement. They graciously understood and moved the silverware to its correct place. My manager observed this interaction and the next day I found a large diagram of correct silverware placement on our bulletin board with big arrows citing *the fork goes here*.

Misinterpretations aren't always so light-hearted. Once, when one of my managers told me she didn't feel good, I suggested she be careful in her dealings with those she supervised, knowing she could be short-tempered when tired. A few minutes later she was livid, believing I thought her incompetent. Another time, our cook stormed out of the kitchen accusing me of not trusting her, after I reviewed the list of orders needing to get out that day. When an ex-employee came in to the Kitchen to chat with me, a current employee worried that I was going to fire her and rehire the old employee.

A good example of asking gone array involves a woman who got so upset during a staff meeting, that the others got up from the table and left. She ranted on and on about how hard she worked and how nobody appreciated her. Having no idea where this was coming from, I finally interrupted her, and said, "What is it you want?" She looked at me in surprised and said, "Well, I want more hours, of course." Could there be a more inappropriate way to ask for more hours?

No doubt, these examples illustrate inappropriate behaviors. They could be interpreted as inexperience with garlic, lentils or table settings. Inexperience, however, doesn't explain the intensity of emotions and deep-seated shame that accompanies these incidents. They are better understood as expressions of inferiority, at the heart of which lie intact patterns of exclusion that for some, result in deep debilitating social pathologies. Statements like, "No one listens to me" or "You better show me some respect" are rather mild examples of rejection we commonly hear. A more incapacitating example is Kathy's proclivity for stealing food from others, which she told me was probably the result of being locked in a closet without food as a child.

Exclusion is just one of the many abuses the women at Christ Kitchen have suffered. Most have backgrounds that include physical violence, neglect, abandonment, rejection, sexual exploitation, and violation. Gilligan states that violations such as these communicate the absence of love. "When we cannot fend off unloving acts, our souls are murdered. A soul empty of love fills with hate," he writes.[8] He goes on to say that violence [among the poor in America] occurs on a scale so extreme, so bizarre, and so frequent that one cannot fail to see that [those] who occupy the extreme end of the continuum of violent behavior in adulthood occupied an equally extreme end of the continuum of violent child abuse earlier in life.[9]

I could not be of service to the women at Christ Kitchen until I understood the motives behind inappropriate behavior. Simply demanding compliance to rules and standards does work for some, but most of the women just give up when they don't measure up, confirming their own worst impressions of themselves: *I'm flawed. I'm despicable. I'm unworthy.* Jesus did not demand compliance of the Samaritan woman. When she insulted him, argued and fought, he offered more of himself. That is what I need to continually learn.

I found James Gilligan's work helpful. I learned to see a continuum of violence ranging from anger and insult to depression and suicide. I learned to understand violence as tragedy; an attempt to achieve justice. Gilligan contends that expressions of shame are the primary or ultimate cause of violence. Violence, acted out by men through physical aggression, or acted inwardly by women through verbal assault and depression, is an attempt to diminish the intensity of shame that rages inside broken people and replace it with pride, self-respect, or self-love.[10]

This may not be self-evident to healthy people because healthy people have resources that tide them over during periods of rejection and loss. Emotional health is not the absence of pain, but rather the capacity to bear painful feelings when they occur.[11] Anderson adds that middle class people have other forms of capital that help mitigate loss: more money, more ways of effectively expressing and caring for themselves, more intact relationships.[12] Having an intact family or culture can provide people with a powerful means by which to bolster their self-esteem and protect themselves from what could otherwise be overwhelming, soul-murdering intensities of shame and humiliation.

This explains why it is hard, at first, for new volunteers at the Kitchen to understand occasional overt and dramatic interpersonal dynamics. For example, several volunteers offered to help one of our women make baskets. She rudely told them they didn't know how to make baskets and would surely ruin them if they tried. She explained to me later that she thought they were going to take her job. Regardless of her motivation, it was traumatic for the volunteers to be on the receiving end of such diatribes.

Serving Effectively

To be effective, mentors for women who've been through unspeakable traumas need to develop methods that counter what Gilligan refers to as the pre-conditions for violence.[13] One precondition is feeling ashamed, usually over matters that seem so small and trivial compared to the magnitude of response that their very triviality creates more shame. A way to counter disgrace is to respect the person but clarify what is important and what is not. "No harm done. Let's just try again," I often say. "Don't worry about that, it's just cookie dough. We can always make more." or "Next time, just say you can't work that day. We'll all understand."

Having no alternative other than violent acting out for diminishing feelings of shame is a second precondition for violence. We teach alternative choices all the time. "Next time you feel like blowing your stack, excuse yourself and go outside. Cool off and then come back in. If you can't do that, you won't be able to work here." Scripture is full of help around this point. "Don't let the sun go down on your anger."[14] "If your [sister] sins against you, go and show her her fault. If she listens to you, you've won your sister over."[15] "Let your yes be yes and your no be no."[16] Modeling and teaching alternatives is perhaps more important than defining consequences.

A third prerequisite for violence is lacking the emotional capacity that normally inhibits violent impulses. This explains why we find so many women involved in multiple moves, relationships and jobs. Without having the emotional competence to deal with things like unpaid bills, suspended children, or annoying neighbors the thinking goes: "If I can just change the environment, I might be able to change the way I feel." No amount of moving or relationships, however, relieves the distress of inner emptiness, deadness and past victimizations. We counter this at Christ Kitchen by showing deep, unconditional love and by believing in their ability to make it through the problem. A safe, loving, prayer-filled environment is an absolute prerequisite for healing. "You can't be here when you're loaded on meth," we might say. "You have to go home now. Come back next week clean, sober, and ready to work. We want you back, but never again high." We constantly discuss choices, attitudes and behaviors to facilitate the employees' ability to think and talk about thoughts and feelings before they get acted out.

Calmly, with great love and even greater self-control, new means of handling interpersonal interactions are modeled every day all day. Some days are longer than others but we need to show up ready to encourage their ability to change and live free. Modeling Jesus' way with clarity, firmness, joy and grace is essential to earning respect from women who might have never seen godly communication. If you try to match anger, intensity or pathology, you'll lose every time. Every once in a while, I've had to raise my voice. Great evil requires great prayer and even greater reliance on God's power. "Out!" I shouted one day at a man who came to harass his girlfriend. "Don't come back or we will call the cops." My intensity startled all of us but came after assessing the situation and praying quickly. Later, the girlfriend said he'd threatened to kill her that morning. We pray often for a hedge of protection around our building.

Trauma and drama are rather common around Christ Kitchen. I likely would never have started the Kitchen, if I knew they happened at all. But this territory comes with getting involved in the lives of the poor, so you have to be prepared. Jesus knew this when he said, "In this world you will have trouble, but take heart, I've overcome the world."[17] He knew he was sending his disciples out as sheep among wolves, so he prepared them. "Be as wise as serpents and innocent as doves."[18]

Perhaps these stories can now put the Samaritan woman's remarks into perspective. When life is a series of tragedies, injustices and bad decisions, we can better understand how free water and fewer chores, or playing the lottery, or getting a free ride might be attractive. It's more about getting a break than it is about laziness, more about gambling that life might get better, than truly believing it will. Life for those caught up in poverty is an endless search to find a spot comfortable enough that they can finally come to rest.

This is where the Saints come in. We are the hands and feet of the Lord on the front line in the battle for the hearts of people on the streets who don't know their Savior. Believe me, Satan is working overtime for their souls. There is no way we could effectively enter the world of the deprived and depraved without help. Only the Lord can equip us to see through the distorted, often tragic presentation of the poor and love them the way he does. The way he prepares us is found in the sixth principle of discipleship: *serving humbly*. He demonstrates what it takes to serve him by performing the lowliest of tasks. We get a clear snapshot of how Jesus did this in the thirteenth chapter of John.

Model of Servanthood

Jesus provides a life-giving and life-sustaining model for servanthood by washing his disciples' feet. It is the classic parable of how Jesus wants to be at our service, giving us a pattern for living. "Now that I, your Lord and Teacher, have washed your feet, you also should wash one another's feet. You see, I have given you a pattern for living: so that what I just did for you, you can do for others."[19] Washing feet is the only way.

Humble servanthood would be impossible without the realities Jesus lays out for us in John 13:3 before he begins washing the feet of his friends. We're told three things that enabled Jesus to perform this most significant act of humility. The text says Jesus knew the Father had put all things under his power and that he had come from God and was returning to God. Jesus knew who he was, whose he was, and where he was going. All three vital elements are available to us: the Father has equipped us with every good thing for doing his will, saved us in Christ, and will reclaim us. Knowing who we are, whose we are, and where we are going, we can work long hours for minimal compensation and welcome into our lives those who want nothing to do with us. We can risk our reputations to stand against injustice. We even can move our families into inner city housing, and quietly, freely, generously offer our money, resources, and lives to those we serve.

It helps to understand the impact of Jesus' act by adding historical perspective. Lincoln observes that foot washing in the ancient world was the menial task of removing dust, mud, animal waste and human excrement. The task was assigned to slaves or servants of low status, particularly females. It was virtually synonymous with slavery. What makes the account of Jesus washing his disciples' feet extraordinary is that there is no parallel in ancient literature for a person of superior status voluntarily washing the feet of someone of inferior status. Jesus' act represents an assault of the usual notions of social hierarchy, a subversion of the normal categories of honor and shame. It is not just an honored teacher who is performing a shameful act but a divine figure with sovereignty over the cosmos who has taken on the role of a slave.[20]

What the disciples are taught by footwashing, states Barbara Reid, is to "emulate not the obligatory service of a slave to a master, nor the altruistic service of one who generously meets the need of another. Both are models of service that necessarily imply inequality and obligation. Rather, the service which Jesus enacts is that of free self-giving of a friend for his friends."[21]

Humble servanthood is a theme we work on constantly at Christ Kitchen. It's probably the most difficult strategy for both volunteers and employees to grasp. They rebel like Peter did when Jesus attempted to wash his feet. They join him in his protestations: "Never will I be so humiliated as to take a position lower than a slave!" It can feel like a life or death proposition to serve those who despise or hurt you. "I spent years kowtowing to a crazy man who blowed off my thumb with a shotgun," complained an employee who was having trouble with this concept. "This turn-the-other-cheek thing will get me killed."

Servanthood is no slight request, no lofty philosophy, to those who've survived by their fists and wit, who prefer physical pain to feeling nothing. Suggesting to souls empty of love, to battered women, women degraded by horrific sexual violence, women exposed to the extreme end of violent abuse in childhood, that it is honorable to assume the posture of a slave is difficult at best. Only extreme love teaches murdered souls such respect. Only repeated evidence proving the superiority of non-violent alternatives assures safety and peace. Only miraculous emancipation from guilt destroys its other remedies. Being loved continually, forgiven repeatedly, respected and valued begins the transformation. To experiential learners, as so many women in poverty are, servanthood is a long, hard sell.

To theoretical learners, like most of the volunteers, humble subservience is also demanding. Many acquiesce to the idea of servanthood taught in Sunday school, but not one forged in experience. One volunteer eloquently describes her lesson in humility when visitors from a local church misidentified her as a Christ Kitchen employee. "They spoke down to me as if I was one of the 'poor' women. For ten seconds, I was insulted. Then I felt immediately ashamed of myself. The greatest gift they gave me was assuring me that I fit in! In a small way, I felt how the women must feel everyday."

I love how one author observes the moral of the foot-washing story. "Let us let ourselves be loved by the Lord. Let Jesus be our Servant-Lord . . . Give in. Be washed, simply because Jesus wants to wash us and not because we think or feel we deserve to be washed."[22] Forgiveness of sins is ultimately the foundation of our relationship with Jesus Christ. This is why he says, "If I can't wash you, you can't have me." This is hard on our Peter-like pride, but it is medicine for the submitting soul.

Our Samaritan woman isn't quite there yet. She misunderstands Jesus' offer, argues with him, and tries to distract him, but she finally asks for the water, even if it is with questionable intentions. That's all Jesus needs to start his very intentional saving work. How he goes about it is surprising.

CHAPTER NINE

Loving Unconditionally

"**G**o," the man said, his kind eyes never changing, "Call your husband and come back."

She was stunned. Speechless. All she could do was shake her head slightly and step back, away from this inexplicable, all-knowing power. Why was he. . . ? How could he . . . ? The blow forced an exasperated sigh. Her shoulders dropped down in defeat.

Husband! The very word brought vomit to the back of her mouth that she forced back down as guilt seared her throat and sent ripples burning into her stomach. Her hand went reflexively to her lifeless womb that sat empty, accusing.

She'd been derailed really, after that filthy jailer. She'd fled to the far side of the village, eating scraps and refuse, hiding in an abandoned house, waiting for Jakum to charge her, punish her. But there must have been some trace of a conscience in the man, for he dropped it flat, like it never happened, like he'd never done anything wrong.

That was when Eliphaz found her. He was just as forsaken as she, but offered the ultimate solution—the elixir of forgetfulness. He wooed her into his wanton world with boisterous revelries and raucous laughter and lots and lots of wine. Why hadn't anyone told her wine could dull pain away most miraculously? You had to keep it up, of course. More and more was required to remedy exponentially expanding heartache.

She really had been fond of Eliphaz: his twinkling eyes and jovial smile. He showed her how to laugh off anything that even hinted of substance or significance; how to live on the edge; how to tempt fate. She *probably married him or at least he said she did. She couldn't remember whether it was true or not. She was so far out on that ledge.*

What she never forgot was his rage the night he found her drunkenly wrapped in the arms of his cousin, Mizzah. Eliphaz actually looked betrayed when he ripped her arm out of its socket pulling her half-dressed body off of his startled cousin. She knew their coupling was just a harmless dalliance, a drunken tryst—something Eliphaz engaged in often himself. Obviously there was a limit to his imperviousness. She should have known his idea of disloyalty was inequitable.

Mizzah tried to protect her after that. He was just a boy really, closer to her age than any man she'd been with, probably kinder too. He was like a puppy infatuated with a neighbor's bigger, meaner dog. No matter how many times she spurned him or hurt him, he just came wagging back for more. Ironic, isn't it? Finally someone acted like he actually loved her and she was so filled with spite she couldn't even respond. He'd insisted they marry out of some kind of disturbed fantasy that played in his head. It wasn't love, though. No one could love the unlovable. She was a loathsome creature, forever and entirely unworthy of love. That's why her mother left her, after all. He should, too.

And that's why she had to get rid of the baby growing inside of her when she discovered she was pregnant a few months later. She had to kill off any life that needed love, any hint of need or innocence, any remembrance of purity. The only midwife who would comply with her demand was as bent on murder as she was. That gnarled old woman slunk into her room, reeking of rotting meat and slaughtered the life out her.

When Mizzah got home and found her hemorrhaging, she laughed deliriously, demanding he leave her alone. When that didn't work, she went for his juggler, insisting her hate for him had killed the baby. Prior assaults had glanced off of him, but that one struck its target, killing the life in him as surely as she'd done to herself. It didn't take long for him to die. Death by broken heart usually takes longer, but he could no longer bear the life he'd saved.

She'd given up after that. Given up everything, really—trying to make it, trying not to, trying to forget. Conscious that she deserved all the agonizing, unremitting pain that the universe could deliver, she wanted nothing to hinder it. She wanted it to burn holes in her soul, knowing death would be too light a sentence. For years she let it rule, plaguing her like a constant shadow.

She spoke to few people through the following years. Like a dry husk, she withered into a non-being, although from the outside, she looked alive. She'd found a calling of sort, tending to pregnant women. That was her penance, she'd decided. She had to suffer again and again through every birth she attended, torturing her conscience with what she'd done. No one knew her brutality from her silent competence and the delicate care she offered babies and their mothers. Her skills were actually quite sought after, even if none of the mothers or village women would acknowledge her later out in public. But that's the way it should be for non-beings. She deserved worse than that.

That's why Omar's affection kind of snuck up on her. He was just a neighbor, who'd lost his wife during the birth of their daughter years before, who occasionally took care of things for her around the room she rented. He admired her skills, wishing they'd been available for his wife. Initially, he just wanted to make life easier for her so that she could take care of other mothers. But he'd grown fond of her and eventually talked her into moving into his house even though she adamantly refused to marry him. There was some deep dark hole inside of her, he could tell, that he knew not to touch. She was kind to him, generous. Sometimes she felt that he tended to her like she cared for pregnant mothers. Omar would make someone a wonderful husband.

And that last thought brought her thundering back to this stranger's comment. Come back with her husband? She didn't know how long she'd paused, but the fight left her. It was as if some gentle breeze had descended over her removing her from battle, so she simply responded, "I have no husband."

"You are right to say you have no husband," he said softly. "The fact is, you've had five husbands, and the man you now live with is not your husband. What you have just said is quite true."

The earth shifted on its axis. The universe shed its deceit. On the far horizon, the sky began to lighten to a delicate pink, as if the sun might dawn.

Jesus, the humble servant, waits to heal the Samaritan woman until she is ready, until she gives her permission. He then begins the exceedingly difficult job of showing her the extent of his love. He loves her too much, too completely, to leave her in her pain and guilt. Jesus is the master of ministering to deep and elusive sin and allows us to witness him at his craft. The antithesis of violence is explored within the seventh lesson in Disciple School: *loving unconditionally*. How Christ Kitchen attempts this hallowed sacrament is presented to serve as an example.

Restoring Gently

Ministering to sin is tough. It's easier to condemn it, punish it, regulate it, legislate against it, control it, or kill it. To do as Scripture directs in Galatians 6:1, to restore the sinner gently, is much, much harder. I love the sound of that Galatians verse if the sinner is me. I will readily point it out to all critics. If the sin is another's, I need help if I am guilty of the same.

We can get all worked up about someone else's sin. Recall David's outrage when Nathan told him the story of the rich man who takes a poor man's only lamb for his dinner instead of taking one from his own vast flock. "The man who did this deserves to die,"[1] David says indignantly, not recognizing his similar guilt with Bathsheba. We need, as Eugene Peterson says, to get around our third-person defenses and compel a second-person recognition, which enables a first person response.[2] Ministering to another's sin is an art, because it entails recognizing and dealing with our own.

Only after we have wrestled with our own sin, can we rejoice in the restoration Paul speaks of in Galatians. *Restore* in Greek means *to set* broken bones or *to mend* fishing nets. This is the ministry of reconciliation that God commits to us because we have been reconciled to him. How do we embark on this ministry? How do we mend unbearable hurt and attend to debilitating sin? To get a handle on it, let's observe how Jesus attended to the woman at the well.

The first thing we notice in Jesus' restoration work with the Samaritan woman is his approach to conviction of sin. "Call your husband and come back," he says simply and directly. It is remarkable what Jesus does *not* do. He does not condemn (*you are a sinner unworthy of my water*), withhold (*you can't have this water until*), bargain (*if you just admit*), or coax (*come on, just do it*). He simply brings up the subject of her greatest pain, her obvious need, her sin.

Jesus is "ministering the Law" to the Samaritan woman. The ministry of the Law applies texts that convict us of our sin. This is different than the ministry of the gospel, which applies texts that offer forgiveness of sin.[3] Both are needed to be truly free. Our Samaritan woman isn't quite ready for the gospel of grace, the free gift of living water. She hasn't come face to face with her need for it. In order to move her to that point, Jesus broaches the subject in one concise sentence: Go get your husband.

In polite society we rarely do this. We are taught through furrowed brows and slight shakes of the head not to bring up transgressions. Oh, we talk about another's sin, but rarely to the sinner, only back home behind closed doors. I am convinced we do this by omission rather than commission. We don't know how to confront well, so we just don't do it at all. But Jesus shows us how to do it well. No drama, no yelling, no anger. Simply saying the facts, bringing up the subject with the intent to restore, is enough.

I admire my husband's ability to confront compassionately. A few years ago, his cousin, whom he hadn't seen in years, came to visit and arrived with a huge black, swollen eye. Rather than ignore the obvious, he asked how he'd gotten it. The answer—something vague about running into a door—didn't dissuade him. "What's this door's name and why were you fighting?" Within minutes of reuniting, his cousin poured out a story about lost jobs, late nights, and lots of beer.

I marvel at how my husband showed his cousin how much he loved him by attending to him bruises and all. Many of us might comment on a black eye, but would have taken the remark about the door as code for not discussing it further. Sadly, most of us comply wordlessly to subtle hints.

A friend of mine came over for dinner and it became quickly obvious that she was drunk, and obnoxiously so. The next time I saw her she apologized for "having had a little bit too much to drink." I threw my arm around her and said, "Girlfriend, you have got to stop drinking. Let's look into treatment, I'll help you." She burst into tears for a few minutes, but then quickly dried her eyes and said that she had it under control. "Call me any time you want to talk," I offered. I haven't yet heard from her. She must not be ready.

It takes courage to minister to guilt and pain. It would be helpful if there were a script or a specific plan that we could follow. But usually, these things ring our doorbells and come to our dinner parties totally unannounced. To restore each other gently, we must mimic Jesus. He learned from his Father. We are told: "He could do nothing by himself, but could only do what he sees his Father doing." How exactly did he see what his Father was doing? "Very early in the morning, before it was light, Jesus got up, left the house, and went off to a solitary place where he prayed." We are assured: "I will lead the blind by ways they have not known, along unfamiliar paths I will guide them; I will turn darkness into light before them and make the rough places smooth."[4] "Morning by morning, he awakens my ear to listen as one being taught."[5] We are taught how to minister in the unknown when we present ourselves for instruction, one prayer at a time.

How did Jesus' gentle start to restoration go over with the Samaritan woman? We get a clue in her response, "I have no husband." Okay, not bad. She doesn't lie, get offended, or run away. She doesn't act surprised by his pointed request to meet her husband, she just states the facts—she is not married. What an artful dodger she is, a clever practitioner of the slight of hand. She reminds me of the many women at Christ Kitchen who introduce me to the man they are living with as their "fiancée." It just sounds better, less sinful, to say they're going to get married, whether they intend to or not. Peterson says that sin isn't essentially a moral term, designating items of wrongdoing; it's a spiritual term, designating our God-avoidance and our god-pretensions.[6] "Fiancée" avoids both God and disapproval.

It is remarkable what Jesus does next. He says, "You are right when you say you have no husband. The fact is, you have had five husbands and the one you have now is not your husband. What you have just said is quite true." He braces his most piercing remark within praises. "You are right" and "You have spoken truth," stand like towers holding up a bridge. She is bracketed on both sides of exposure, like the angel of God and the pillar of cloud that supported the Israelites fleeing Egypt. He strikes deep, while holding her up on both sides with compliments. He is the Master of speaking truth in love.

At Christ Kitchen, we bracket tough love with nurture and support. The very fact that we hire women with felonies, mental illness, disabilities, and spotty job histories braces them from the moment they walk in the door. They create community with friends from their past, other parolees, struggling single-moms, and kindred spirits. Overtime they become stable as we train them with marketable skills that eventually will supply local businesses with retooled, transformed, industrious employees. The end goal buttresses their efforts. In between those struts lies discipleship—personalized mentoring, prayerful support, clear accountability, high expectations and tough love.

Terri's story is a good example. Terri came dragging into the Kitchen fifteen days clean after eleven years of running hard, selling drugs, three marriages and four kids. She had lost custody of all of her kids, but was in a new relationship with Roy, who she described as "hot." She fell in love with Jesus and was committed to turning her life around. One morning before work, I found her intently reading her Bible and asked what she was up to. "I'm trying to find where it says it's okay to have sex before marriage. I know it's in here somewhere."

"Hmmm. . ." I said considering how to respond. "Well, keep look-ing," I encouraged her. I could have huffed, "Good luck with that." I could have told her she wouldn't find any such Scripture. I could have pointed her to all the verses on purity. I knew, however, that Terri was very bright and I realized that she was on a mission, with a come-to-Jesus meeting on her horizon. She had my support on one end and the Bible on the other. Truth was to be found in between.

That evening, Terri called me somewhat miffed. "I only found verses that say sex is okay within marriage."

"Uh huh," I said. This is my fallback line learned from years of raising teenagers. "Hmmm" or "Uh huh" are lifesaver lines that assure I'm listening, I'm interested in what you have to say, you have no idea what I'm thinking and I'm open to hearing more. This is very hard to do and takes a great deal of practice.

"Soooo . . . I guess this means I can't have sex anymore with Roy," she said. I could just see the grimace on her face, expecting condemnation.

But I am trying to mimic Jesus so all I say is, "Wow," hoping my victory dance couldn't be heard through the phone line. "How do you think that's going to go over with him?"

"Well he probably won't like it, but I think he'll be okay with it." She's always been so idealistic.

"You might want to get ready for a stronger reaction from him. He might say that's fine, but find another girlfriend. . . like next week."

"Oh, he's committed to me. I don't expect him to do that."

It took two weeks for Roy to leave her and six weeks for her to discover she was pregnant. She desperately needed support all around her after that. Deep, abiding faith developed in the course of this experience that I could never have taught her. She had a meeting at the well with Jesus and he showed her exactly which way to go.

A key Scriptural passage for this work is 2 Timothy 4:2: Preach the Word; be prepared in season and out of season; correct, rebuke, and encourage—with great patience and careful instruction. Notice how correction and admonition are cushioned between the Word and patient instruction. It takes a lot of hard work, much study and prayer to be prepared and equipped to deal with dilemmas like Terri's and other events that occur every day.

Here are some examples. To employees locked in conflict, we refer to Matthew's means of reconciling (18:15). To a donor unhappy with the political leanings of a volunteer, we studied disputable matters (Romans 14:1). To an employee sabotaging the new organizational plan, we talked about making every effort to do what leads to peace and to mutual edification (Romans 14:19). That didn't work as well as appealing to her position as an older woman whose job it is to train younger women (Titus 2:4). Being a good steward of money was the Scriptural precedent I relied on when an employee's husband asked to borrow $5,000. That is what "preaching the Word" entails around Christ Kitchen. It is a relevant, spontaneous application of godly thought to each situation.

I want to grow to the point where I view every conversation as an act of reconciliation. This church-y word, often quoted in complex theological discussions, was displayed in all its simplicity and beauty recently in a conversation I had with Ronda. She had been accused of stealing by another employee, but vehemently denied it. Not knowing what to believe, I sent her home to pray about what to do. "You need to deal with God about this," I told her without much hope that she would.

I wasn't optimistic because over the past fifteen years not one of our employees has ever admitted to stealing, even when the evidence was clear and right in front of us. I was discouraged because Ronda is a great worker and I'd hate to lose her. I prayed all weekend that she would know that forgiveness was available. I prayed God would intervene. "Please, please, please, do something, Lord! Show her what to do, how to come back; show her how Truth offers freedom."

She didn't call on Tuesday when we'd arranged to talk. My worst fears played havoc with prayer. Had she conceded to discouragement, old habits and beliefs? Would this deride her newfound stability and sobriety? Oh! I can get morose thinking I know the future.

Wednesday morning she called. "I've been reading my Bible," she said, "all weekend actually. I wasn't ready to call you yesterday; I had to keep reading. A chaplain friend told me to find verses that would help me. So I've been reading about being a thief. Did you know there's a lot of verses about that? And, well, I don't want to be one. There's this verse in Ephesians that says if you used to steal, don't do it anymore but work and do something useful. And that's what I want to do, Jan. I want you to respect me. I love Christ Kitchen and I want to work there. Do you forgive me?"

Ah, sweet Jesus. Reconciliation simply means making peace with God when all the barriers are removed. God accomplishes this when he sheds his grace on us, the fallen, the oh-so-messed-up, the discouraged. It's an invitation to accept God's astounding provision in exchange for our dismal attitudes, bleak perspectives and deadly habits. Ronda, my rookie theologian, spoke hope right over the phone line to my discouraged heart. She joyfully revealed God's mighty power to change the world one soul at a time.

A common thread within the stories I've used as examples is that we have no idea how God will work. We pray, we hope, we encourage, but we don't know how it's going to turn out. Jesus, on the other hand, knew everything about the Samaritan woman he just met at the well. She can count herself among the many people in the Gospels about whom Jesus *knew* everything. Jesus knew the hypocrites' evil intent, the Pharisees lack of love, the crowd's desire to make him king, and the disciples' quest for greatness. Jesus knew his disciples' confusion, their desire to ask him questions, which of them did not believe in him and who was going to betray him. Jesus knows our deeds, hard work, perseverance, poverty and tribulation. He knows the intention of our hearts, our thoughts before they come into our heads. And he died for us anyway.

It is a great relief to me that I have no such ability, that I am dependent on Christ to know another's intent. I want to be content to rely on his ability alone to heal wounds and deal with sin. I rely on the verse, "He himself bore our sins in his body on the tree, so that we might die to sins and live for righteousness; by his wounds you have been healed."[7] Both sins and wounds are covered by his radical grace. My part is to stand firm in that truth with those who aren't so sure. Oswald Chambers says, "Until others learn to draw on the life of the Lord Jesus directly, they will have to draw on His life through you. You must literally be their source of supply, until they learn to take their nourishment from God."[8]

Love One Another

To stand firm, to support others while they learn great lessons, requires unconditional love. The seventh lesson in Jesus' School of Discipleship, *loving unconditionally*, is the scaffolding around discipleship. Jesus loved his disciples with a radical love and commanded them to love one another. The phrase "love one another" is quoted twenty-six times in the New Testament.[9] It is a *new* command, Jesus tells his disciples in John 13:34: "Love one another. As I have loved you, so you must love one another." Richards calls these "familiar yet strange words."[10] Love is nothing new; the Old Testament speaks often of love and commands, "love your neighbor."[11]

But love of neighbor in the Old Testament becomes, "love one another as you love yourself" in the New Testament. Later, in John's gospel, Jesus tells the disciples to love one another "as I have loved you"— love with a love that sacrifices self, that puts sister, brother, neighbor before one's own well being. This command is new (*kainen*), meaning "that which is unaccustomed or unused, not new in time or different, but fresh."[12] When the saints move into an impoverished neighborhood and begin thriving ministries in the inner city,[13] love begins to have a fresh, new impact on the world. When a pastor leaves the pulpit and starts ministering to the much neglected restaurant community,[14] love begins. When the saints begin walking the downtown streets looking to befriend homeless teenagers,[15] the impact begins to change lives one at a time. Only Jesus' living presence can explain such love.

The seventh lesson in Jesus' School of discipleship, *loving uncon-ditionally*, is a goal, a seemingly impossible moving target, a daily triumph at Christ Kitchen. To love as Jesus loves can feel overwhelming or out of reach. Who could practice such sacrificial, selfless love when it's rarely been witnessed? No wonder the Samaritan woman was baffled and suspicious when Jesus asked her for a drink. "I would have thought the guy nuts," commented one woman at the Kitchen when asked how she would have felt if she was the Samaritan woman. "I'd have thought he was selling Amway," said another.

In order to love like Jesus does, it helps to identify God-acts when they happen. It helps to tell stories about Holy Spirit cleansing and new life realities, to put words to situations of unmerited favor and to identify God as the change agent of the smallest detail. "God is good," we say when praises are shared. "Mmmm, child, He has you under His wing" the older women muse when triumphs prevail. "He'll see you through," we say when tragedy threatens. Intentional identification of God's holy work in the mundane details of life helps us recognize sacrificial love. Witnessing it in others helps us practice it ourselves.

The women at Christ Kitchen readily understand *phileo* (friendship) love and can go on for hours about *eros* (sexual) love. However, they crave learning and talking about *agape* (unmerited, selfless) love. Favorite stories recounting undeserved healing are requested over and over. They say, "Tell the one about the woman caught in adultery." "Tell the one about the blind guy at the pool." They can readily identify such love, but seem to have hazy understandings of it. Once, for example, when a volunteer brought her daughter in to decorate cookies, the catering manager, Esther, observed how gently the volunteer helped her daughter apply frosting correctly. She mused, "Well, would you look at that? That little girl is so lucky to have her mom show her stuff." Esther saw love in action and understood the intrinsic value of this small act, but she also seemed amazed by it.

With searing honesty, many women at the Kitchen will attest to the source of their confusion when they tell stories of being loved as children while also experiencing horrendous parental abuse and neglect. "It screws you up, dude," concluded one woman as she recounted her alcoholic, abusive father's declaration of love. "I think I just raised myself," said another.

There are many "one another" verses in the New Testament that teach us specifically how to love. A condensed review of them teaches us to be devoted to one another; to prefer one another; to be of the same mind; to contribute to, rejoice, weep, and be at peace with one another. We are to show forbearance, speak truth, be kind, tender-hearted and forgiving to each other. We are to teach, admonish, sing, comfort, and build each other up. We are to warn, stir up, not speak against, judge, or complain to one another; but, rather, confess, pray, and fervently love one another from the heart. Finally and always, fervently love. Learning how to love requires frequent, intentional practice.

The volunteers at Christ Kitchen are caring, warm women who have been, for the most part, loved and valued in their lives. They pass on that love when they show broad acceptance of our employees with all their shortcomings and foibles. They model Christ's love. It is common, for example, to find a volunteer spending hours working next to an employee who is having a difficult time. It is a wonder to see a volunteer come alongside a woman and offer just the right word of encouragement. Some volunteers take women to doctor's appointments or shopping and help them get appointments with specialists. Some offer free haircuts, massages, and manicures. Many share gently used clothes and house wares. They remember birthdays, clean dates, and special occasions with cards and presents. Several baby-sit for the women's children, take their children to special events, sponsor camp registrations, and make home-made baby food together. Ironically, most volunteers say that they get much more out of doing these simple acts than they could ever give. Many admit they've rarely felt so appreciated or accepted as they do by the women at Christ Kitchen. "They are kinder to me than most of my friends," admitted one. "They always seem genuinely glad to see me," said another.

Loving unconditionally takes practice, proximity, and perseverance. It is a life-long pursuit. Jesus seems to have all the time in the world for Samaritan women. We have to show up every day, model Christ's methods, and expect nothing back. We have to spend time with Jesus at the well, so that we are amply supplied for the long, circuitous journey.

The journey for our Samaritan woman has a few more twists and turns. She hasn't yet fully accepted Christ's unconditional love. She still has to go a few more rounds until her life is totally transformed.

CHAPTER TEN

Being Committed and Patient

*H*e knew! He knew it all—the men, the babies, the beatings, the unspeakable acts, the desires, the torment, and the deaths. She could see it somehow in his eyes that he recognized every act, every part of her, as if he'd actually been there when she'd committed sin after sin. She recognized that some deep, sad part of him even knew all the shameful dark deeds done to her, like he could count the lashes. Lament seeped out of his soul and seemed to cover hers.

Her eyes were drawn to his hands and then to his feet, as if the wounds of this wretched world would be written there. But she found only the rough hands of a carpenter and the dirty feet of a wayfarer. She heaved a heavy sigh as something started to break open. She pictured that little girl leaning against her mother's body, but this time it wasn't her mother; it was something stronger, something unblemished, complete.

"Sir," the woman stammered, "I can see you are a prophet," for she knew no other word to describe him. "Prophet" fell short and didn't begin to give shape to the power or authority or supremacy that exuded from this gentle stranger.

A slight breeze caught the sand at her feet and swirled it around her legs catching her attention. She looked down as the tiny grains battered her ankles, like little spears attacking her skin. As she adjusted her skirt like she'd done thousands of times to thwart the relentless sand, she shook slightly, like she was waking up from a dream. What was she thinking? How was it possible that this man was a prophet? And why, if he was, would he have anything to do with her?

All that is contrary to Spirit rose up to defend its grip on her heart.

The melee commenced. Shame and wickedness took their seats for the prosecution, introducing her evil acts, her faults and lies as evidence of unworthiness to the official masquerading as a judge. Disgrace presented her dead baby to the jury, humiliation offered her multiple husbands, and dishonor proceeded through every impure, black thought and deed she'd ever considered. There was talk at the sidebar that she deserved the father of lies, that she would be sifted like wheat.

The prince of this world pranced around her, taunting and threatening. "He's just a Jew," he sniggered in her ear. "You're even considering his words? You traitor! You know your people worshiped for centuries right here on this mountain. You dare to betray them?" he accused as hot, putrid breath slimed out of his mouth.

"Our fathers worshiped on this mountain," she mumbled, embarrassed at her feebleness, but too confused to sort it out.

"Go ahead," the accuser dared her, "you have a right to worship here. It wasn't too good for your people. Are you better than they are?"

Chaos reigned as she heard her voice accuse this perfect being . . . "but you Jews claim that the place where we must worship is Jerusalem." Am I mad, absolutely insane, she wondered? This gentle soul just wanted to give me eternal life-water and I am picking a fight with him over the right place to worship? Why do I do this—always fight, always contend? She gave up, knowing he would annihilate her now, knowing she deserved it.

Some secret thought, though, made its way through the blackness to the edge of her heart, hoping he could handle this, too.

Unconditional love takes a long time to mature. We are baffled when the Samaritan women in our own lives rebuff our efforts to help. Isn't help just what they need? We discover reasons for this resistance as we observe the Samaritan woman's adroit sidesteps to Jesus' confrontation. As she plunges into hot debate about appropriateness of worship, we recognize sophisticated, learned patterns of avoidance. The dance steps of the abused, disenfranchised poor are chaotic, but serve a definite function. Examples of detours in the lives of the women at Christ Kitchen illustrate our eighth principle in relevant discipleship: the need for *commitment and patience.*

It looks like the Samaritan woman is making progress when she perceives Jesus to be a prophet. In AD 303, Ephrem the Syrian cited her progression. "First she caught sight of a thirsty man, then a Jew, then a Rabbi, afterward a prophet, last of all the Messiah. She tried to get the better of the thirsty man, she showed her dislike of the Jew, she heckled the Rabbi, she was swept off her feet by the prophet, and she adored the Christ.[1]

Detours, Delays, and Distractions

Before he becomes her Christ, the Samaritan woman makes one more detour in their discussion. Commentators have debated her sudden and surprising shift in conversation from prophet to worship. Some commentators think the woman, having perceived Jesus to be a prophet, takes the opportunity to settle the dispute about where to worship that had raged for centuries between her people and his.[2] Others believe she is raising a theological red herring, much like some rebut Christian witness with comments about the starving children in China, Christian hypocrisy, or politics.

I think the Samaritan woman throws out the worship debate as a distraction from Jesus' ability to know her heart and anxious thoughts. Much like Nicodemus, the Pharisee who praises Jesus as a "teacher from God,"[3] she first compliments Jesus as a prophet and then tries to divert his attention away from sin toward the mountains, away from conviction toward contention. This side trip on the journey toward wholeness serves a definite function in her old battle gear, but until its surrendered, makes the process difficult and demanding.

Loving women living in poverty into health and stability takes a long time. Pastor John Perkins, a distinguished evangelical voice for racial reconciliation, leadership development, and Christian community development, believes it takes at least fifteen years.[4] I remember when I heard him say this I pumped both fists in the air and gave a great, "Thank you! Jesus!" After working at Christ Kitchen for five years, I was impatient to see significant changes in the women's lives. Some women had gotten off of drugs and alcohol, some were feeling more confident in themselves and some were establishing healthy relationships. I'd written many letters of reference, and helped women get jobs in local businesses, but too often would hear that the job hadn't worked out, or that they'd returned to addictions, jail, shelters or another bad relationship. Few had secured full time jobs or started going to church. *My* measures of success hadn't been attained and I was discouraged. So I was relieved to hear John Perkins, who'd been in the people-restoration business in inner-city Chicago for fifty years, say significant change takes a long time. If it takes fifteen years, then we were right on schedule.

I remember comparing this progress to my own daughter who was fifteen years old at the time. I estimated that if my husband and I died and she was left with nothing, she would be able to survive. She would have the where-with-all to find a safe place to live, apply for scholarships, get a good job and create a reasonable life for herself. Having been very loved and nurtured for fifteen years, she had become stable enough to make it on her own.

This capability is referred to as "linking social capital" by sociologists. It is the ability—taken for granted by the non-poor—to make connections with people and institutions that wield significant societal power, influence, or control as a source of information, guidance, referral, or support.[5] Women raised in poverty, unlike my daughter, are much less likely to have access to these kinds of seemingly incidental, but profoundly important elements of social mobility and support.[6] They also have the additional burden of dealing with years of neglect, trauma, and abuse.

So why was I frustrated at the extended time it seemed to take for a woman off the streets to become stable? I was comparing her improvement to my middle class expectations of progress and success. I was assuming she would know how to take full advantage of the love and opportunities people like me and others wanted to offer. It took a while to understand the ingrained patterns of dependence, resistance, and pain that I had not seen in my eighteen years as a therapist in private practice. I had to learn how to minister within this dance of distractions, difficulties, and dependence.

Jember Teffera, who works with desperately poor women in Ethiopia, explains that it takes a long time for those raised in conditions unfit for human beings to gain a sense of dignity. "We must work at their pace," she warns. "In our eagerness, we want to change things fast. We want to use our knowledge and power to change the poor. Donors in particular, want things fixed quickly."[7]

If we don't separate personal expectations from experience, we can lose a sense of efficacy and personal accomplishment becoming cynical and exhausted in the process. "Burn out," as many call it, happens in the mission field when our plans supersede God's. I have a friend, for example, who referred to his disappointment when projects he started in the inner city failed as "compassion fatigue." Oswald Chambers says that exhaustion is a result of being devoted to a cause, belief, or doctrine, instead of to Christ himself. He writes, "Our Lord's primary obedience was to the will of his father, not to the needs of people—the saving of people was the natural outcome of his obedience to the father."[8] Putting prayer at the top of the to-do list, when we're confronted with so much suffering, takes guts (and a total belief that God is better at this than you are).

Psychological Research

When I started Christ Kitchen, I could find nothing in the professional psychological literature on treatment strategies for issues facing the poor. The abysmal history of psychotherapy with the poor parallels that of the contemporary church. In the 1950s and 60s, psychotherapists held the belief that most poor people did not have the skills to engage the therapeutic process.[9] In the 1970s, community mental health centers opened their doors to the poor with more culturally aware interpretations of treatment difficulty, but in the 80s, psychologists' attention shifted away from psychological consequences of poverty toward biology, neurology, and genetics of mental disorders. By 2003, Moreira deplored the "medicalization of poverty," a worldwide tendency to relegate mental health treatment of the poor to hospitals and psychiatrists.[10] In 2005, Smith suggested that psychotherapists' unexamined classist assumptions constitute significant barriers to working with the poor due to the therapists' blind spots, classist stereotyping, and feeling overwhelmed by their issues.[11]

With little help from my profession, I become a student of poverty from the experts—my patients at Christ Clinic. As I listen carefully to their life stories, I learned about the consequences of poverty. The more I learned, the more passionate I became to teach them about Jesus. I also knew we needed to target the consequences of poverty directly if they were to live free of its restraints. Developing a business together seemed like a practical way to address physical, mental, emotional, and spiritual needs. Health in all four categories would be necessary if they were to learn to love the Lord with all their heart, mind, soul, and strength. Learning to love and serve the Lord would expand the scope of pragmatic, emotional, and spiritual resources for coping with the stress and adversity that I heard about daily in my therapy office.

It wasn't until later that research began appearing in the psychology literature that confirmed Christ Kitchen's approach to increasing stability of low-income women. In 2007, research into utilization of mental health services by the poor suggested low-income women had limited access to therapeutic services due to cost, difficulties with childcare and transportation, distrust, an expectation of stigma, and provider's lack of sensitivity to her socio-cultural context.[12] We tried to avoid these barriers at Christ Kitchen by creating a friendly, accommodating atmosphere in which dignity and godly self-esteem would flourish.

In 2010, relevant research conducted by Goodman, Smyth, and Banyard confirmed our experience showing that mainstream mental health interventions were not sufficient to meet the complex needs of poor women, despite the rather large body of research showing poverty strongly associated with mental health deficiencies. As an example, they cite cognitive behavioral therapy, a type of therapy based on the assumption that emotional reactions are caused by dysfunctional thoughts and attitudes. They found that this symptom-focused intervention is simply insufficient or even inappropriate to an isolated, anxious woman who may, for example, be without a safe place for her children to sleep or contending with an abusive husband.[13]

In their research, Goodman et al. found economic deprivation to be the cause of a level of hardship characterized by stress, pervasive powerlessness, social isolation, and exclusion—all powerful contributors to emotional distress and key mediators of the relationship between poverty and mental health. They concluded that emotional well being of low-income women increases with intervention strategies aimed to reduce stressors, increase control and choice, and increase the size and utility of social networks.[14]

I knew if we could create a welcoming, godly, joyous atmosphere at Christ Kitchen, women would want to come to work instead of stay home. It would get them in the door and would be enough to start them onto the road to recovery. One of our employees, looking back on the first day she came to the Kitchen said, "It felt like I stepped from chaos in to peace." We have to pray every day for the Lord to bless us with that peace, faithfulness, and kindness. Some days are better than others.

There is other research that helps explain the prolonged and convoluted healing process for low-income women. Extensive research on the biology of stress now shows that healthy development can be derailed by excessive or prolonged activation of stress response systems in the body with damaging effects on learning, behavior, and health across the lifespan. Disruptive impacts of toxic stress are clearly found to link early adversity associated with poverty, discrimination, and maltreatment to later impairments in behavior, physical and mental health.[15]

Harvard pediatrician, Jack Shonkoff, explains that early experiences are literally built into our bodies. Learning to cope with adversity is an important part of healthy child development. When threatened, our bodies prepare us to respond by increasing heart rate, blood pressure, and stress hormones such as cortisol. When a child's stress response systems are activated within an environment of supportive relationships with adults, these physiological effects are buffered and brought back down to baseline. The result is the development of a healthy stress response system. However, if the stress response is extreme and long lasting, and if buffering relationships are unavailable to the child, the result can be damaged, weakened systems, and brain architecture with lifelong repercussions.

This new research addresses an uncomfortable truth: the roots of impairment and underachievement are biologically embedded, but preventable. "You can modify behavior later, but you can't rewire disrupted brain circuits," notes Shonkoff, a leader in this field of study. "We're beginning to get a pretty compelling biological model of why kids who have experienced adversity have trouble learning." [16]

The science is still accumulating, but this convincing message from biology is that if we want to chip away at poverty and improve educational and health outcomes, we have to start early. For many children, damage has been suffered before the first day of school. As Frederick Douglass noted, "It is easier to build strong children than to repair broken men."[17]

The biological evidence convincingly coincides with strong correlations found between adverse childhood experiences and psychopathology,[18] poor health,[19] sensitivity to current life stressors,[20] and high-risk behaviors such as alcohol and drug abuse. All of these stressors have been found to negatively impact long-term labor force participation. [21]

These findings help explain episodic work histories of the women at Christ Kitchen—their lack of skills, limited work experience, limited understanding of appropriate work behaviors and the prevalence and severity of mental illness and substance abuse.[22] They suggest that solutions to poverty that focus only on job skills, training, and placement miss significant issues which render the poor population unable to participate in programs designed around work and job training. They also suggest a need for early childhood abuse prevention, intervention, and appropriate trauma treatment in order to produce future adults with abilities to maintain health and employment.

Successful Employment

The business practices of Christ Kitchen were developed with an appreciation for our particular employees in mind. We understand that in order to help women move out of poverty into stability—or even into a place in which they might take advantage of other available programs like GED training—we need to provide employment and job-training that also encourages spiritual, emotional and physical stability, healthy relationships, and citizenship. Our central tenet reflects these values. It is based on the word *resurrection,* which is used in the New Testament to mean "a rising up" or "causing to stand." Our mission statement reads: "The ministry of Christ Kitchen is founded upon the essential principles of Christ's life and seeks to aid homeless, abused, poor, or disenfranchised women in their rising up out of poverty, ultimately to stand on their own feet with the security of Christ."

We understand that low-income women initially come to Christ Kitchen for money. They don't come for freedom, for community, for training, or for Jesus. They come for cash. They've heard through friends, agencies, or social workers that we pay minimum wage and have minimal requirements (specifically, they must be clean and sober and work reasonably well with other women). Some women come to earn enough to pay off a bill, make rent money or buy medical prescriptions, diapers or cigarettes. Others admit they originally came for money to get high. We don't judge the original motivation for appearing at our door; we just want them to come in the door and welcome them as they are.

A unique feature of our business is that we pay our employees to come to Bible study. We tried everything to attract them to the discipleship well, but nothing seemed to work. Nothing attracted them to Bible study until our work program happened to include a voluntary, hour-long, once-a-week Bible study within paid hours. Paying for Bible study is as unconventional as Jesus proclaiming the gospel on Samaritan turf. The Pharisees insist its sacrilege; the disciples are wondering why, and the damaged suspect foul play. We, however, view our workplace as a well where disenfranchised women and thirsty travelers stop for a drink. Most would come unsuspecting were it not for the obvious sign over the door that says *Christ* Kitchen. We named the project purposely to presume informed consent among those who enter. Christ Kitchen is a thriving small business, a legitimate employer. We also conduct a Bible study during work hours. It's legal. It works.

Martha's story exemplifies the success of this model. Martha and her husband had been meth addicts until he blew off her thumb with a shotgun in front of their six-month-old son. Her husband went to jail and she went to treatment, eventually moving with her son into a Habitat for Humanity house around the corner from the church in which Christ Kitchen was located. Her mother read a newspaper article about Christ Kitchen and suggested Martha try it out. She later told me that she'd never stepped into a church before and was sure the roof would fall in on her if she did. When she walked in that first day and saw Bibles on the tables, she almost walked out. Too embarrassed to leave just then, she sat down, thinking she'd sneak out at the break. "But I didn't mind it too much, so I came back the next week," she said. The more she listened, the more intrigued she became with the message.

Martha would have never stepped foot inside a church because she was sure she was absolutely unfit to attend. Because our Bible study was voluntary and paid, she tried it out. Slowly, she settled in. "I just tied knots in raffia in a corner for four months," she recalls. "I'd been so messed up, hurt and confused, I didn't even think I could work. But I just came every week and sat there and found I could do this simple job. Later, when Barb asked me to join the food table, I figured I could measure ingredients, so I tried that. The women on the food table actually liked me, and I started to think maybe I could work after all. We laughed and chatted and I started to feel human again." Now, nine years later, Martha is the kitchen manager supervising eight employees.

Martha's past history of childhood trauma, drug abuse, and domestic violence left her isolated and scared with a sense that she was incapable of productive work. Mainstream mental health interventions were insufficient to meet her complex needs, but she assures me, she wouldn't have gone to "no head-shrinker" anyway. "I wasn't crazy," she says, "I just needed help and had no idea where to even start." Going to church was totally out of the question, but as she says, "Sitting through Bible study all those months, Jesus just came to me. The other women had more faith in me than I had in myself. But slowly, I got what they meant. I am a loved child of God." Through *patience and commitment* to helping her succeed, the women at Christ Kitchen loved her into a life that Jesus transformed.

All aspects of Christ Kitchen and our staff are committed to helping women like Martha encounter Christ and change their lives. Foundational to Christ Kitchen's business practices is a theology of work[23] that prioritizes dependence on God, service to others, and self-sufficiency. Its model for business has at its core respect, responsibility, and accountability. Christ Kitchen has attempted to create a workplace where every employee feels needed, valued, and capable of upholding the model. Input, suggestions, and corrections from all participants are encouraged and requested formally through evaluations and informally through conversations and periodic employee meetings. Our motto—"At the foot of the cross, the ground is level"—communicates the Christ Kitchen commitment to rectify power imbalances within arbitrary class, race, and socioeconomic divisions. Because our employees come with a vast range of experience in areas of dependence and dominance, we intentionally orchestrated the design of the workplace and practices to encourage physical, emotional, and spiritual health and balance. We understand that developing praiseworthy business practices on every level of the organization creatively transforms each individual as well as the community.

Hiring practices, personnel decisions, and job-training procedures take into account unique factors inherent in the lives of low-income women. Lack of confidence, self-worth, and training often inhibit them, especially those with backgrounds of abuse, addiction or criminal history, from seeking employment or utilizing employment placement agencies. Many are not only unemployed, but also feel unemployable. Disabilities, age, handicaps, injuries related to violence, emotional and physical disorders, and mental illness often discourage other employers from hiring them. Christ Kitchen is unique in that it recognizes the myriad of issues that hinder women living in poverty from achieving self-sufficiency, and offers an individualized work setting in which any willing woman can gain skills in competence, self-image, and productivity.

We also take into account complications from relationships, financial aid, and unhealthy work environments that have been deleterious to our employees' successful employment in the past. An example would be their tendency to base personal and work-related decisions on issues concerning personal relationships instead of job security. Unlike women in the middle and upper classes, who tend to prioritize self-sufficiency, personal identity, and achievement,[24] low-income women tend to leave jobs when they encounter conflict, family emergencies or relationships. Unlike their more educated sisters, who base decisions on career aspirations, lifestyle, and financial obligations, decisions to terminate employment are rarely completely thought through and are often detrimental to their long-term well-being. A common example would be a woman moving out of a stable living situation to live with a man who promises love, rent, and care, only to find herself within a few weeks penniless, jobless, battered, homeless, and/or back on drugs. Abruptly and angrily leaving work after confrontations or misunderstandings is another common occurrence. Group support, friendships with women, testimonies of others, mentoring, and Bible study help women make better decisions, practice new behaviors, and satisfy their need for healthy relationships.

Successful employment for this population is also hindered by the lack of healthy work settings. Many have a desire to return to work but find the atmosphere of minimum wage jobs emotionally draining and devastating, if not dangerous. They describe abruptly quitting jobs due to sexual harassment, petulant bosses, and fractious interactions. Some secure jobs on graveyard shifts in high crime areas in high-risk settings because they are readily hired, work while their children sleep, or live close by.

The emotional toll of such work can have deleterious effects. A woman named Maureen, for example, suffered a mental breakdown after being robbed for a third time at her job at a convenience store. No longer able to care for her four-year-old and six-year-old grandchildren, they had to return to their drug-addicted mother, but were later removed to foster care when found unattended in a grocery store at four in the morning. Maureen, like many single parents and grandparents in poverty, was the sole emotional and financial support of the family and was totally overwhelmed by circumstantial events out of her control. Another woman, Ivy, was fired after missing only one work shift because her twenty-four-year-old daughter, who was in the terminal stages of Lupus, needed her help after surgeons removed the wrong tear duct from her one-year-old granddaughter's eye.

The emotional sacrifice of leaving children, friends, and family to make minimum wage becomes an overwhelming sacrifice. It is understandable how governmental aid becomes an attractive alternative because it offers dollars *and* time to care for significant relationships. Even an unhealthy relationship with a man who has an income source can seem desirable when it is compared to the risk of losing one's family to neighborhood crime, illness, or poor decisions.

Christ Kitchen woos women to work by offering a nurturing,

healthy, caring environment in which women earn money *and* meet relational needs. It provides a community within which women can grow, learn, give, be held accountable and receive support. Our commitment to patience to walk together with our employees over the long term is integral to every aspect of employee relations, policies, and practices.

It's not too hard to imagine why the Samaritan woman attempts to distract Jesus away from her past, its complications and hopelessness. Fear of the unknown can feel more paralyzing than being stuck in old habits and behaviors. Jesus is about to change all that. "A time is coming . . ." he assures her, when the way out is revealed.

CHAPTER ELEVEN

True Worship

"**W**oman," he said, in a way no man had ever done before. It drew her attention as she searched for hidden notes of condescension, lechery or regret but found nothing she expected. She could only sense her own shame from her last comments reflecting back to her in disgrace. She wondered what it was in her that was so drawn to him yet resisted him so vehemently.

"Believe me," he continued, "a time is coming when you will worship the Father neither on this mountain nor in Jerusalem. You Samaritans worship what you do not know; we worship what we do know for salvation is from the Jews."

She listened intently. He spoke to her like he would a friend or colleague, like she had value. His tone was cordial, but under no circumstances did she presume he exaggerated or spoke falsely. On the contrary, she knew in the depth of her being that he spoke truth. Clearly his words were not up for debate; he spoke as one who knew times and mountains and salvation.

All of her pretense fell away. Her habit in discussion to dispute, defeat or cajole vanished. There was no discussion here. She understood implicitly that she had no knowledge of the mysteries unfolding in his words, that she, the most inferior student, was in the presence of a master. It was true what he said that she, a Samaritan, had never worshiped, not the way his whole being made use of the word. Adoration, reverence, praise was due his Father. Nothing less. She had never known such veneration. She could not imagine the authority and power with which he predicted her forthcoming worship of the Father. She fell *silent, attentive, mesmerized. She felt whole in his presence, tranquil, full; ready to accept his words as her own. "Who is this man?" she pondered, waiting for it to be revealed.*

"A time is coming," he went on, "Indeed it's happening right now, when the true worshipers will worship the Father in spirit and truth, for they are the kind of worshipers the Father seeks."

All she could think of was that she wanted to be one of those worshipers. Every fiber in her longed to be one, a true worshiper, in whom there was nothing false, only pure spirit and truth. If the time he referred to has not yet come, perhaps she could become one. If it's happening right now, she suspected it had everything to do with this man and his father. She yearned for a father, but the kind this man spoke of could not be from this world. Just imagine: a father who knew what was true. Her eyes lifted to the heavens. This Father is seeking her. She was certain of it.

"God is spirit," he said knowing her thoughts, "and his worshipers must worship in spirit and truth."

Truth was what she had sought all her life, but it was a tawdry thing in the hands of humans. Within the context of worshiping this seeking-God, however, it is precious. Somehow this man, his father, and spirit must enable such adoration. It was right at her fingertips, she could feel it. She longed for it like nothing else in her life. There was no point to life without it. She had changed in an instant; there was no going back.

But how could she say any of this in a way the man would understand? She searched for words to relate. A thought formed in the back of her mind that had been there since she was a small girl. She remembered it from times her Baba and Uma took her to the temple on Mt. Gerizim. "Messiah is coming," the priest had said over and over again. Messiah. She mulled the word over and somehow it seemed to fit, like a last piece in a complicated puzzle.

Tentatively, she said, almost too low to be heard, as if to herself, "I know that Messiah is coming. When he comes, he will explain everything to us." She searched her memory, sure that that is what her people believed. She must have heard it often, though no specific occasion

came to mind, because the sentences rolled off her tongue in a practiced
sort of way.

Then the man declared, "I am He."

As Jesus unveils the way of salvation, the Samaritan woman's
heart moves upward to faith in the living truth, as the first "I Am"
in the Gospel is granted her. Lessons learned within the School of
Discipleship at Christ Kitchen confirm that as the dispossessed and
dispirited find their Lord, they become stable, they begin to feel loved,
and their ability to learn and change blossoms.

Sweet, sweet Jesus. Recognizing the Samaritan woman's artful dodge from prophet to contesting the correct place to worship,
he could have dragged her back to reality, to her sin, her five husbands. "We aren't done here," he could have said with wagging finger.
"Where you worship really isn't the point right now," he could have
corrected her. "Mountains are not the issue," he could have insisted.
But no, Jesus directs her to what is most important. He explains the
completeness of Father, Son, and Holy Spirit. He shows her the ninth
lesson in discipleship: *true worship.*

It is critical when visiting the foreign country of American poverty to concentrate on what is most important. We can get very distracted by historical or doctrinal mountains or by lesser things like
what you look like, what you eat, if you go to church, or what to wear
when you get there. There is much to distract us when we're new to a
culture. Carol, a first time volunteer, for example, couldn't get over the
fact that so many employees at Christ Kitchen were overweight. Carol
had been raised in an upper middle class home and had never ventured into the poorer parts of town. So she was stunned by the stark
differences in body weights between the women she worked out with
at the Spokane Club and the women who worked at Christ Kitchen.
"For some reason," she admitted candidly, "I thought they'd be mal-
nourished and starving, not obese." Carol was distracted by an image
of what she assumed a poor person would look like. I explained how

the poor often shop at neighborhood convenience stores and eat high caloric, high fat food in order to feel full. "I guess when I'm depressed I eat a lot of unhealthy things also," she said with growing understanding. From that day on, Carol brought a healthy well-balanced lunch once a month for all the women.

Other details distract volunteers. One day when I was handing out paychecks, an employee named Trish exclaimed that she couldn't wait to cash her paycheck so that she could get her nails painted green for St. Patrick's Day. Hearing this, two older volunteers asked me privately if I might suggest to Trish not to waste her money. I understood their concern, but said, "I'm just really glad she's not using it for beer." I explained how we try to celebrate the baby steps women make toward wholeness. "Well," one of them said, "I guess I shouldn't expect her to start an IRA with her $23 paycheck." I suggested the volunteers take Trish out for coffee and get to know her a little better. Before long, they'd made a regular weekly coffee date with Trish.

When we're committed to loving others like Jesus did, we find ways to set aside disputable matters in favor of more important ones, at least for the time being. This is not easy because details catch our attention and drag us into their silly world. Differences seem magnified when we're new to a foreign culture. Focusing on what is vitally important instead of the obvious takes practice, patience and prayer. Watch how Jesus moves the Samaritan woman from mountains to true worship.

"Ah woman," Jesus says in effect, "it is not mountains that make worship authentic. Very soon, worship will be changed forever. God is a seeking God. He is looking for those who honor his Son and his Spirit." He is throwing heavy Trinitarian theology at this most unlikely student—an outcast, a Samaritan, a woman. He picks her of all people in John's gospel to be shown the doctrine of the Trinity. Their conversation is not for the slight of heart as Jesus explains how the Spirit goes down deep into human hearts, moves us upward to faith in the living truth, and then brings us spiritually to the heart's

true goal: to God the Father.[1] This is the purpose of his seeking—
to free us from the bonds of details, doctrines, and differences—and
allow us to recognize his infinite value. When we do, we fall down at
his feet and worship.

What a promise! God is looking for worshippers and all he asks
is that we turn our hearts toward him and come to him without pretense. "Come as you are," he beckons, "no need to hide your flaws." The
Samaritan woman knows the truth about herself and has just discovered that Jesus knows every bit of it also. He loves her anyway; he *still*
seeks her. God waits for her to turn her heart toward heaven. That's it.

"Ah, woman," I hear my Christ say when our women go out to the
alley to smoke or when one jumps on a motorcycle without a helmet,
"keep your eyes on me. Show them the extent of my love," he tells me
when one stays out all night at the casino or another goes back to the
man with a terrible temper. "I am the only way, the very truth, the
ultimate light. They will find me when they seek me with all their
heart. Teach them my precepts and the right way to live. My Spirit is
at work." I must work alongside my seeking Father waiting for them
to *become* willing to be found.

Waiting on maturity may be the hardest thing we do. Nadia, for
example, worked for us through a Work First project that paid for
her schooling in return for internship hours at the Kitchen. She was
twenty-two years old with five children, had gotten clean and fled her
last husband and old lifestyle. Everyone commented on what a great
worker she was. She started going to church with some of the women
and beamed the day she gave her life to the Lord and was baptized.
One day, in what seemed to me a casual chat, she told me she was concerned that the Spirit had left her, because she didn't feel guilty when
she had sex last night with her neighbor.

"Hmmm . . . " I said, looking at her directly, trying to keep the *are
you kidding me?* look off my face. These kinds of bombshell declarations always concern me, but I'm trying to be like Jesus, so I'm trying
to stick with her and not put her off by my reaction. I'm working on

the calm "you've-had-five-husbands-and-the-one-you're-living-with-is-not-your-husband," type of Jesus remark instead of the smack-my-palm-to-my-forehead *you did what??!!* type of reaction that seems much more satisfying.

"Yeah," she goes on as if I really want to know more about this, "before I felt guilty and that made me stop. But the guilt never came last night, so I just went ahead with it. Does that mean I lost the spirit?" I am instantly concerned about baby number six, about vene-real disease, about her girls waking up to find a strange man in their apartment. She, however, is wondering why guilt or a spirit didn't stop her. Like the Samaritan woman, she gets the prophet part of Jesus, but is still worshipping what she does not know. She is at a precipice and I recognize its significance. "You cannot lose the Holy Spirit," I say, "but you can grieve him. I don't think that's the issue, though, Nadia. Satan is going to throw everything he's got at you to destroy your life. If feeling guilty worked the first time, then he's going to make sure it doesn't the next. Guilt is not what will keep you safe, God is. He is faithful and will never let you down, will never let you be pushed past your limit. He will actually provide the way out of these situations. The real question to consider is if you will trust him to do that, to take care of you, your needs, your loneliness, your desires? He is able to do immeasurably more than you can imagine." We prayed that Christ would strengthen her heart to rely on him entirely.

"Were you using birth control?" I added. I couldn't help myself.

Surrender

I must remember that I am not in this enterprise alone. All three members of the Trinity are at work actively seeking and creating true worshipers. My job is to clear my distractions, trust him, obey what I hear, and focus on what is most important in the mission field he has placed right in front of me. His job is to save the world.

Surrendering to God's way takes practice. In a Bible series on the fruit of the Spirit, we had just studied the subject of self-control, when

Margaret got a chance to practice it. She got a call from her son's elementary school requesting she take her son home for fighting on the playground. Margaret started slamming the mop around the floor in furious strokes like it had never been cleaned before. "What are you doing?" I asked, thinking she should get over to the school.

"I am trying have some f!!zlx*g! self-control before I go kill someone!" she said, in all seriousness. Well, I burst out laughing in that kind of way you can't stop, when your eyes tear up and you double over in fits. It was the funniest thing I think I'd ever heard. She looked at me like I was the one she was going to kill, which made me laugh even harder. Finally, she started smiling, her shoulders relaxed, and she, too, started laughing and crying alternately. I hugged her for a long time and praised her and prayed for her little boy and the peace that transcends understanding to cover her trip to the principal's office. The next day she said the school secretary complimented her on how well she handled the interaction.

To the willing he is faithful. From the moment we seek to find him, our prayers are heard and he comes in response to them.[2] It isn't always pretty, but it's perfect.

The Samaritan woman is almost there. She's been impertinent, insulting, incredulous, and insistent. She's tried to ignore him, sparred with him, done her thing, strutted her stuff, all to no avail. Truth is dawning. Spirit is drawing. Finally, she is astounded. She searches for the concept, for the words that might fit this apprehension. The word appears on the periphery of her awareness and she considers it, cautiously—Messiah!

Sychar Sunday School, catechism's lessons and confirmation's instructions pay off! The saying, "Messiah is coming," which she learned to repeat on demand as a child and mindlessly acknowledged as a teen, now, magnificently takes on bodily form and is standing right in front of her, staring her in the face.

"I am HE."

"Yes!" we can just hear her Spirit say in response to his Holy one.

Fireworks! All the angels in heaven who have been bending their ear awaiting that yes! explode in joy, pumping their fists and high-fiving each other. The heavens rejoice! The hallelujah chorus resounds from the great company of heavenly hosts. "Glory to God in the highest and on earth peace to this woman on whom his favor rests!"

But we can't quite wipe the sweat from our brow and brush the crumbs off our aprons like good Jewish grandmas, saying, "Oy vey. Finally. Finally she comes. Now we can get back to making dinner." There's more work to do, for the disciples are returning and they missed the hallelujah chorus. They need help.

CHAPTER TWELVE

Being Honest

A grand, triumphant "Yes!" escaped her. The long awaited One, the One prayed about and hoped for and dreamed of by all peoples for all time is here. Like a subtle shift in the cosmos, everything found its place. Deep abiding love, tender and pure, washed through her. Fear and condemnation fled. In their place, an inexplicable peace remained, a perfect peace.

Joy filled his face and flooded onto hers. She knew he understood what had occurred and that he was its author. There was no doubt or ambiguity about worshiping in spirit and truth. Her whole being took to it like it was the most natural thing in the world. Her spirit joined the chorus of angels rejoicing with the Father that she was now found.

Ah, so this is living water. The consuming dread she'd carried ever since she could remember was gone. Her countenance lightened and her shoulders relaxed. She no longer carried the weight of the world, he did. A divine transfer had taken place. Without a word between them, she understood this was his intent all along—life without thirst. The spring was welling up and ready to overflow.

His eyes moved just past hers as she heard voices behind her. She did not want this moment to ever end but the sound drew closer. He refocused on her, smiling, knowing what she was now preparing to do. She understood and smiled back.

The chattering disciples crested the hill. She could tell by the silence that passed from one to the other as they each realized she was talking with Messiah that they were amazed. "Not more than me," she could have told them with a laugh, a new laugh filled with assurance. She

*turned to look at them and noted that her usual defiance she would
have enlisted for defense a few moments ago was unneeded. None of
them asked what she wanted or what she was doing. They seemed too
surprised for the thought to have occurred.*

*She turned back and looked at her Messiah. His gentle eyes seemed
to say, "See? I am your rock. I will guard your heart. No need to worry or
be afraid." She understood. She had power now to stand firm, to not get
tossed about. The living water covered everything she would ever need.*

*The wellspring began to overflow. Her people had to meet him.
His disciples brought him food and he might be leaving soon. Urgency
gripped her. She should hurry to town and tell them about him. They
must come see him before he leaves. She gathered her skirt ready to
leave and glanced at him one last time. He gave a slight nod as if he
approved of her plan.*

It's a moment of high drama in our story. We can hardly wait to
hear the Samaritan woman's response to Jesus' rare declaration that
he is the Messiah. Just when the dramatic tension is at its height, just
when she is poised to react, the scene cuts to—what?—the disciples
returning from the market? We were just high five-ing with angels,
soaring on an evangelical high, and then our attention is directed to
baffled, dusty disciples who've no idea what's going on. What an anti-
climax. Critics would pan the film right about now. "Hmmm . . . a
little too close to home," hints our disappointed conscience, "because
I'm a little baffled myself." We can't just leave the Samaritan woman
without knowing what she does with the invitation. No, no. If I were
directing this film, I would tie up all the loose ends before changing
plot lines. She would say something like; "I've seen the light! I'm off to
pass out tracts in Sychar!"

But no, like it or not, the Samaritan woman fades into the background for a moment while the cameras scan to the scene of the disciples' return. We've all but forgotten about the disciples. They were
mentioned parenthetically nineteen verses ago advising us they'd

gone into town to buy food. Interesting that they are off buying food from Samaritans, people with whom they do not associate. How often the privileged find the ability to buy food from their foes, but not the other way around. Now the disciples are back and most inconveniently interrupt our celebration narrative.

Interruptions like this occur so often around Christ Kitchen. Just when a woman gets back on her feet, something happens to discourage her. She finally gets settled in an apartment and then her daughter runs off leaving her with three grandkids. She finally dedicates her life to the Lord and then discovers she's pregnant. She gets up the courage to leave her abusive husband, but can't find anyone to babysit. We get so excited and then, wham, the stagehands are on set changing the scenery.

Oh, that devil prowls like a roaring lion. "Don't be afraid, don't be discouraged," we pray and encourage in the manner of Moses, Isaiah and Elijah. Our community of women knows what it's like to experience setback after setback. We stand firm for each other, praying that faith will not fail when everything else has, lending support to get through the dark night. June, for example, had finally stopped drinking and moved into a little apartment over a restaurant downtown. She didn't mind the noise and smells because she was at peace in her own place. Four months later the building burned down and she lost everything. When her fellow employees heard the news, they gathered everything she needed to set up another apartment from their own meager supply and second-hand stores. They brought it to her that same day with a brand new Bible on top of the pile.

Interruptions seem more the norm than the exception. Just when life is about to start looking up, twelve noisy disciples arrive at your door. Can you just see the twelve of them coming up the hill toward Jesus, yakking away, fast food bags in hand? Peter is no doubt distributing orders: fries to Phillip and Bartholomew, Boanerges Burgers to the Zebedee brothers, and drinks to Matthew and Simon. Thomas is likely doubting he got the right order, Nathaniel is sure nothing good can come from Sychar, Judas is counting the change thinking they've been overcharged, and John is urging everyone to pray before digging in. Then . . . freeze action! What in the world? Jesus is not alone. He is talking to *a woman*!

"We only left him for a little while," they must be thinking. "How can he get into trouble all by himself? Has anyone seen our rabbi talking to a woman? People will talk. We've got to keep a cap on it. Any way to spin this to our advantage?" They become uncharacteristically silent. Not one of them asks why he is talking to her. They know him only too well. "Here we go again," they mutter.

They know only too well that Jesus is the master of surprise. He has been ever since he was twelve, astonishing his parents when he stayed in Jerusalem at the temple courts among the teachers of the law instead of returning to Nazareth. His startling deeds irked the Pharisees when he ate with sinners and tax collectors, didn't wash before the meal and bested them at every turn. These twelve bewildered disciples are used to his antics. They've spent months with him. They gasped when he broke social traditions, shook when he spoke truth to power, worried when his words offended, cried out when he rocked the boat. He flipped hierarchical order on its head saying things like, "Blessed are the meek," or "The first will be last and the last will be first." Try as they might to steer him away from demon-possessed lunatics, innocent children, crowds of hungry people and sinful women like this one, they can't seem to divert his attention away from outcasts and misfits. "Settle in," their eyes say to one another as they take in the view of Jewish rabbi and Samaritan woman. "We might be here a while."

Honesty

It is interesting to note the Samaritan woman's forthrightness in her conversation with Jesus compared to the disciple's reluctance here to question or challenge him. It reminds me of the refreshing candor and honesty I find among women at Christ Kitchen. They instruct me daily in our tenth lesson in discipleship: *being honest.* Compared to my reluctance to disclose weakness, they are shining examples of forthrightness.

My own hesitancy to use the word *poverty* is a case in point. Several women and I were designing the outdoor sign that stands on the street corner advertising our business. It was agreed that the Christ Kitchen logo would go on top, but I mentioned my reluctance to put our byline, "A Place of Hope for Women in Poverty," underneath. The women looked at me with blank stares. "I'm not sure we should use the word poverty," I said, not sure how to explain the discomfort I felt.

"Why?" one of them asked. "We *are* poor." I realized she was simply describing a fact in her life, one to which I had attached negative value. "Isn't that why you started this place, Jan?" What could I say? "Yes, I know you're poor but we aren't supposed to talk about it?" What kind of duplicitous nonsense is that?

Well, I'll tell you what it is. It's fear. Like the disciples, I worry about how my words will be received and fear disapproval from the women. I was as reluctant to use the word poverty, as the disciples were to ask, "Why are you talking to *that* woman?" We have a filter system, an impression management scheme, which prevents unacceptable words from escaping our mouths. The irony here is that the thought is acted upon whether said out loud or not. Jesus searches our hearts, examines our minds and knows our thoughts. He said, "Out of the overflow of the heart, the mouth speaks."[1] I pray for a courageously honest heart in which every motive and intention are surrendered to God so that it overflows with goodness, not negativity and judgment.

Karen, a brassy, tough gal who worked for us in the early years, felt called to be my teacher in these matters. She and some women had worked very hard writing a grant for self-development funds from a regional denomination. I facilitated the discussion, but the grant specified that recipients, not an administrator or grant writer, write the grant themselves. After weeks of work, they submitted a handwritten document to the local office with each of their hand-written answers attached to the form.

When the administrator reviewed the grant, he asked to talk with me. It was clear that he believed I had written the grant instead of the Kitchen employees. He simply could not believe that the women could write so passionately about extending Bible study and job training to more low-income women. When I recounted this with Karen and the others, she gasped in exasperation, "We're poor! We're not stupid!" Honesty is jarring when it reveals truth.

"Well, it *is* surprising to find them so articulate," explained a journalist friend who understood the grantor's incredulity that women living in poverty were intelligent and thoughtful enough to have accomplished the task of writing a grant. Erroneous assumptions, like the poor are unintelligent, or poverty should go unnamed, frustrate our ability to help.

Karen's forthrightness was spot on, but candor isn't always advisable. I had to explain to Cindy, for instance, that volunteers consider it impolite when she asks them if they are rich. Debby, a volunteer who babysat an employee's five-year-old at her condo, told me the child counted the number of televisions in her house and declared, "I want to be rich like you one day and have seven TVs also." What might be endearing in a child, is not always so in an adult.

Learning a degree of appropriateness is important to be able to work within the middle class. Matters of dress, for example, are a frequent discussion at Christ Kitchen, particularly among the older women, who feel called to help the younger ones. They comment on how much skin, cleavage, or leg is exposed, how high the heel, how tight the jean. We work on ways to comment sensitively (why don't you put on a sweater?) instead of bluntly (well, you look like a whore) to encourage change.

The ability to be searingly honest in spiritual matters, however, is an area where the Christ Kitchen women are expert teachers to the rest of our community. Their ability to present themselves unadorned in front of their Lord instructs me daily. I rejoice in the frequent statements we hear, like the following: "I am thankful every day that Jesus rescued me from my drug addiction," and "When I was in jail, God taught me to praise him," and "I was a heroin addict for thirty years until I found Jesus," and "I don't know how he could love a sinner like me, but I'm grateful." Their candor teaches us to face painful realities with courage.

I never knew, for example, that my friend of twenty years struggled with an alcoholic son until she asked the Kitchen women to pray for him. A visitor, who listened to stories of living with addictions, abuse and failure, felt able to share her own battles with alcohol after she visited the Kitchen. For the first time in her life, she began to relinquish years of shame. Visitors and volunteers are constantly surprised, as I continue to be, at how the Lord ministers to us through the honesty and sincerity of the women at Christ Kitchen. James' words ring true: Has not God chosen the poor in the eyes of the world to be rich in faith and to inherit the kingdom he promised those who love him?[2] I never expected to find heroines in the guise of the homeless, mentors clad in second-hand clothes, teachers among the disabled, but I am humbled every day by their honesty, courage and resiliency; I am challenged to become more like them.

The Samaritan woman's refreshing candor is not so admired by the disciples back at the well, however. Their interruption ends her remarkable conversation with Jesus, but clearly not its effect. Upon seeing the disciples, she leaves her water jar and hurries back to town with, what Frank Spina calls, the issue of messiahship uppermost in her mind.[3]

CHAPTER THIRTEEN

Being Transparent

She hadn't run in a very long time. It made her laugh as she fairly flew down the hill toward town. She hadn't run like this since she was a girl. The hot sun, beaming with the same intensity as it always had, didn't exhaust her or slow her feet.

It occurred to her suddenly that she'd forgotten her water jar. Such an essential, costly item was never left unattended. It was back at the well, now surrounded by all the men. She supposed it was safe until she returned. "What were they thinking about me?" she wondered, knowing they must be watching her flight. All of it—her talking with a man, her sprint toward home—was such a breach in etiquette, so out of the ordinary. They must be talking about her. It would have bothered her before that they would be staring at her, even from behind. It would have made her turn red with shame or rage. But now, even that was gone because she had total trust in Messiah who was among them. He would deal with it, with them.

As she approached town, she realized she hadn't thought about where she was going specifically, or what she would do. The mission, the passion was just to tell her people that this man, the Messiah, was at their well. The men sitting at the city gate looked up as she came into view becoming alert when they realized she was running. She swept by them, not bothering to stop or answer their questions. That made some curious and others annoyed, so they got up and followed her. Like a pied piper, she continued on toward the village square with a crowd beginning to gather behind her.

She knew now who she was looking for—Tirzah. At this time of day the young girl would probably be with the other new mothers chatting *around the clay griddles making their bread for the evening meal. She spotted a group of women working near the fire pit and headed there. It didn't occur to her what she was going to say until she stopped, bending over with hands to knees, to catch her breath.*

When she raised her head, an audible gasp went up through the sizeable crowd that now gathered around her. Her face beamed, literally shone with new light. She knew they saw it, as surely as if she was surrounded by sparkling stars. Her eyes were clear and bright as she looked about the crowd. These were her people; she knew every one of them. The scales of hatred, fear and spite seemed to have fallen from her eyes as she looked on them with compassion. She saw in an instant from how they carried their weary bodies and worried expressions, that they were no different than she was. She understood their exhaustion and burdens and troubles. She had felt similar not twenty minutes earlier.

As she caught her breath, a smile broke out all over her face. "Come!" she sputtered between gasps of air, "Come, see a man who told me everything I ever did." She said it so openly, so candidly, the people hesitated, curious. Their expressions changed from suspicious to interested as they stared at her.

She knew this was a bit much for them, her people who were not used to being astonished, who had known few miracles. "Could it be . . ." she said haltingly, wondering how they might react and then plunged ahead, "Could it be the Christ?"

A collective gasp went up from the crowd. Wonder seized them. Now they turned to each other in awe. What? The Christ? The long awaited Messiah? There was certainly something amazing that had happened to her, their eyes seemed to say as they looked from each other back to her. They began to chatter with each other and a few began looking around as if the miracle was somewhere close by. She pointed toward the well. The astonished people turned in that direction and, like a flock herded by angels, began to make their way out of town and toward the well.

Jesus' Way is pure, clear and immediate. The Samaritan woman, like so many poor who grace the doors of Christ Kitchen, becomes an immediate emissary for Christ. Having nothing to lose, she is incredibly honest, real, and even self-critical. It yields immediate results: her transformation is clearly evident to the townspeople as her enthusiasm piques their interest. Honest, transparent, joyful evangelism from converted lives at Christ Kitchen illustrate the eleventh principle in discipleship: *being transparent.*

Our Master storyteller begins to get creative in the Samaritan tale. He splits the screen to give us a glimpse of an even greater plot at hand, allowing us to see two concurring stories taking place at the same time. On one screen, *Return to Sychar* is showing, starring the Samaritan woman. In the theater next door, *Missions Possible* stars Jesus himself. Both are unique studies on evangelism and mission.

In the last scene, we left the Samaritan woman as she returns to home. The camera follows her into Sychar and records her transformation into an instantly effective evangelist. "Come and see," she calls to all the townspeople, " a man who told me everything I ever did. Could this be the Christ?" Ironically, the woman who just lectured Jesus on the inappropriateness of speaking to a lone man, now brazenly summons a whole city of them. The only explanation for her renovation is the very thing Jesus promised—his spilling-over, living water—a spring in her life welling up to eternal life.

The blessings of Jacob arrive! The long awaited messianic leader, predicted by the Samaritan's prophet, Moses, has come as promised.

> I will pour water on the thirsty land,
> and streams on the dry ground.
> I will pour out my Spirit on your offspring,
> and my blessings on your descendants.
> They will spring up like grass in a meadow,
> like poplar trees by flowing streams.[1]

How amazing it is that the offspring chosen, the channel from well to town, should be this woman! This outsider, demonized by both Samaritans and Jews, becomes the conduit of faith for a whole town. How very much like God, who sent a baby to save the world and picked twelve ragtag nobodies to tell the story, to bring great news through such a raw, implausible source. What's even more remarkable is that the Sycharites take her, their promiscuous outcast, at her word. The next thing we know, the people leave the city and head straight for the well without question or hesitation.

"Come and see," our Samaritan evangelist says in the tradition of her well-teacher. Jesus had recently used those same words when he invited two disciples to "Come and see" his accommodations. They ended up hanging out with him for the rest of the day and then for the rest of their lives. Phillip repeated the words, "Come and see" to Nathanael when he questioned where Messiah was from. "Check it out," Phillip says in effect. It's not a pushy, "Go see for yourself," but an inviting, "Come along with me, come join me, as we investigate this Messiah-thing together." Jesus, Phillip, and now our Samaritan woman take their time wooing their friends. They courteously respect caution and skepticism, but urge them on toward their Messiah.

The women of Christ Kitchen are the best good news bearers. Barbara, an employee on her way to work, found a woman crying on the bus and she brought her along to Bible study. "You don't have to say anything," she told her new acquaintance. "Just come have a cup of coffee and sit with me. You'll feel better." Donna gathers pajamas for women sheltered at a downtown mission because she remembers being homeless and sleeping in her clothes; she gives them out with an invitation to Christ Kitchen's Bible study. "Nothing's going to change, 'till you get changed," she tells them. Our "church" looks a little different than the Sunday-morning variety, which is probably why the guilt-ridden and anguished dare to enter.

What visitors to Christ Kitchen see when they step in the door is something close to what the Samaritan woman admits to her towns-folk: "A man who told me everything I ever did." Clear confessions of sin might not be the tipping point that gets you to church or encourages you to open a Bible, but it works around our place. I remember what Sheryl said about her first impression of Christ Kitchen:

> It took me about an hour to feel comfortable that first day. I hadn't wanted to come because I hadn't worked in eight years, didn't know if I still could. It seemed crazy to risk "church people" after years of getting loaded. I was scared, but I trusted Lori's opinion that we needed more fellowship than Narcotics Anonymous offered and more Bible study to grow our faith. I felt God's peace in the Kitchen right away. I knew He had brought me here, because nobody judged me or looked at me different. Every woman in there was trying to change her life just like me. They were looking at Jesus looking for a new way.

"Could this be the Christ?" the Samaritan woman asks her townspeople. More literally, her question was, "This couldn't be the Messiah, could it?"

"Her question expected a tentative negative answer," explain commentators Walvoord and Zuck. They believe she framed the question this way because she knew the people would not respond favorably to a dogmatic assertion from a woman, especially one of her reputation.[2] This is similar to what I find at Christ Kitchen; the women have no expectation that others will listen to them. It takes deep love and a long time to develop dignity to believe one is worthy of being listened to. Jesus had captured her attention with curiosity and she piques their interest with the same. The whole town decides to see why she's beaming.

A rather short little unimpressive sermon for such a massive response, don't you think? Her two-sentence sermon begins with her own sin and ends with a doubtful question. You're never supposed to end a sermon like that. You're supposed to be confidant, convincing and controlled, winning souls and converting sinners, not wondering aloud about who Christ might be. But there she stands in all her simplicity and obvious sparkle with faith as small as a mustard seed moving mountains.

Commentators are abuzz. Matthew Henry notices, "She fastens upon that part of Christ's discourse which one would think she would have been most shy of repeating.[3] Frances Gench writes, "Her example reminds us that faith that is tentative, full of questions and not yet mature can bear witness and do so effectively."[4] John the Evangelist is teaching us that our words don't have to be flowery, ornate, or even eloquent to be effective. They just need to be honest, real and centered in Jesus himself.[5]

If the Sycharites are anything like visitors to Christ Kitchen, the Samaritan woman's honesty is perhaps the very reason they believe. Her transformation is obvious; there is no earthly explanation for it. What other than a completely transformed life could engage so many people?

Transformation means *to remodel or alter, to change into another form.* The people of Sychar saw that the woman had changed. What they may not quite understand, is that God had removed the veil from her eyes enabling her to recognize him. She is free now, her face reflecting the brightness of his face. So altered, her life becomes brighter and more beautiful as she becomes more like him.[6] With such hope, comes boldness, we are told in 2 Corinthians 3:12. As Peterson puts it, "With that kind of hope to excite us, nothing holds us back."[7]

It is the excitement of changed lives that attracts people to Christ Kitchen. We pray constantly that each person who enters our doors will sense the Spirit of God. Our women see themselves as emissaries of his miraculous work. It is not unusual to hear them testifying to the UPS man, their bus drivers, restaurant patrons, and food delivery people. Lest you cringe, worrying about the appropriateness of such witness, let me assure you their hope and joy is infectious. It attracts the most unlikely souls: businessmen, tattoo artists, real estate agents, drug dealers, and even our Vietnamese tailor next door ask them for prayer. They seem to be considered a safe alternative to more conventional means of discussing faith issues. Ah, Lord, your ways are mysterious. We join the saints in exclaiming, "Can you fathom the mysteries of God?"[8]

It is clear that Jesus' true worshipers seminar is already taking effect. The Spirit has gone down deep into the heart of one flawed but willing woman, moved her to faith in the Son of truth, and brought her to God the Father, her heart's true goal. Completely transformed and utterly transparent, she in turn, seeks others. Her call to "come and see" is a call to worship her Father in spirit and truth. The people listening are clearly convinced by her new ability to transcend "everything she ever did." The time has literally come when the kind of worshipers the Father seeks begin making their way up the hill to his son.

CHAPTER FOURTEEN

Sowing His Word

*T*hey all passed by her, hurrying now to the well. The same collective mindset that had caused them to shun her now instigated urgency to see the man, the phenomenon, which had so dramatically changed their outcast. They looked at her as they passed, searching her for clues as to what could possibly have caused the transformation. Perplexed, the village women, many whom she'd help in their deliveries, the snippy ones and the kind ones, smiled slightly from what she sensed was relief that they their strained relations were over. The men who had alternately ignored or leered at her straightened and cleared their throats when they found her watching them join the mass movement up the hill. She saw neighbors, shop owners, elders and carpenters hiking up their tunics ready to make the short journey. Young girls helped their grandmas, mothers gathered their little ones and men stroked their beards as all ascended the hill.

A sweet affection welled up in her for her townspeople, these harassed and helpless souls. Such a strange feeling, she noted, one she'd never had before. They were so needy, she realized from somewhere deep within, so desperate. Their outward appearance and behaviors were nothing more than veneer hiding secret hurt and shame. It all became clear as they passed in front of her that they were just like her, toughened shells protecting fragile cores. She experienced a sense of release as that awareness settled in her thoughts. How could she describe this sensation? It was the same as she'd felt while talking with Messiah. She searched for a word that captured it. Then it came to her—forgiveness. Forgiveness rang true like a bell heard throughout the village. Forgiveness is what *transpired between her and Messiah and now forgiveness was unifying her with her judges and prosecutors. Freedom took the place of condemnation. Mercy replaced scorn. So this is what a spring of water welling up to eternity was all about.*

Finally she spotted Tirzah, off to the side attempting to juggle a newborn with a young boy pulling on her skirt wanting to be carried. She made her way over to them through the dispersing crowd and reached down to pick up the boy. The toddler stiffened at the unfamiliar touch until he saw his mother's face brighten when she saw who'd come to her aid. They smiled at each other, a moment of truth passed between them. "Finally," the woman's face seemed to say, "we can walk together, because truth is at hand, justice is dawning, healing awaits." But words were not necessary, only a knowing look on the older woman's face that formed trust in the younger one. Tirzah patted her son as he snuggled his head into the woman's neck. She adjusted the sleeping baby in her shawl as they joined the last of the townspeople making their way to the well. She would make sure Tirzah met Messiah, she would introduce her to him.

As they passed the city gate, she noticed not everyone in her village joined them. A few priests were arguing with each other about the meaning of this exodus. Some merchants, worried about leaving their wares unattended, were hurriedly packing them up. One of the town officials was actually trying to get people to turn around. From the corner of her eye she spotted her ex-husband, the jailer, Tirzah's abuser. She was surprised at how even more disfigured he became, as she watched him muttering to himself, deviously collecting items left in haste by the people. She sighed, looking over at Tirzah, hoping she hadn't seen him, but the girl was preoccupied with the baby and hadn't noticed. It occurred to the woman that not everyone wanted to change or be freed from his or her shackles. It was sad, really. Her hatred of the man actually took on a note of pity. Amazing. She'd have to think about that one later.

There was so much to be joyful about! She hadn't seen her people excitedly clamoring together like this in, well, forever. Their expectation was palpable. A few people looked back to see if she was coming with them. She acknowledged them with a quick smile when they saw her. As they drew nearer to the well, however, she focused entirely on the Messiah still sitting with his friends, watching them approach. It was as if he'd been expecting them. Her heart leapt, confirming what she knew to be true. He was waiting for them, all of them, waiting to give them a taste of living water.

Jesus defines our twelfth discipleship lesson to the disciples by explaining that *sowing his Word* is not about food; it's about doing the will of God. In this lesson, Jesus offers instruction in farming: sowing, reaping and harvesting. Jesus encourages us to take a good look at what the unlikely Samaritan evangelist has already sowed. What encouragement to the church that the Spirit is working in ways we can't imagine.

As the townspeople of Sychar begin their trek to the well, the master storyteller returns our attention once again to the disciples' story playing out in the theater next door. Another anti-climax! Just when the townspeople are on the verge of discovery, the camera scans back to what's happening at the well. We're beginning to get the picture now; this is like a movie where you know the two protagonists are bound to find each other, but their lives haven't intersected yet. The storyteller must have some big finale planned for the time when the Gentile, uncircumcised, foreigner, with-out-hope Samaritans finally meet the circumcised, citizens-of-the-covenant, members-of-God's-household disciples. Goodness. If these two groups are ever going to get along, the Apostle Paul is going to have to write long epistles and treatises about peace and destroying dividing walls of hostility.

A well placed *meanwhile* moves us back to the ongoing discussion between Jesus and his disciples. And what are they talking about? Food, of course! "Eat something, Rabbi," the worrywarts urge. So focused are the disciples on food and shopping, the mundane and minute, that we can't help but identify with them. Details often cloud the bigger picture. It only seems natural to concentrate on grocery lists, gas prices, and grass clippings, the happenings and worries of life, when something momentous is at hand. Just like Martha, Mary's sister, the disciples are busy cleaning the dishes, mopping the floor, straightening up for company, and getting a wee bit peeved that no one is helping. We can just hear them say with a hint of their Jewish grandmas' irritation, "We walked all the way into that Podunk town and bought dinner from people we aren't even supposed to associate with, and you won't do us the courtesy of even taking a bite?"

They do notice, however, that something is different. They left a tired, thirsty Rabbi and came back to someone filled, nourished and satisfied. Even so they don't understand his metaphor. "I have food to eat that you know nothing about." What?! The grandmas are alarmed. "Someone already brought him food?" they exclaim, as if this is the most important item on the agenda.

We have to militate against minutia in missions work. How easy it is to become focused on the program over the people, the plan over the purpose. We have to continually balance our ministry goals with the business at hand, adjusting details to comply with the mission statement. Right before one of our big annual events, for example, I reminded the volunteers to stay focused. "When in doubt," I prompted, "choose people over program. It's going to get busy, but remember, the whole reason we're doing this is to mentor women in Kingdom living, even in the stressful hustle and bustle of a huge event."

One of the volunteers told me later if I hadn't said that, she would have lost her temper at the woman working next to her, grabbed the spatula right out of her hand and scooped the brownies out herself. "There is something evil in me," she concluded. But I assured her with the words of Lilla Watson, an Australian aboriginal woman who said, "If you have come to help me, you are wasting your time. But if you have come because your liberation is bound up with mine, then let us walk together."[1]

We, volunteers and employees, Gentiles and Jews, discover that all of us are bumbling disciples together on the same long journey. There is rarely a defined teacher or prescribed student. Those roles fluctuate. Sometimes we mentor and sometimes we become the mentee. God, however, is always teaching, counseling, exhorting, and correcting. Just begin to think you've got it going on and he'll put the slowest worker next to your brownies to spoil your glowing image of yourself. Eugene Peterson says, "Life is full of starts and stops, blind alleys, disappointing detours, and bad guesses. Eventually, by God's grace, we find our way into acts of obedience, acts of praise. But along the way we spend considerable time extricating ourselves from brambles and scratching our heads."[2] Arloa Sutter adds, "God beckons us to reciprocal relationships with the poor. Urban pilgrims receive the blessing of escaping controlling powers [as] they learn an outward focus in their walk with Jesus."[3]

Solicitously using the disciples' current food obsession as illustration, Jesus continues his lecture to them. "My food is to do the will of him who sent me and accomplish his work." His whole soul filled with the coming of the woman to her God. No meal could satisfy like that. Spina underscores the emphatic nature of what transpired. "Jesus sees the significance of his conversation with the woman in terms of his most basic mission."[4] Jesus is teaching his disciples here to *do* the will of God, that in itself nourishes the doer. He might be wondering right about now if they missed the manna lecture in Hebrew school. "Man does not live on bread alone, but on every word that comes from the mouth of the Lord."[5] Remember?

Mutual Ministry

As Christians throughout America, we must remember our most basic mission. Doing the Father's will not only feeds our souls, but extends the Kingdom beyond the bit of soil where we've been commissioned. It's not that we haven't been amply warned about the hazards that disrupt the mission. We understand that the worries of this life can strangle little faith-seeds preciously planted in our soil. We get that wealth offers fraudulent enticements that consume our energy, time and attention. We know the warnings not to put our hope in wealth or store up treasures where thieves, moth and rust destroy. We get it.

But will we do it? Will we leave our precious water jugs—symbols of our sustenance and toil—in the Lord's hands and rush to town to share the News? Oh! Church, there are so many Samaritan women and men in your towns who need *you* to care about them, to befriend them and help carry the load, to cheer their recovery and bless their progress. In doing so God promises he will richly provide you with everything for your enjoyment![6] Can you believe it? Not only does being generous and willing to share bring treasure, it actually creates pleasure and delight. Ultimately, we are assured a filled and full soul, the ultimate power breakfast.

Like the disciples, however, we are slow-witted and in need of further explanation. So Jesus goes on by insisting that there are miracles in the message, power in the Word. The simple gospel message, he explains, is enough to bring people to the Lord, sometimes immediately, like we've just seen with the Samaritan woman. "Don't conform any longer to the pattern of this world," we can just hear Jesus plead to his sometimes-remedial students, "and forget the focus-on-food thing." That old Jewish proverb, "It's still four months till harvest," is equivalent to "Rome wasn't built in a day,"[7] but Jesus is insisting those proverbs aren't true in this case; actually, just the opposite. "Just look! Open your eyes. See the ripe harvest fields!" Jesus says as he directs their attention to the whole ripe town of Sychar making its way to the well. Miracle!

If someone were to ask an employee of Christ Kitchen for our secret to success, I have no doubt they would say prayer. "We pray about everything and miracles just happen," one of our employees told a news reporter doing a story on Christ Kitchen. "Oh yes," she said, intending to impress the poor man, "our Bible studies go on and on."

"Really?" he asked me doubtfully. I wasn't sure if he was asking is it true you see miracles, or why in the world would you have Bible studies that go on and on? Regardless, he wasn't impressed. (Just to set the record straight, our Bible study lasts about an hour and fifteen minutes. That's not really *on and on*.)

The journalist's question points to the fact that some people prefer *The Five Minute Devotional: Meditations for a Busy Woman*[8] and some spend an hour with Kay Arthur's *Precept Upon Precept*.[9] We saints can get off track, self-absorbed actually, believing others want to hear the sermons *we* like, sing worship songs *we* love, listen to preachers *we* admire. Bible studies that go "on and on" may not be your cup of tea because, perhaps, you've had plenty of tea. You've had so much tea, in fact, that you can't believe anyone else can possibly drink tea anymore. If you are an academic learner, you might enjoy an Earl Grey type of Bible study, one that is more restrained and steeped in traditions, one that has just the right amount milk and sugar for you to go home and apply the lesson in the privacy of your own home. A Red Zinger type of study might appeal to more experiential learners: those who like to raise and praise, get down with the choir, and shout "Amen!" in agreement with the pastor. At Christ Kitchen, I teach an Earl Zinger study, full of deep, thought provoking leaves with lots and lots of sugar. I make a point of asking guests with different styles, methods, and voices to conduct Bible study when I am away. It illustrates the many varieties of tea available.

One of my dearest employees, Cora, who is African-American, pondered these differences when she commented on variations in church music. In all sincerity she asked me why white people's church music has to be so bad. "Well, *they* don't think its bad," I said, "They love it." She couldn't wrap her head around that, so I explained my theory that Christians, who are well fed, who have good jobs and can pay their bills, whose needs are mostly met, seem to like music that is often serious and thoughtful. Their music is reflecting who they are, reminding them that God is sovereign, that there are others in need, that there is much to do in the world. The suffering church, on the other hand, spends Sunday mornings trying to forget how rotten things are in and around their worlds. Their music is passion-ate, adoring, and free, reflecting what they need—their petition for help and assurance that God has not forgotten them. "Hmm . . ." Cora grumbled, only half buying it. "I think those serious ones would feel a whole lot better if they got up and moved their booties." That girl makes my day.

Prayer

There is no doubt that we pray a lot around Christ Kitchen. We pray a lot because there is so much to pray for. The lives of the women are too often desperate, chaotic, unpredictable and tragic. They get sick without health care, their teeth abscess, their trucks break down, they get into fights with each other, their kids get put in jail, their men lose their jobs. There is very little else we can do most of the time *but* pray. We need that daily bread daily.

"Before they call, I will answer; while they are still speaking I will hear," Isaiah 65:24 promises and we count on it. As a result, we see miracle after miracle. A woman walked in our doors one morning in desperate shape. She recounted a tragic story of nursing her hus-band through a long grueling death to cancer. He had dealt with the money and bills, but after he was gone, she discovered the money was too. She was franticly applying for food stamps and medical care. She hadn't worked in thirty years and needed a job, but we didn't have a position available. She started to cry. Though she said she wasn't really a "churchgoer," she let us pray for her and promised to come back the next day for Bible study.

About a half hour later, a man walked in looking a bit befuddled and asked if we were an organization that helped widows. He was a construction worker driving to work when he heard God say very specifically that there was a widow in need of help and he should stop at Christ Kitchen and give her some money. He took a hundred dol-lars from his wallet as Kari burst into tears and told him the story of the woman who'd just left. He simply nodded, still rather baffled, and drove away. We prayed and prayed the woman would come back the next day. When she walked in the door, she was met resounding joy and praise and a hundred dollars.

Another time, our bookkeeper and office manager discussed whether they should tell me our financial reserves were perilously low. They both knew that I could get consumed worrying about finances, so I had instructed them to alert me only if our bank account went under $3,000. Kari, my sweet, protective office manager went home that Friday and prayed and fasted all weekend. On Monday morning, three ladies walked in to the Kitchen with a check for $10,000 from their church. He heard before I even knew to call.

Another time, our Operations Committee determined that we needed marketing help but none of us knew anyone in the field. The next day a man came in saying that he had awoken at two o'clock in the morning a few days before and heard God say that he should volunteer at Christ Kitchen. We weren't sure what we could find for him to do. Having him tie knots in raffia just didn't seem appropriate, so I asked his background. He said, "Marketing." Before we called, the Lord had answered.

The middle of the night seems to be a good time for God to reveal miracles. Last Christmas the Kitchen was so busy we barely had enough product to meet demand. I knew we needed help organizing our production, but didn't have a clue how to go about it. One night in January, I woke up in the dead of night with the thought "Have Jen do it." Now, I never wake up in the night, so I paid attention. The only Jen I knew was an athletic trainer who volunteered to exercise with the women. I made an appointment with her the next day and explained my dream and our production needs. When I saw tears well up in her eyes, I knew we were on holy ground. Jen had been meaning to ask me if she should apply for a job she'd seen in the paper for a medical assistant at Christ Clinic. "I think God has a job for you at Christ Kitchen," I told her. Since she's come on board, our production has increased three hundred percent.

Miracles

Miracles knit God's converging movie scenes into an integrated whole for the glory of his kingdom. People with money or talent deliver their offering before the need they will fulfill is even identified. Disciples are learning about harvesting while that harvest is walking up the hill. Oswald Chambers describes these miracles as ways we see God at work. He says, "If we obey Jesus Christ in the seemingly random circumstances of life, they become pinholes through which we see the face of God.[10] Miracles are daily God-experiences of the obedient.

Harvest time is gospel time. In the spiritual realm there is no long wait for crops to ripen; miracles are happening all the time. In spiritual matters we don't have to wait because Jesus, the sower, is here—all that is needed is spiritual vision and perception.[11] Open your eyes! Look! See! The Samaritan woman is reaping what Jesus sowed in her—a citywide evangelistic movement. There is life-changing power in the Word.

Lydia had sat silently through several Bible studies with furrowed brows and a bit of a scowl on her face. She'd had a hard life raising an autistic son while her husband molested their three daughters. When she learned what was happening, she left him. She was then faced with all the damage done to her girls and the responsibility of getting food on the table. She'd gotten so distressed at one point that she'd considered drowning her son. Scowls were the least of her problems. I could tell something was marinating in her as she listened at Bible study. Finally, one day she said with as much disdain as she could muster, "What is with you people? Your lives suck as bad as mine, but I've been watching you, and I think you are genuinely happy. I don't think you're faking it." Gentle smiles met her derision as several testified to the Holy Spirit's work in their lives. At break, Kelly asked her if she would want Jesus to come into her life, too? "Yes, I just want to be happy, too," she sobbed. It took years for Lydia's heartbreak to heal, but slowly she began to trust again and even started to smile. The power of the Word broke down strongholds of pain and defense.

C.S. Lewis said, "Miracles are a retelling in small letters of the very same story which is written across the whole world in letters too large for some of us to see."[12] This is what Jesus is trying to explain with his analogy of reaper and sower. Others have been at work with small letters sowing Samaritan fields. Old Testament prophets, and perhaps even John the Baptist prepared the soil. No doubt the disciples would have forgotten this as they approached the city of Sychar believing there could be no harvest there. "These people despise us Jews and would have no use for our message," we hear them fret. But just the opposite was true: the harvest was ready and only needed faithful workers to claim it. The disciples went into the village to get food for themselves, but they did no evangelizing. The woman took their place![13] Small letters of the most surprising saints are a version of the larger narrative God is writing throughout the world.

We are learning a valuable lesson along with the disciples. We are not alone in the work of the Lord and must never look on any opportunity for witness as wasted time and energy. It takes faith to plow the soil and plant the seed, but God promises a harvest. When we spread Word seeds, we may not see the harvest, but those who come behind us who do the reaping will see it and give thanks for our faithful labor. In a few years, Phillip, Peter and John will preach, pray and heal among the Samaritan people and many more will believe with great joy.[14]

We know this to be true at Christ Kitchen. By the time a worker walks in our door, we know the saints have been praying for her for years. Some women arrive quite mature in their faith, and are simply looking for work, friends or money. Others are like the fig tree in Luke 13:6 that has had no fruit in years. Their faith, grown hollow or knurled, needs fertilizer and tending. Some are so full of aphids and blight they walk in simply because the saints have prayed. We rejoice with the sowers who did the hard work at prior times that brought each of them to our doors.

Similarly, when any of our women leave prematurely, we have to trust that the Word goes with them and that they will hunger and find nourishment in some other field. We pray for the little faith they have gained with us to sustain them against dark forces at work to wreak havoc in their lives. We pray they will not be attracted to what Timothy refers to as treacherous and brash men who "worm their way into homes and gain control over weak-willed women."[15] A few return but we don't hold our breath. We pray the saints will join us in these prayers and will become the field offering sustenance for the next part of her journey.

There is great joy among planters of seeds and harvesters of crops! The Samaritan woman has joined the assembly of saints, neophyte though she is. Her denomination may not yet be registered in the disciples' association of evangelicals, but her people are on their way to the convention. The angels are perched on the edge of their seats awaiting the grand finale.

CHAPTER FIFTEEN

Savior of the World

*T*he Samaritans gathered around the man sitting at their well, mingling with each other and his friends, although most felt awkward at first. As she crested the hill, she watched his disciples begin to fan out meeting her people with genuine smiles and expressions of greeting. "My goodness," she thought to herself, "It's as if two neighboring villages are sharing a meal, like they've done this for years." The child in her arms had fallen asleep and she adjusted his little form as she put a hand on Tirzah's back. The young girl's eyes were glued on the Master.

The woman motioned to her to hand her the baby as she sat down on the ground near the Messiah. She moved the sleeping boy onto her lap and reached up to get the baby. She motioned with a quick nod that she would take care of the children if Tirzah wanted to move closer to the Teacher. Covered in babies, she watched as Tirzah not only moved closer, but fell on her knees at his feet. Her heart ached for her as Tirzah began sobbing. Deep agonizing cries released the grip of tightly bound sinews of pain.

The woman wanted to rush to her, this girl with whom she felt a deep bond. Today was the first time they'd ever really spoken, but she realized she had kept an eye on the girl ever since that horrible day they'd met. She hadn't wanted to acknowledge it, because the girl reminded her too much of herself. And now, Tirzah was at the feet of the Healer. He would know what to do; she trusted him completely.

She watched as he slowly placed his hand under Tirzah's chin and raised her face to meet his. He spoke quietly to her for a while and her body began to relax. The women couldn't hear what was said, but she *knew he was speaking truth, pouring living water over her ravaged soul. She watched him smile that beautiful, gentle smile and saw Tirzah nod in agreement, gathering her skirts as she stood.*

When she turned back toward the woman and her children, her face was at peace, exhausted, like she'd just been through a battle, but at peace. Slowly, her red, swollen eyes began to turn up at the corners forming a sad, sweet smile that broadened over her face. When Tirzah's eyes met the woman's, she dissolved again into tears, but this time in sweet joy. Tirzah ran to her and joined the children on her lap. The woman made room for her among the sleeping babies and somehow gathered all three of them into her arms. Her own silent tears wept with longing for this precious closeness she'd missed out on all her life. She rocked them, thanking Messiah in the depth of her being for creating these little bundles lying in a heap on her lap. Glancing his way, she saw him smile warmly.

After a while, she watched many others have their own personal conversations with Messiah. His disciples delved into serious dialogue with leaders from her village and she saw heads nodding in agreement, handshakes, and smiles. Her people listened to the Master's teaching and talked together in small groups. Occasionally, she would hear someone comment about her, about her radical transformation and testimony that she'd met the Messiah who knew everything about her. They would glance over at her then and smile, nodding their heads in thanks. She smiled shyly back, amazed at being acknowledged and relishing this new sense of community.

As it grew late, her people urged the Master to come back to their town and stay with them for a while. She was as surprised as his disciples that he actually agreed. She had the profound sense that the Father and all of heaven were rejoicing over what was taking place in her village. A Jewish rabbi and his followers were walking and talking with Samaritans like this was a normal event, like it had been planned for eons. Under the Master's care, her neighbors were conversing intensely, seeing miracles in their midst, believing in the author of wonder. Many became believers right then and there. She could tell by the changed light in their eyes.

He stayed with them for two days. There was feasting, dancing, and laughing. There were in-depth, theological discussions, heated debates, and thoughtful discourse. There were individual conversions and an overall mass transformation of centuries-old animosity between their people. Above all they prayed. They prayed prayers that rang all the way into the heavens and back again into hearts' darkest regions. They prayed and worshiped and rejoiced. A deep peace settled in Sychar then that lasted for as long as anyone could remember.

She had left the well with Tirzah and the children and Tirzah had begged her to come back to her home with them. She longed to do just that. With all the excitement, she hadn't really thought about returning to Omar's home. It was tainted now. As kind as he'd been, there was no way she could go back to him or to their way of life. She hadn't seen him at the well, but she hoped he'd been there. No matter, she would tell him all about Messiah some day soon. He had a good heart and she knew he would believe.

So Tirzah's invitation was welcomed. She was thrilled actually. Babies and a new daughter! How could she possibly deserve such bounty? Why, only this morning she was a lost wretch and within a few hours, she had a new life, a family, and Messiah. "Amazing grace," rang out in rhythm to a new beat in her heart, "how sweet the sound!"

Tirzah's place was near the center of the village, so they got to hear Messiah's teachings and the words of life he offered everyone who came to him over the next few days. Along with the other village women, they made meals for him and his disciples and made sure they had plenty to eat and drink. Many of the women from the village made a point of thanking her, some with a gentle pat on the arm, some with broad hugs. Several actually apologized for not talking with her over the years. She changed topics quickly when this happened, because she didn't want to spoil the tranquil, joyful atmosphere that had settled over all of them. But to a few she said, "Oh no, sister, it is I that apologize." Although neither really understood exactly what that meant, it was enough to put away the past and begin anew.

The Master's words were like a salve on her people's souls. The morning he prepared to leave, they all gathered to him for one last time of worship and prayer. No one wanted him to go or to end the meaningful connections they'd made with his disciples. They walked with him as far as the well, wanting to spend every last second in his presence. At the well, he knelt and prayed as they all wept and embraced him. As he rose to go, the woman walked up to him with such contented joy in her eyes. He smiled back and placed his hand on her head in blessing. That is exactly how she felt—blessed.

His departure was bittersweet for the villagers. They were quiet as they watched him and his disciples begin their journey north. And then slowly, the import of all he'd done began to crackle like lightening around them. The village leader, directed the town's attention toward her, and with sincere appreciation said, "We no longer believe just because of what you said; now we have heard for ourselves." Murmurs of agreement rose from every villager. "We now know," he went on, "that this man really is the Savior of the world!"

Their voices joined together in shouts of praise and jubilant rejoicing. The Messiah, the Savior of the world, lavished living water on one insignificant little woman and the results could be heard throughout heaven and earth. From far off, Messiah and the disciples heard the great roar of exultation and, filled with joy, thanked the Father. Thousands upon thousands of angels, a great company of the heavenly host, joined their voices with the joyful assembly giving glory to God in the highest. The Samaritan woman joined her people in deepest thanks for the free gift fully bestowed—her Savior.

An incredible mutuality of ministry develops at Christ Kitchen as women from the streets testify to and befriend women from the church. As a community of women from very different walks of life study Scripture together, share their stories, and minister to each others' needs, the Lord begins to heal arbitrary, unnecessary divisions and shows us real transformation.

The anticipated climax of outsider-Samaritans meeting insider-Jews transpires around the well with Jesus at the center. The camera lenses converge into one concentric view as Jesus' purpose becomes clear: to create one people out of two, one new kind of community. The mystery of Christ is about to unfold before our very eyes. The union of two disparate peoples, separated for centuries by hostility and suspicion, is at hand. We have a front row seat among the angels waiting for the cue to explode in thunderous applause.

Our story has been masterfully orchestrated so that the seekers arrive once the workers are ready to receive them. Jesus preached peace to those who were far away in Sychar by sending them one of their own made new. On the testimony and transformation of one woman, her people set out to find the source of such power. Jesus, meanwhile, preached peace to those who were standing right next to him, explaining that the reaper isn't waiting for the traditions of men or for the law code that had become so clogged with fine print and footnotes that it hindered more than it helped.[1] Jesus treated Samaritan and Jew as equals, making them equal. His imminent death on the cross will soon unleash Holy Spirit power for these two groups to embrace each other on their own, but until then, he brings them together in his presence. Both will soon then have access to the Father. Both are becoming true worshipers, those whom the Father seeks.

We are told that many of the Samaritans believed in Jesus solely because of the woman's simple statement, "He told me everything I ever did." What an unusual courier of the gospel message, we think, until we remember that soon Jesus will commission other women—Mary Magdalene, Salome, and Mary, the mother of James—as first witnesses of the resurrection. When the men betray him, deny him, and fall asleep in the Garden, these faithful, humble women stand by the cross, keep vigil through the night, watch, wait, and weep. As the men kept their distance, safely huddled behind closed doors,[2] the women bring anointing spices to the tomb at dawn. It is the women who are comforted by angels when they can't find his body and are first to be told that their Christ has risen. "Come and see," the angels tell the women, using the Samaritan woman's words. "Go and tell," they are instructed.

In the manner of her sister-disciples, the Samaritan woman beckons others to her Christ. She had mistaken Jesus as a thirsty sojourner just as Mary mistook him to be the gardener. Both women, however, leave their encounters with Christ in joyous expectation to share their news. "I have seen the Lord!" Mary tells the disciples and, though most considered it an idle tale, Peter and John come running. "Come and see!" her Samaritan sister echoes the angels and her town turns out in force.

When the townspeople of Sychar arrive at the well, the first thing they do is ask Jesus to stay with them awhile. Asking seems to be a central theme in this tale. The story began with Jesus asking for a drink. The woman questions his asking and is told she would have received living water if she'd only asked the asker. The disciples specifically don't ask Jesus why he is talking with a woman and now the Samaritans ask him to stay with them a few days. Clearly, asking, even imperfect asking, elicits Jesus' response. In their asking the Samaritans are given belief; in their seeking they find him; when they knock the door opens, he walks in and stays for two days.

Perhaps it is a good idea that the disciples remain quiet, refraining from asking the many questions that must be occurring to them. "We're *staying* in Podunk? With the half-breeds? For several days?!" Or maybe the sower-reaper lecture by their beloved teacher has softened their hearts. Maybe, like Peter, who received a vision to eat food considered unclean, they are revising their understanding of who's in and who's out: catching sight of a new Kingdom made up of Samaritans, centurions like Cornelius, and all who God has made clean. Perhaps the disciples remain quiet because they are in awe, glimpsing Jesus' joy at having two precious days with people who really want to hear what he has to say. In contrast to their fellow Jews, who refuse to acknowledge him, endlessly dickering, suspiciously testing, jealously disputing, treacherously plotting his death, these Samaritans invite him to dinner, listen to his sermons, catch the vision, and become donors to the cause. "Here, then," write commentators Jamieson, Fausset, and Brown, "would He solace His already wounded spirit and have, in this outfield village triumph of His grace, a sublime fore-taste of the inbringing of the whole Gentile world into the Church."[3]

Pure irony, isn't it, that the insider-Pharisees call Jesus a demon-possessed Samaritan and remain outsiders with their father the devil, while the outsider-Samaritan become insiders because they believe the Father's words? The latter ask him to stay, the former ask him to go. Believers, regardless who they were before Hope dawned, receive living water, understand the great I AM to be in their midst, and joy-ously abide with him.

The Samaritan Tutorial

There are a number of lessons the church in our present day must take from this Samaritan tutorial.

- We must learn from the disciples' reluctance to follow Jesus into Samaritan country that we likely won't feel comfortable venturing into poverty stricken areas of our cities, but we should go anyway.

- We may find the dearest souls or the most unkempt, inappro-priate, dismal, hurting souls who want to have nothing to do with us, but we can strike up conversations anyway.

- We might not know what to say to people from cultures and classes foreign to us, but we can listen to their lives anyway.

- We can provide things that will support their stability—jobs, health care, housing, transportation, babysitting, kindness, friendship—whether anyone returns to thank us anyway.

- We might come from vastly different races, colors, creeds, backgrounds, or bank accounts, but we can find mutual interests anyway.

- We may not have any experience offering our free gift of living water, but we can learn to do it anyway.

- We may not think they'll want what we have to give, but we can offer it anyway.

- We may be put off by lifestyles, habits, addictions, parenting practices, or live-in fiancées, but we can learn to love them anyway.

- Our achievement orientation and obsession with money might put them off, but we can value them and learn from them anyway.

- We might be surprised at what we find them talking about, but we can watch and learn how Jesus works with them anyway.

- We might find, in fact, that they are more receptive, more interested, more eager to abide with Jesus than anyone we've ever met, but they might befriend us anyway.

We are working on these things at Christ Kitchen. We are a very imperfect community of women who gather daily at the well around our Lord, praising him that we have another day to live into his glory. Some of us have backgrounds like Mary Magdalene and others have had blessings like Joanna, but all of us know we've been redeemed from the empty way of life handed down to us from our forefathers.[4] Some of us have faced darkness too shameful even to mention,[5] but know the Lord is close to the brokenhearted and saves those who are crushed in spirit.[6] Many of us have guilt so overwhelming it is a burden too heavy to bear,[7] but trust the Lord is able to cleanse our guilty conscience[8] and restore our soul.[9] We are learning to live in the assurance of 1 Peter 2:24 that Christ bore our sins in his body on the tree and by his wounds we have been healed.

The people who join the Christ Kitchen women as volunteers vary from long-time believers who grew up in church to brand new seekers disillusioned with established religion. Together they serve lunch, serve the ministry, and serve our women. Students from private universities join those from local community colleges to work on annual fundraisers and daily projects. We have volunteers who are school principals, disabled workers, business owners, and those completing court-ordered community service hours. Volunteers spray weeds, conduct Bible studies, clean the parking lot, create spreadsheets, make sandwiches, and improve our overall appearance. Catholics, Seventh-Day Adventists, Baptists, and Presbyterians lift their hearts in prayer and praise with women who don't know what a denomination is. Many come to bathe in the simplicity and honesty of Kitchen women. Many come for prayer themselves. Some have sat at Jesus' feet for decades while others are from towns like Sychar who've heard the testimony of changed lives and wonder what its about. Though they come to help the poor, they often find they, too, are poor in spirit and need the care, wisdom, and faith offered by those who gather at our well.

The crowd at Christ Kitchen's well seems quite similar to that at the Sychar well thousands of years ago. All of us—the richest and poorest in town, insiders and outsiders, people of color and people of means, drunks and teetotalers, extroverts and introverts, the sanctimonious and the sinner, those who speak in tongues and those who sit on their hands, those sure of their salvation and those sure of nothing—gather together because we've heard the Lord's call. We congregate at the well, surprised to find the others, but like the disciples, quietly watching what the Lord will do with us. We learn at his feet, attempt to follow his steps, weep as he washes ours, and humbly turn to do the same to our friends and to our enemies.

We all recognize traits of the Samaritan woman in us and, like her, have a deep passion to bring our friends and family to the well. We pray for her courage to shout with joy and wonder, "Come and see the man!" We rejoice in the spring of living water we find overflowing in our lives and say with conviction to those still thirsty, "If only you knew the gift of God!" We bow in gratitude and adoration with the Samaritan woman, joining her as we exclaim, "This man really is the Savior of the world!"

Cue the thunderous applause.

Suggestions to Begin an Acquaintance with Christian Traditions

Discipleship

- Reclaim the word *discipleship* by studying it, using it, doing it. Start a discipleship study group at your church and prayerfully begin.

- Develop a committed personal relationship with someone who is willing to disciple you.

- Practice accountability with a friend.

- Attend AA or talk with someone in recovery to learn how he/she practices mentoring and accountability.

- Find discipleship ministries and get involved.

Hospitality

- Invite people to eat with you. Practice sharing a table. Practice sharing what the Lord is doing in your life. Be natural, warm, inviting.

- Invite friends over to watch the movie *Babette's Feast*[1] and discuss hospitality in light of the film's message.

- Invite missionaries to stay in your home.

- Volunteer in a hospital or local Hospice organization.

- Organize weekly potlucks at your church and invite people from local shelters.

- Volunteer at inner city missions.

- Examine discomfort while participating in the above. Talk about it.

- Examine how you developed your stands on social/public policy. Do they square with Scripture? Find specific Scriptural precedents for the views you hold.

- Research every Scripture that deals with the poor.

- Begin a specific ritual of generosity.

- Create an "Elijah's Room" in your home for those needing a place to stay.

Missional women

- Commit to finding role models of women and men serving the poor.

- Read books about missionaries and mission organizations.

- Volunteer at an inner city mission.

- Correspond with a current missionary.

- Find women with hearts for missions and join their efforts or start one.

- Ask questions. Probe Scripture. Listen to the Holy Spirit.

- Let Jesus be your role model.

---

1. Isak Dinesen, *Anecdotes of Destiny* (Vintage, 1988). *Babette's Feast* was first published in the *Ladies Home Journal*, and later it appeared in Isak Dinesen's *Anecdotes of Destiny*, published in 1958. The movie, directed by Gabriel Axel, received the Academy Award in 1986 for Best Foreign Film.

Starting a Job-Training Microenterprise

Things to consider for initial start up of a job-training project like Christ Kitchen

A. Prayer

Prayer is the essential ingredient to stay on track with God's plan. Discouragement is the enemy's tool (just wait until you read about health permits!) Perhaps you could get a prayer group together and get many people praying. Accountability, support and advice from prayerful, mature, supportive believers are so helpful. When Christ Kitchen began, we had a prayer board made up of faithful women with strong support of its mission, who also had expertise in specific areas such as ministry, business, church leadership, small group leadership, psychotherapy, law, marketing, small business, food handling, and catering.

B. Familiarity with issues involving poverty

There are great books and many people from which you can learn about the population you want to serve. Make appointments with missionaries in your town and pick their brains. Ask them for good book recommendations.

C. Need analysis

There is always a need for prayer support, Bible study, and fellowship for women living in poverty. Many programs attending to the needs of this population of women provide housing, food, clothing, counsel, and training, often under the umbrella of a church or para-church organization. It is interesting to find out if they are also preaching, teaching, studying the Word of God. There is no need to alter the spiritual component of your program for fear of losing funding sources. God will open doors.

D. Product selection

When you select a product to be made by the people you will employ, pick something you feel comfortable making, that is not highly technical or difficult to put together. Many subsequent decisions and plans will evolve around the type of product you select. For example, if you select a food product, a facility capable of passing health inspection is required as well as permits specific to food.

E. Location

Having a facility with easy access for workers is helpful. Consider locating near a bus line or downtown area where potential workers might live. You could also consider being near or in relationship with existing women's shelters or programs. Otherwise, you could provide transportation to the facility.

F. Licenses and Permits (check state and city ordinances particular to your location)

Business licenses are usually required in order to sell a product to the public. A quick call to your local business licensing bureau requesting information will get you started. I have found them to be most helpful. City or state governments often have bureaus that help small businesses get started. Depending on the product you produce, the facility must be able to accommodate production of your product while meeting city, county, and fire codes. For example, manufacturing of food products requires state health department inspection, qualification, and permit. In Washington State, dry product sales are licensed by the Department of Agriculture. Wholesale sales require additional licensure.

Cooked food products require a licensed commercial kitchen in which to cook food products if food is to be sold to the public. Specific appliances, food preparation surfaces, dishwashing equipment, etc. are necessary in order to obtain this license. Don't let this discourage you. It's just the cost of doing business.

G. Insurance

Coverage for your facility, product, workers, and liability may be necessary. It may be helpful to join with an existing ministry and increase coverage on their insurance plan.

H. Accounting/Tax Issues

Monthly documentation of earnings, payroll, and taxes is required by most states. In the state of Washington, Christ Kitchen pays: Federal Tax Deposit (monthly payment of Medicare and Social Security for workers based on hours worked); Labor and Industries (a quarterly payment for workers injured on job); Employment Security (a quarterly payment for unemployment that can be altered for non-profits); and Excise tax (only paid on non food product sales).

I. Rent or mortgage payments

This may be an additional cost. I have heard many stories, however, of buildings being donated to a ministry or money mysteriously showing up for building costs.

J. Be encouraged

Be strong and courageous. Do not be terrified; do not be not be discouraged, for the Lord your God with be with you wherever you go. (Joshua 1:9)

Don't let details discourage you or leave you feeling overwhelmed so that you don't proceed. That is the enemy's work.

He doesn't want women living in poverty, in crisis, need, or transition, and women who may never otherwise go to church to hear the Word of God, to surrender to Christ as their Savior, to begin living through Him, to improve every aspect of their lives. This is what is at stake. Without God's plan, his will, his way, without tapping into his power, the project will be difficult if not impossible. Consider how Abraham, Moses, David, and the disciples persevered in order to lead their people. Think about Jesus' ultimate sacrifice. It makes slogging through the process of obtaining health permits or business licenses seem miniscule. Lives are at stake, so stay prayed up and get on with it.

Initial Work in Starting a Job-Training Microenterprise

#1 Write a Business Plan

Purpose: to develop your business practices
Include:
1. Company Information
2. Goals
3. Substantiation of project
4. Competitive and Partnership Analysis
     Product Description,
        Features
     Comparisons
     Product Literature
     Market Analysis
     Industry Analysis
     Keys to Success
     Market Forecast
5. Business Strategy and Implementation
     Marketing Strategy
     Sales Plan
     Sales Force
     Strategic Alliances
     Service
6. Organization
     Organizational Structure
     Management Team
     Management Team
        Gaps
     Other Team Considerations
     Employees
7. Financial Analysis
     Financial Plan
     Financial Assumptions
     Start-up Costs and
        Capitalization
     Pro Forma Income
        Statement
     Break-Even Analysis
8. Appendix
     Objectives
     Start up Phase
     Production Phase
     Expansion Phase
9. Substantiate each business practice with appropriate Scripture.

#2 Write a Mission Strategy

Purpose: to develop your ministry practices
1. Questions to Consider:
    a. What is the purpose of the ministry?
    b. How did the purpose develop?
    c. What population will you serve?
    d. Explain why that specific population?
    e. Have you felt "called" to that population?
    f. What do you know about that group?
    g. What training or experience have you had with this group?
    h. Have you spent time with the population?
    i. Have you been transformed by them?
    j. Have you submitted your initial theories on what you plan to do to the Lord for revision?
    k. How flexible are you?
    l. Where are your limits? What don't you want to do?
    m. Will your funding sources, location, or partnerships compromise your ministry?
    n. Who is on your advisory board?
    o. Who holds you accountable?
    p. Have you found others to mentor you through this journey?
    q. How did Jesus do this same work?
2. State your mission strategy in 30 words or less.

#3 Revise your business plan to accommodate and advise your ministry strategy

Location & Mailing Address:
2410 N. Monroe St
Spokane, WA 99205
Phone: 509-325-4343   **Fax:** 509-448-1438
Email: sales@christkitchen.org
Website: www.christkitchen.org

Shop Hours:
Monday through Friday (9:00am – 5:00pm)
Saturday (10:00am – 4:00pm)

Director:
Jan Bowes Martinez, DMin

Christ Kitchen Mission Statement

Christ Kitchen is a Christ-centered, nondenominational ministry providing work, job training, discipleship, support, and fellowship for women living in poverty in the Spokane area. Through the production and sales of gourmet dried food products, this ministry enables women to learn to work, to become employable and, eventually, to support themselves and their families without reliance on government programs or destructive relationships.

Our Beliefs

We believe people want to feel better and to be more self-sufficient yearning ultimately for Christ Himself. Therefore, Christ Kitchen's strategy is directed to a hungry community—the poor in need of employment and others in need of Provision.

This is how we understand discipleship, being Christ's hands and feet to a hurting world. Creating jobs and job training for women living in poverty, promoting self-sufficiency instead of government dependency, and promoting Christ-sufficiency in all things are supportable goals and are within the reach of women wanting to participate.

Our Mission

Resurrection, a central tenet of Christianity, is used in the New Testament to mean "a rising up" or "causing to stand." The ministry of Christ Kitchen is founded upon the essential principles of Christ's life and seeks to aid homeless, abused, poor, or disenfranchised women in their rising up out of poverty, ultimately to stand on their own feet with the security of Christ. Our mission is to reveal Christ and make known the facts of the gospel through group support and fellowship, individual discipleship, and job training. We seek to enable women trapped in poverty to improve, renew, heal, and maintain spiritual, mental, emotional, and physical health.

Ministry of Reconciliation

So from now on we don't evaluate people from a worldly point of view, by what they have or how they look. We now look inside, and what we see is that anyone united with the Messiah gets a fresh start, they're created new. The old life is gone; a new life burgeons! Look at it! All this comes from the God who settled the relationship between us and him, and then called us to settle our relationships with each other. God put the world square with himself through the Messiah, giving the world a fresh start by offering forgiveness of sins. God has given us the task of telling everyone what he is doing. We're Christ's representatives. God uses us to persuade men and women to drop their differences and enter into God's work of making things right between them (2 Corinthians 5:20, *The Message*).

Christ Kitchen Products

Gourmet Mixes:

Benevolent Brownies 20 oz
Blessed Bean Soup (Sm) 14 oz
Blessed Bean Soup (Lg) 24 oz
Blue Corn Bread of Life 14 oz
Chariots of Chile (Lg) 24 oz
Chariots of Chile (Sm) 12 oz
Converted Rice   14 oz
Corn Bread of Life   14 oz
Cookies 23 oz M&M_ Mac_
Disciple (12 Bean) Soup 24 oz
Disciple Soup for Two 6 oz
Exalted Espresso Beans 3 oz
Faithful French Lentil Soup 15oz
Heavenly Blue Hotcakes 12oz
Heavenly Cocoa 8 oz
Jumpin' Jubilee Popcorn 8 oz
Living Lentil Salad 15oz
Mercy Mint Lentils 3 oz
Naomi Bars 16 oz
Obedient Oatmeal Cookies24oz
Omega Oatmeal 12 oz
Prayerful Pintos   24 oz
Soulful Cider Spice Mix .5oz
Spicy Hallelujah Popcorn 12oz
Tabitha's Tabouli 8 oz
Testament Tea 10 oz
Victorious Vegetable Soup 7oz

Holiday Items:

Joyous Gingersnaps 16 oz
Peppermint Brownies 19 oz
Peppermint Cocoa 9 oz

Taxable Items:

Aprons
Hats
T-shirts
Beggars Dog Bones (sm) (lg)
Goliath Granola
Single Frosted Cookie
Cookie Bouquet

Gift Baskets:

Dinner
Christmas Joy
Fun at Heart
Little One

Chile Night
Vegetarian
King Soups
Breakfast
Abba Java
Kit'n'Kaboodle

Please contact Christ Kitchen for a current list of products and pricing:

Christ Kitchen
www.christkitchen.org
2410 N. Monroe; Spokane, WA 99205
509-325-4343 Fax: 509-448-1438
E-mail: sales@christkitchen.org

Each Christ Kitchen product includes a Scripture verse relating to the particular name of that product. It is our prayer that His Word would go out from our business to you and on into the world. May His Seed find good soil.

Job Phase System

Phase I

Duration:	Minimum 4 weeks
Work Hours	3.5 hours/day
Hourly Wage	$9.19/hour (Minimum wage in Washington State in 2013)
Requirements:	Demonstrate perfect attendance and punctuality
	Demonstrate ability to correctly clock in/out
	Demonstrate ability to perform at least three production skills
	Demonstrate ability to work well with other employees
	Acquire a Food Handler Permit from Department of Health Production
Skills Gained	Assemble packaging of products in various phases of production
Opportunities:	Participate in Bible study
	Participate in support and fellowship

Phase II

Duration:	As long as needed
Work Hours:	3.5 hours/day
	Additional hours as they become available
Hourly Wage:	$9.19/hour
Requirements:	Demonstrate perfect daily attendance and punctuality
	Master production skills in all areas of assembly
	Demonstrate ability to assemble zero-defect products
	Demonstrate ability to learn basic kitchen skills
	Demonstrate ability to work on food assembly line
	Demonstrate ability to clean kitchen according to standards
	Demonstrate cooperation within work team
	Continued mastery of Phase I skills
Production Skills Gained:	Mastery of appropriate chef assistant skills
Opportunities:	Participate in Christian support/Bible groups (Bible study, life skills)
	Extra hours available

Phase III

Duration:	As long as needed
Work Hours:	5 hours/day
	Additional workdays/week
Hourly Wage:	$9.50/hour
Requirements:	Demonstrate perfect daily attendance and punctuality
	Demonstrate ability to teach production skills
	Demonstrate ability to work independently
	Demonstrate ability to make and cook products
	Continued mastery of Phase I, Phase II
Production Skills Gained:	Mastery of cooking skills
Opportunities:	Participate in Christian support/Bible groups (Bible study, life skills)
	Participate in staff education group
	Participate in leadership training
	Take opportunity to lead Bible study in staff training

Phase IV

Duration: As long as needed
Work Hours: Full or part-time
Hourly Wage: $10.00/hour or above

Requirements: Demonstrate ability to manage employees
                  Demonstrate ability to run production line
                  Demonstrate ability to order and stock ingredients
                  Demonstrate ability to maintain accurate accounting of production
                  Demonstrate ability to inspire excellence in work team
                  Demonstrate ability to lead team meetings
                  Continued mastery of Phase I, Phase II, Phase III

Production Skills
Gained: Mastery of organizational skills
                  Mastery of leadership skills

Opportunities: Participate in Christian support/Bible groups (Bible study, life skills)
                  Participate in staff education group
                  Participate in leadership training
                  Lead Bible study in staff training
                  Participate in leadership of Christ Kitchen

Ministry Goals of Christ Kitchen

- **Stability**
  Spiritually
  Emotionally
  Mentally
  Physically

- **Work**
  Provide Jobs
  Skills training

  Healthy Work Environment

  Supportive Work Environment

- **Relationships**
  Work
  Interpersonal
  Family
  Marital
  Church Community

- **Citizenship**
  Healthy and Contributing
    Community Member

- **Accomplished Through:**
  Bible Study, discipleship, fellowship,
    life-skills development, mentoring,
    healthy role modeling/meals

- **Accomplished Through**
  Product sales, donations
  Assemble products, demonstrate
    proficiency, supervision, increasing
    responsibility
  Prayerful obedience, daily devotions,
    thinking scripturally
  Staff training, mentoring, hard work daily

- **Accomplished Through**
  Bible Study, mentoring, evaluation,
    supervision, conflict resolution,
    role modeling, classes, sacrificial
    living, honoring commitments, wise
    decision making, relationships
    w/volunteers

- **Accomplished Through**
  Membership in CK community founded in
    Scripture, mentoring, paying bills,
    saving money, wise decision making,
    dealing w/ past commitments, reconciling
    past (judicial, recovery, family)

Christ Kitchen Financials

1998
Income

	Donations	10,257
	Sales	14,973
Cost of Goods Sold		(5,022)
	Gross Profit	20,208

Expenses

	Payroll	8,099
	Payroll tax	2,237
	Other	320
	Total expense	16,316
	Net Income	8,914

2012
Income

	Donations	158,323
	Sales	200,800
Cost of Goods Sold		(88,470)
	Other	43,054
	Gross Profit	313,707

Expenses

	Payroll	162,193
	Payroll tax	23,064
	Other	118,543
	Total expense	303,800
	Net Income*	36,792

*less depreciation

Employees/Year

1998	1999	2000	2001	2002	2003	2004	2005	2006	2007	2008	2009	2010	2011	2012
36	28	59	117	126	73	76	74	83	48	45	36	36	42	37

From February 1998 through August 2006, Christ Kitchen rented a church kitchen and fellowship hall in a small Presbyterian church. We paid $50/month rent in 1998, which increased to $100 by the time we moved out. Because expenses were so low, we hired every woman who sought work. When we moved into our new facility in August 2006, we limited hiring to accommodate increased expenses.

In 2011, Christ Kitchen purchased a garage next door for the purpose of increased storage and long-term growth potential. God willing, we will build a production facility on the new property and make a larger restaurant in the current building. The goal of expansion is to enable more low-income women to be hired to help them become Christ-dependent and self-sufficient.

Christ Clinic/Christ Kitchen is a non-profit organization serving the working poor of Spokane. We are dedicated to sharing the love of Christ through medical care and job training. Our Mission Statement reads as follows:

Throughout the Bible, the people of God are told to defend the cause of the poor and needy. Christ's life exemplifies this command. Because His offer of new life is often associated with physical and psychological healing and the restoration of personal, familial, and occupational function, we commit ourselves to following His example.

Many of our neighbors are without work, financial reserves, health insurance coverage, and access to essential primary health care. As believers, we have the opportunity to obey Christ's commands and follow his example by using our gifts to help meet our neighbors' needs in an affordable and respectful way. We also recognize this as a unique opportunity to help rehabilitate broken people, restore function, encourage stability and self-sufficiency, and promote the Good News of the gospel.

We believe that complete health includes the total person and therefore commit ourselves to addressing the spiritual, psychological, physical, and vocational needs of our patients and employees. We believe that as people grow and heal they become contributing members of the community, and therefore we commit ourselves to working in conjunction with local believers to unite them in relationships and ministries that are beneficial to both and that further the Kingdom.

Christ Clinic:
Sharing the Love of God Through Medicine

Christ Clinic is a non-profit medical clinic serving the needs of Spokane's working poor. Christ Clinic began in 1991 as the vision of four Christian physicians who recognized that rising health care costs were forcing uninsured individuals and families to use the emergency room for health-related needs. They began a primary care clinic, staffed primarily by Christian volunteers, to serve the medical and spiritual needs of the uninsured, working poor.

Endnotes

Introduction: Notes

[1] Robert Louis Wilken, *The Spirit of Early Christian Thought* (New Haven, Conn.: Yale University Press, 2003). 166-180. I am indebted to Jerry Sittser for pointing the way to Wilken in Gerald L. Sittser, *Water from a Deep Well: Christian Spirituality from Early Martyrs to Modern Missionaries* (Downers Grove: InterVarsity Press, 2007), 20

[2] Frederick Dale Bruner, *Matthew: A Commentary*, vol. Volume 2: The Churchbook; Matthew 13-28 (Grand Rapids: Eerdmans Publishing Company, 2004). I love how Dale Bruner pronounces Jesus' metaphorical instruction on becoming a disciple as attending his "School of Discipleship." See pages 148-163. I use this metaphor with great thanks to my mentor, Dr. Bruner.

Prologue: Notes

[1] Psalm 34:18

[2] Psalm 91:4

[3] Ecclesiastes 12:14

[4] Philippians 4:7

[5] 2 Corinthians 1:4

[6] Christ Clinic is a medical clinic serving the working poor in Spokane. See page 223.

[7] Luke 8:1-3

[8] 1 Peter 1:18

Prologue: Digging Deeper

1. Have you ever read through the whole Bible? You might consider it. I suggest you get a good 365-day devotional and try it. If you miss a few days, don't get discouraged, just pick up on the reading for the day. My favorite devotional is: *A 365-Day Devotional Commentary* by L.O. Richards. (See bibliography.)

2. Write out your faith history. Who has prayed for you for years?

3. Read the stories of Sarah and Hagar (Genesis 16; 21:1-21) and Mary Magdalene and Joanna (Luke 8:1-3). How do the relationships between the women compare?

Prologue: For those Digging a Well

1. Have you been called to a particular people or ministry? How do you know? List specific experiences confirming the call on your life. Develop them into a story you will be able to share with others. (Believe me, you will be asked to share it often.)

2. Who do you consider your "village"? Is that community supportive of your mission and does it share your passion, or will you have to teach them to be supportive?

3. How did you learn about poverty? Was it first-hand experience or through others' perspectives? How valid is that perspective?

4. Make a list of verses that affirm your passion for this particular group.

Chapter 1: Notes

[1] John 4:10

[2] Frances Taylor Gench, Back to the Well, 110.

Chapter 1: Digging Deeper

1. Read the story of the Samaritan woman (John 4:4-42) in different Bible translations. In your own words tell the story to a friend. What do you think is the main point?

2. Why do you think Jesus phrases his question about living water (John 4:10) the way he does?

3. What do you learn from the following verses about guidance and being instructed? Proverbs 2:2,6; 3:5-6; Psalm 32:8; Isaiah 28:9-10; 30:21; 58:11; Jeremiah 10:23

Chapter 1: For those Digging a Well

1. What experiences have you had hurdling obstacles of culture, class, race, or economics? Write down what you learned about yourself in these experiences.

2. Make a list of people you'd like to be a part of your ministry. Make appointments with them, sit down over coffee and review your mission/plan/heart with them. Afterward, write down what you learn.

3. What "safe waters" do you need to leave in order to launch your idea?

4. What is the difference between running a charity and building relationships?

Chapter 2: Notes

[1] Bruner, *Matthew: A Commentary*. Volume 2: The Churchbook; Matthew 13-28.

[2] TANF stands for Temporary Assistance to Needy Families.

[3] Spokane Regional Health District, *Facing Spokane Poverty - A Community Health Assessment Resource* (Spokane, WA: Spokane Regional Health District, 2002). Available at http://www.assessnow.info/publications/epubs.2006-03-03.8465302252 (accessed March 2, 2009).

[4] Matthew 28:18

[5] Mark 16:15

[6] Matthew 28:18, Eugene H. Peterson, *The Message:The Bible in Contemporary Language* Colorado Springs: NavPress, 2003.

[7] Mark 16:18

[8] Frederick Dale Bruner, *Matthew: A Commentary*, vol. Volume 2: The Churchbook; Matthew 13-28. 805, 816, 824.

[9] Ibid., 815.

[10] Ibid., 143.

[11] Matthew 28:20

[12] Hebrews 13:21

[13] Mark 16:20

[14] Acts 1:8

[15] Bruner, 817.

[16] Dale Bruner refers to Pharisees as "the serious" and to Sadducees as "the sophisticated." p. 90. It makes me laugh.

[17] Coggins, R.J. *Samaritans and Jews*. (Oxford: Blackwell), 1975.

[18] J.F. Walvoord, R.B Zuck, and Dallas Theological seminary, *The Bible Knowledge Commentary: An Exposition of the Scriptures* (Victor Books: Wheaton, IL), 1983.

[19] Ibid.

[20] John 8:48

[21] Luke 17:7

[22] Luke 10:25-37

[23] Frederick Dale Bruner, "John: A Commentary," (2008). Unfinished manuscript on John Chapter 4 sent to author.

[24] John 4:26

Chapter 2: Digging Deeper

1. Read the various ways Jesus commissions his disciples in Matthew 28:18-20; Mark 16:15-18; Luke 4:18-19; and John 20:21-23. What does this teach you?

2. Do a word study on the word "church." Look it up in a Bible dictionary and see what you find. How does this help you?

3. Read Acts 1:1-8. Who/where is the Jerusalem, Judea, and Samaria of your world? Make a list of verses that sustain you among "enemies." Read stories that involve Samaritans (Luke 10:25-37; John 4:26.) What do they teach you about "enemies"?

4. Consider the word "Go" in Genesis 12:1-8 and in Luke 10:1-4. What strikes you about those directions? Discussing "going" with someone you trust.

Chapter 2: For those Digging a Well

1. Who was influential in your life in helping you get to know the Lord? What characteristics do you admire about that person(s). How might you implement those attributes into your ministry?

2. Write down the goals of your project/mission. Formulate the goals into a mission statement. (This should be only a few sentences. Think of it as an "elevator speech," something you can tell others in a few minutes that explains the whole project.

3. Write separate goals for the business and for the ministry. Do they confirm and encourage the other or are they at odds? Share the goals with some of the people you hope to employ/work with. Consider revising the goals.

4. Make a list of people who know the population of people you want to work with. Make appointments to talk with or write to them. Ray Bakke suggests asking, "What are the signs of hope you see in this [neighborhood]?" This helps them tell you about what's working.

Chapter 3: Notes

[1] Isaiah 6:8

[2] Oswald Chambers, *My Utmost for His Highest: An Updated Edition in Today's Language: The Golden Book of Oswald Chambers* (Grand Rapids: Discovery House Publishers, 1992).

[3] Genesis 12:1

[4] Chambers, *My Utmost.* April 25

[5] Luke 10:2

[6] 2 Timothy 4:2

Chapter 3: Digging Deeper

1. Do you have a favorite verse? Is it applicable to your new work setting, neighborhood, or place in life?

2. What is the "harvest" (Luke 10:2) in your world right now?

3. Regardless of vocation or station in life, we are each given the charge in 2 Timothy 4:1-5. Have you ever considered this as a personal call on your life?

Chapter 3: For those Digging a Well

1. Have you ever considered yourself a missionary? What comes to mind when you think about it? Read some great stories about missionaries throughout history and the world to encourage you. List qualities of the missionaries you admire.

2. What is the "Samaritan" part of your town? What do you know about it from hearsay or casual conversations? Compare this with facts you gather from your local library, or from church leaders, missionaries, teachers, police officers working in those areas, or newspaper stories.

3. Have you ever led a Bible study? Start preparing for a casual conversation or a formal group of 50. You can Google-search "How to lead a Bible study" and find many resources.

Chapter 4: Notes

[1] Luke 10:39-42

[2] Matthew 11:28

[3] Psalm 51:6

[4] John 8:31-32

[5] Bruner, *Matthew: A Commentary*, Volume 2: The Churchbook; Matthew 13-28. 143.

[6] Chambers, *My Utmost*. January 5.

[7] Dietrich Bonhoeffer, *Discipleship* (Minneapolis: Fortress Press, 2003), 62.

[8] Romans 12:2

[9] Ephesians 4:22-24 (*The Message*)

[10] Ephesians 4:14

[11] Ephesians 2:19

[12] Bruner, 145.

[13] For more on middle-class American values, read Ruby Payne's exposition of the issue in Ruby K. Payne and Don L. Krabill, *Hidden Rules of Class at Work* (Highlands, Texas: aha! Process, Inc., 2002), and Ruby K. Payne, *A Framework for Understanding Poverty*, Revised Edition (Highlands, TX: aha! Process, 1998).

[14] Timothy Keller, *Blessed are the Poor*. Sermon series Hope for New York at Redeemer Presbyterian Church, New York City, April 5, 1998.

[15] Original author unknown

[16] 1 Peter 4:10

Chapter 4: Digging Deeper

1. Look up verses that deal with "being known" by God. Do these comfort you? How might they help others? (Psalm 139:1, 23; 44:21; Jeremiah 24:7; John 7:28; 10:14; Acts 1:24; Matthew 6:8; 2 Timothy 2:19).

2. Compare the different ways Peter might have understood the word "follow" in Matthew 4:19 versus 26:69-75.

3. Start a list of verses that help you understand God's heart for the poor (or poor in spirit.) Gather books (see bibliography for suggestions) that help you understand poverty and justice from the Lord's perspective.

Chapter 4: For those Digging a Well

1. Make a list of the hidden rules with which you were raised. Discuss these with people raised in very different circumstances.

2. Is anyone really prepared to suffer? Should we expect it? What do you need to get ready? Even if you don't think preparation is important, you might want to do it anyway.

3. Who are your role models for the specific work you want to do? Make appointments online, on the phone, or in person to talk with them. Their expertise and experience is invaluable. Remember, however, the way the Lord leads you might be very different.

4. Ask your role model about suffering in this work.

Chapter 5: Notes

[1] Mother Teresa

[2] *Webster's Third New International Dictionary.*

[3] Daniel J. Hill and Randal G. Rauser, *Christian Philosophy A-Z* (Edinburgh: Edinburgh University Press, 2006), p. 200.

[4] Sigmund Freud, "The Question of a Weltanschauung," in *New Introductory Lectures in Psycho-Analysis* (1933). As quoted in Ken Funk, "What Is a Worldview?" (2001). http://web.engr.oregonstate.edu/~funkk/Personal/worldview.html.

[5] Romans 12:1

[6] Peterson, *The Message.*

[7] *Webster's Third New International Dictionary.*

[8] John E. Schwartz, *Freedom Reclaimed: Rediscovering the American Vision* (Baltimore: G-University Press, 2005), 37.

[9] US Census Bureau, Poverty: 2007 Highlights, ed. Housing and Household Economic Statistics Division US Census Bureau, http://www.census.gov/hhes/www/poverty/poverty07/pov07hi.html. Available at http://aspe.hhs.gov/poverty/12poverty.shtml/#thresholds. Accessed July 2012.

[10] 2012 Health and Human Services Poverty Guidelines. The Census Bureau uses a set of monetary income thresholds that vary by family size and composition to determine who is poor. According to federal standards (which are now fifty-five years old), the "absolute poverty line" is the threshold below which families or individuals are considered to be lacking the resources to meet the basic needs for healthy living. http://aspe.hhs.gov/poverty/12poverty.shtml/#thresholds. Accessed July 2012.

[11] Bryant L. Myers, *Walking with the Poor: Principles and Practices of Transformational Development* (Maryknoll: Orbis Books and World Vision, 1999), 66.

[12] Ruby K. Payne, Philip E. DeVol, and Terie Dreussi Smith, *Bridges out of Poverty: Strategies for Professionals and Communities* (Highlands, TX: aha! Process, Inc., 2005), 11.

[13] Oscar Lewis, "Culture of Poverty," in *On Understanding Poverty: Perspectives from the Social Sciences*, ed. Daniel P Moynihan (New York: Basic Books, 1969).

[14] Robert C. Linthicum, *Empowering the Poor* (Monrovia: MARC Books, 1991), 10; Ibid.

[15] John Friedman, *Empowerment: The Politics of Alternative Development* (Cambridge, MA: Blackwell, 1992). Quoted in Myers, 69.

[16] Robert Chambers, "Rural Development: Putting the Lat First," (London: Longman Group, 1983), 103. Quoted in Myers, 66.

[17] Myers, 72.

[18] Robert Putnam, *Bowling Alone: The Collapse and Revival of American Community* (Simon and Schuster, 2000), 12. See also http://www.bowlingalone.com/data.htm.

[19] Tex Sample, *US Lifestyles and Mainline Churches* (Louisville: Westminster John Knox Press, 1990), 59-62.

[20] Tex Sample, *Hard Living People & Mainline Christians* (Nashville: Abingdon Press, 1993). See chapter 3.

[21] Sample, *US Lifestyles and Mainline Churches*, 61.

[22] See demographic information on Christ Kitchen employees.

[23] Elijah Anderson, *The Code of the Street: Decency, Violence, and the Moral Life of the Inner City* (New York: WW Norton and Co., 1999), 35-44.

[24] Ibid., 45.

[25] James Gilligan, *Violence: Reflections on a National Epidemic* (New York: Vintage Random House, 1997), 191.

[26] Kit Danley, interview by author. Spokane, WA, January 5, 2009.

[27] Gilligan, 201.

[28] Ibid.

[29] Maya Angelou, *Even the Stars Look Lonesome* (New York: Random House, 1997), 107-108.

[30] W.E. Vine, *Vine's Expository Dictionary of Old and New Testament Words* (Old Tappan, New Jersey: Fleming H. Revell Company, 1981).

[31] Ibid., 109.

[32] Ronald Sider, *Rich Christians in an Age of Hunger: Moving from Affluence to Generosity* (Nashville: W Publishing Group, 1997), 41.

[33] P. J Achtemeier, *Harper's Bible Dictionary*, 1st ed. (San Francisco: Harper & Row, 1985).

[34] See Proverbs 13:18

[35] See Proverbs 20:13

[36] Achtemeier.

[37] R.C. Sproul, "Who Are the Poor?" *Tabletalk* 3, no. 6 (1979).

[38] See Proverbs 13:23

[39] Achtemeier.

[40] Sider, 62.

[41] Read Deuteronomy 5:9-10. It says the sins of the father will visit the children to the third and fourth generation *for those who hate me,* but for *those who love me,* I will *shower with blessing.* The question, of course, is how will Ida come to love the Lord and thus break this cycle?

[42] Deuteronomy 15:7, 8, 10, 4

[43] Psalm 82:3

[44] Deuteronomy 15:5

[45] Matthew 25:40

[46] Eugene H. Peterson, *A Long Obedience in the Same Direction: Discipleship in an Instant Society* (Downers Grove: InterVarsity Press, 1980), 13.

[47] Dennis McCallum and Jessica Lowery, *Organic Disciplemaking: Mentoring Others into Spiritual Maturity and Leadership* (Houston: Touch Publications, 2006), 34.

[48] Ibid., 25.

[49] Ibid., 26.

[50] Ibid., 27.

[51] Ibid., 28.

[52] Titus 2:3-4

[53] McCallum and Lowery, 32.

[54] Ibid., 31, 33.

[55] Ibid., 34.

[56] Henri Nouwen, *Reaching Out: The Three Movements of the Spiritual Life* (New York: Image Books, 1975), 66.

[57] Christine D. Pohl, *Making Room; Recovering Hospitality as a Christian Tradition* (Grand Rapids: William B Eerdmans Publishing Co., 1999), 5.

[58] Ibid., 6.

[59] Ibid., 8.

[60] Ibid., 6.

[61] Ibid.

[62] Ibid. 8.

[63] Ibid.

[64] D.R.W. Wood and I.H. Marshall, *New Bible Dictionary.*, electronic ed. of 3rd ed. ed. (Downers Grove: InterVarsity Press., 1996), 267.

[65] Heidi A. Peterson, "Clothed with Compassion," *The Christian Century* 118, no. 13 (2001).

[66] Joyce Hollyday, *Clothed with the Sun: Biblical Women, Social Justice, and Us* (Louisville: Westminster John Knox Press, 1994), 176. Deuteronomy 24:17 says, "You shall not deprive a resident alien or an orphan of justice; you shall not take a widow's garment in pledge."

[67] Ibid.

[68] Ibid.

[69] Susan Smith, *Women in Mission: From the New Testament to Today* (Maryknoll: Orbis Books, 2007).

[70] Justo L. Gonzales, *The Story of Christianity*, 2 vols., vol. 1: The Early Church to the Dawn of the Reformation (San Francisco: HarperCollins, 1984), 99.

[71] Henry Bettenson, ed. *Documents of the Christian Church*, 2nd ed. (London: Oxford University Press, 1963). Quoted in Gerald L. Sittser, *Water from a Deep Well: Christian Spirituality from Early Martyrs to Modern Missionaries* (Downers Grove: InterVarsity Press, 2007), 56.

[72] Sittser, 57.

[73] Ibid.

[74] Gonzales, 51.

[75] Hollyday, 177.

[76] Romans 12:2

[77] 1 Corinthians 1:21-25

[78] Smith, 79.

[79] Sittser, 87.

[80] Pohl, 107.

[81] Ibid.

[82] Ibid.

[83] Pohl, 108.

[84] Timothy Keller, "Grace and Money."

[85] Sittser, 86.

[86] Romans 8:28

[87] Smith, 114.

[88] Ibid., 116.

[89] Charles Duhigg, *The Power of Habit: Why We Do What We Do in Life and Business* (New York City: Random House, 2012), 69.

[90] Ruth A. Tucker and Walter Liefeld, *Daughters of the Church: Women and Ministry from New Testament Times to the Present* (Grand Rapids: Zondervan, 1987), 243.

[91] Ibid., 247.

[92] Ibid.

[93] Smith, 126.

[94] Tucker and Liefeld.

[95] Ibid., 291.

[96] Smith, 126.

[97] Mark A. Noll, *A History of Christianity in the United States and Canada* (Grand Rapids: Eerdmands Publishing Company, 1992), 278.

[98] Tucker and Liefeld, 248.

[99] Noll, 184.

[100] Tucker and Liefeld, 276.

[101] Ibid, 266.

[102] Tucker and Liefeld, 291.

[103] Laura Swan, ed. *The Forgotten Desert Mothers* (New York: Paulist Press, 2001). Quoted in Sittser, 85.

[104] Justo L. Gonzales, *The Story of Christianity*, 2 vols., vol. 2: The Reformation to the Present Day (San Francisco: Harper, 1985), 308.

[105] Noll, 124.

[106] Tucker and Liefield, 258.

[107] Gonzales, *The Story of Christianity*, 334.

[108] Ibid.

[109] Anderson, 110-111.

[110] Gonzales, *The Story of Christianity*, 381.

[111] Noll,

[112] Tucker and Liefeld, 399.

[113] Jember Teffera, "Transformational Leadership" *Overture I* (lecture, Bakke Graduate University, Seattle, WA. June 8, 2004).

[114] Philippians 2:15

Chapter 5: Digging Deeper

1. Study Romans 12:1-2 and look into commentators' opinions about the verses. How have you gotten "adjusted" to pain, suffering, violence, and poverty in this country? What specific things can you do to "not conform any longer" to those patterns?

2. Jesus had quite a lot to say about violence. He doesn't let us get away with restricting the 6th Commandment (Thou shalt not kill) to those who slit throats or blow off heads. Read Deuteronomy 5:17 and Matthew 5:21. What do you learn about anger? Murder is obviously a highly visible, full-blown sin, but beneath the final act are lesser acts, and beneath that lies a corrupt heart. Scripture is tough on us for these lesser acts, these sins of the tongue and poisons of relationships.

3. Read through the Gospel of Luke and make a list of how Jesus welcomes the stranger, the outcast, the poor, the outsider. How many times does his encounter involve eating together?

Chapter 5: For those Digging a Well

1. Ask your friends and family about why they think "poverty" is a controversial subject in the US today.

2. What are some "uninformed" views of poverty that you've held or heard? How do facts, research, and Scripture change that?

3. Consider Ida's story. How do you foresee her future? Read her story to some folks quite unfamiliar with the life she's been handed. Ask them how it expands their understanding of poverty.

4. Make a plan for how will you investigate the history, lifestyles, priorities, strengths, and weaknesses of the people you serve. Who will you enlist as mentors?

5. What do you make of the state of domestic missions in our cities today based on the history presented in this chapter?

Chapter 6: Notes

[1] John 8:31-32

[2] Matthew 14:16

[3] Luke 14:12-14

[4] Luke 7:42

[5] 1 John 3:17-18

[6] Matthew 25:41

[7] *The Poverty and Justice Bible*, (New York: American Bible Society, 1995).

[8] Millard Erickson, *Christian Theology* (Grand Rapids, MI: Baker Book House, 1983), 641.

[9] Ibid.

[10] Ibid., 64.

[11] "Joining the Reality-Based Community or How I Learned to Stop Loving the Bombs and Start Worrying," *TomDispatch,* ed. Jeremiah Goulka, http://www.tomdispatch.com/blog/175590/.

[12] Ruby K. Payne, *A Framework for Understanding Poverty,* Revised Edition (Highlands, TX: aha! Process, 1998), 44-45.

[13] Ruby K. Payne, Philip E. DeVol, and Terie Dreussi Smith, *Bridges out of Poverty: Strategies for Professionals and Communities* (Highlands, TX: aha! Process, Inc., 2005).

[14] Erickson.

[15] Joe Nocera, "Subprime and the Banks: Guilty as Charged," *New York TImes,* October 14, 2009 2009.

[16] J. Allison, *Raising Abel: The Recovery of the Eschatological Imagination* (Crossroad Publishing: New York), 21.

[17] John 11:50

[18] See Proverbs 12:16; 1 Peter 3:9

[19] James Alison, *Raising Abel: The Recovery of the Eschatological Imagination* (New York,: Crossroad, 2000).

[20] Jeremiah 31:33-34, Hebrews 8:10-11

[21] Hebrews 9:14

[22] Hebrews 4:16

[23] 2 Cor. 1:4

[24] Elijah Anderson, *Code of the Street; Decency, Violence, and the Moral Life of the Inner City* (New York: W.W. Norton, 1999), 186.

[25] James 2:6-7

[26] James 2:5

[27] Chambers, *My Utmost for His Highest: An Updated Edition in Today's Language: The Golden Book of Oswald Chambers* (Grand Rapids: Discovery House Publishers, 1992), 1131.

[28] Psalm 119:22-23

[29] Proverbs 11:9

[30] Yonce Shelton, "Overcoming Poverty Is Both/And," *The Clergy Journal,* April 2007.

[31] Bo Boshers and Judson Poling, "Jesus-Style Mentoring," *Group* 32, no. 1 (2005).

[32] CCDA Mission, "Christian Community Development Association — Mission,"

Christian Community Development Association http://www.ccda.org/mission. "The mission of CCDA is to inspire and train Christians who seek to bear witness to the Kingdom of God by reclaiming and restoring under-resourced communities.

[33] Wayne Gordon, "The Eight Components of Christian Community Development," http://www.ccda.org.

[34] Horace R Pratt, "Pastoral Strategies for Ministering to Poor Black Single Mothers," (1988).

[35] Timothy Wilson Hobbs, "Solidarity with the Poor as an Expression of Faithful Discipleship to the Vision of Christ," *Colombia Theological Seminary* (1999). http://rim.atla.com/scripts/starfinder.exe/5500/rimmarc.txt.

[36] Gerald O. West, *The Academy of the Poor: Toward a Dialogical Reading of the Bible* (Sheffield: Academic Press, 1999), 16-17.

[37] Murphy Davis, "Breaking the Bread of Solidarity: Prayer in the Activist Community," *Hospitality* 27, no. 9 (2008).

[38] Barbara E. Reid, "The Cross and Cycles of Violence," *Interpretation* 58, no. 4 (2004).

[39] Dorothy Day, "Loaves and Fishes: The Inspiring Story of the Catholic Worker Movement," (Maryknoll: Orbis Books, 1997).

[40] Kristen Bargeron, "Fruit That Will Last," 19, no. 8 (2000). http://www.opendoor-community.org/fruit.htm.

[41] Dennis McCallum and Jessica Lowery, *Organic Disciplemaking: Mentoring Others into Spiritual Maturity and Leadership* (Houston: Touch Publications, 2006), 88.

[42] Ron Belsterling, "The Mentoring Approach of Jesus as Demonstrated in John 13," *Journal of Youth Ministry* 5, no. 1 (2006), 77.

[43] J. Carruthers, "The Principles and Practices of Mentoring," in *The Return of the Mentor*, ed. B.J. Caldwell and E.M. Carter (London: Falmer Press, 1993).

[44] Lynn Anderson, "Is Spiritual Mentoring a Biblical Idea?," *HEARTLIGHT® Magazine* (1999). http://www.heartlight.org/hope/hope990407mentoring.html. HEARTLIGHT® Magazine can be accessed at http://www.heartlight.org/. Anderson's article is available at http://www.heartlight.org/hope/hope_990407_mentoring.html.

[45] Ibid.

[46] Elana Dorfman, "Ayelet Program: Mentoring Women Leaving the Cycle of Violence," *Journal of Religion & Abuse* 6, no. 3/4 (2004).

[47] Joel Brown, Bonnie Benard, and Marianne D'Emidio-Caston, *Resiliency Education* (Corwin, 2001).

[48] Waln K Brown, "Resiliency and the Mentoring Factor," *Reclaiming Children and Youth* 13, no. 2 (2004).

[49] Mary Cagney, "Mentoring and Modeling Great Aspirations," *Christianity Today* 42, no. 4 (1998).

[50] Lynn Anderson.

[51] Esther Burroughs, *A Garden Path to Mentoring: Planting Your Life in Another and Releasing the Fragrance of Christ* (Birmingham: Woman's Missionary Union 1997).

[52] Keith R. Anderson and Randy D. Reese, *Spiritual Mentoring: A Guide for Seeking and Giving Direction* (Downers Grove: InterVarsity Press, 1999).38.

[53] Payne, DeVol, and Smith, *Bridges out of Poverty: Strategies for Professionals and Communities*, 84.

[54] Ibid.

[55] Ibid., 102.

[56] Ibid., 44.

[57] Wendy S. McClanahan, "Mentoring Ex-Prisoners in the Ready4work Reentry Initiative," *Public/Private Ventures Preview* (2007). http://www.ppv.org/ppv/publications/assets/212_publication.pdf. Available at Public/Private Ventures website: www.ppv.org.

Chapter 6: Digging Deeper

1. Read about scapegoats in Leviticus 16. Does this differ from our contemporary understanding of scapegoat?

2. Read the story of the rich young ruler in Luke 18:18-30 with people from a very different socioeconomic class than yours. What do you learn?

3. Read 1 John 3:24. Although the word *mentor* doesn't appear in Scripture, its root *menō* does. In this verse, *menō* has been translated "resides" because this verse refers to the mutual, reciprocal and permanence of relationship between God and the believer. How does this verse help you understand the concept of *mentoring*?

4. Look at James 1:27. What kind of religion do you have?

Chapter 6: For those Digging a Well

1. How well do you handle criticism? How about when it's false?

2. What areas of your life need to be "converted from below" or "de-schooled"? List a few things you will do specifically to improve those areas.

3. There are many good books on mentoring or perhaps some experts in your town. What if you asked a group at your church to study mentoring with you in preparation for your work? Maybe a few will be interested in helping your ministry!

4. Consider the evolution of my dad's Bible study. How might that be a template for facilitating change in your church, small group or family?

Chapter 7: Notes

[1] Matthew 11:28 (*The Message*).

[2] Bruner, *Matthew: A Commentary,* vol. Volume 1: The Christbook; Matthew 1-12 (Grand Rapids: Eerdmans Publishing Company, 2004), 538.

[3] Ibid.

[4] "The Seeker-Friendly Purpose Driven Church Growth Movement," ed. Don Koenig, http://www.thepropheticyears.com/comments/Seeker%20friendly.htm.

[5] C. Draper C. Brand, A. England, S. Bond, E. R. Clendenen, T. C. Butler & B. Latta, ed. *Holman Illustrated Bible Dictionary* (Nashville: Holman Bible Publishers, 2003).

[6] Elijah Anderson, *Code of the Street; Decency, Violence, and the Moral Life of the Inner City* (New York: W.W. Norton, 1999), 77.

[7] Ibid., 9.

[8] Ibid., 34.

[9] Ibid., 72.

[10] Ibid., 33.

[11] Frederick Dale Bruner, *The Gospel of John: A Commentary* (Grand Rapids: William B Eerdmans Publishing Company, 2012), 245.

12 William Temple, *Readings in St. John's Gospel* (1945), 66. Quoted in Bruner, *The Gospel of John: A Commentary,* 254.

13 Asset-Based Community Development Institute, 2009. School of Education and Social Policy; Northwestern University.

14 Elizabeth Elliot, *Through Gates of Splendor* (Carol Stream: Tyndale House Publishers, Rev Upd 1981). Unfortunately, when the missionaries attempted to meet the Huaorani, they were killed. The deaths of the men galvanized the missionary effort in the US in the 1950s, sparking an outpouring of funding for evangelization efforts around the world.

15 Best Practice is an idea asserting that there are *methods* and *techniques* that have consistently shown results superior to those achieved by other *means* and used as *benchmarks* for which to strive. Best practices are the most efficient and effective ways of accomplishing a task, based on repeatable procedures that have proven themselves over time for large numbers of people. See Businessdictionary.com, ed. WebFinance Inc, in the WebFinance, Inc, http://www.businessdictionary. com/definition/best-practice.html.

16 Jan Martinez, "Discipleship with Women Living in Poverty," (Bakke Graduate University, 2009). For more information, see dissertation details.

17 Mary Ellen Bowman, director, Christian Women's Job Corps, Wilmington, North Carolina. As quoted in her returned questionnaire.

18 Elaine Dickson, director, CWJS, Huntsville, Alabama. As quoted in her returned questionnaire.

19 *Lifeguide Bible Study* (Downers Grove, IL: InterVarsity Press).

20 *Fisherman Bible Study Series* (Colorado Springs: Shaw Books).

21 See, for example, Jack Kuhatschek, *Self-Esteem: Seeing Ourselves as God Sees Us,* A Lifeguide Bible Study (Downers Grove: InterVarsity Press, 2002). This nine-week series studies issues such as being God's masterpiece (Psalm 139), yet fallen (Romans 3:9–20), forgiven Hebrews 10:1–18), eternally loved (Romans 8:28–39), being blessed (Ephesians 1:3–14), new in Christ (Ephesians 4:17–32), God's power to remove weakness (2 Corinthians 12:1–10), being rich in Christ (1 Corinthians 4:8–13; 2 Corinthians 6:3–10), and dying in Christ (1 Corinthians 15:35–58).

22 Ephesians 4:22-24

23 Deuteronomy 24:15

24 Matthew 18:15

[25] Romans 14:19

[26] 2 Timothy 2:14

[27] Philippians 2:3

[28] Psalm 127:1

[29] Luke 12:31

[30] Proof texting is the practice of using decontextualized quotations from a document to establish a proposition rhetorically through an appeal to authority. Critics of the technique note that often the document, when read as a whole, may not in fact support the proposition. For more information see http://en.wikipedia.org/wiki/Prooftext.

[31] http://www.crossroadskitchen.org/

[32] Tom Gorman, "Government's Role in Wealth & Poverty," *InfoPlease* (2003). http://www.infoplease.com/cig/economics/government-role.html.

[33] Tammy Tam, Cheryl Zlotnick, and Marjorie Robertston, "Longitudinal Perspective: Adverse Childhood Events, Substance Use, and Labor Force Participation among Homeless Adults," *American Journal of Drug and Alcohol Abuse* 29, no. 4 (2003), 2. Adverse childhood events (ACE) refers to experiences prior to age 18 such as foster care, out-of-home placement, sexual abuse, physical abuse, running away, being arrested, homelessness, early regular alcohol or drug use, witnessing maternal battering, family malfunction.

[34] Tina Rosenberg, "A Payoff out of Poverty," *New York Times*, 12/21/08 2008; ibid. *New York Times Magazine* Available at http://www.nytimes.com/2008/12/21/magazine/21cash-t.html?pagewanted=1&_r=1&th&emc=th.

[35] Religion and Ethics Newsweekly, 2003. "Perspectives: Jim Towey: Faith-Based Initiative," *Current Stories*, http://www.pbs.org/wnet/religionandethics/week635/perspectives.html.

Chapter 7: Digging Deeper

1. Explain how the Sermon on the Mount (Matthew chapters 5-7) is the yoke Jesus speaks of in Matthew 11:28-30.

2. Study Ephesians 4:22-24. How do you relate to it personally? How might the verse and your own experience help you understand the process of change in others?

3. Proof texting is using a Bible passage out of context in order to support a personal opinion or view. Consider how you or others have done this in the past. (For example, Ephesians 6:5 was used to justify slavery.) Understanding the context of a passage and the intention of the writer can prevent it.

Chapter 7: For those Digging a Well

1. Make a step-by-step plan for how you will engage your target population. Include as many details as you can. Explain each step: Why *this* well? Why will they want what you have to offer? Will they come voluntarily? How will you pay them?

2. Convert your plan into a business plan. You can obtain templates for business plans online or ask to use the plan of a business similar to yours. Ask local business people or students in business programs to help you. Take advantage of every service learning opportunity.

3. Assess the assets of your target population. What can they do well and not so well? How does this affect your business plan? Will you need to rely on experts for various aspects of the work? Will your experts volunteer their time?

4. Interview experts in your field of interest. What do they advise you in preparing for your mission/business?

5. Find Scripture verses that support each aspect of your mission.

Chapter 8: Notes

[1] W.W. Wiersbe, *Wiersbe's Expository Outlines on the New Testament.* (Victor Books: Wheaton, IL) 1997.

[2] R. B. Hughes, J. C. Laney, & R. B. Hughes, (2001). *Tyndale Concise Bible Commentary.* Rev. ed. of: New Bible companion. 1990; Includes index. The Tyndale reference library (p. 470), Wheaton, IL: Tyndale House Publishers.

[3] Walvoord, Zuck, and Dallas Theological Seminary, *The Bible Knowledge Commentary: An Exposition of the Scriptures.*

[4] W. W. Wiersbe, (1997, c1992). *Wiersbe's Expository Outlines on the New Testament* (p. 221). Wheaton, IL: Victor Books.

[5] John Calvin, *John*, 3rd ed., vol. 2 vol (1564). As quoted in Frederick Dale Bruner, *The Gospel of John: A Commentary* (Grand Rapids: William B Eerdmans Publishing Company, 2012), 257.

[6] A.T. Lincoln, *John* (Nashville: Thomas Nelson, 2005). As quoted in Bruner, 258.

[7] Bruner, 252.

[8] James Gilligan, *Violence: Reflections on a National Epidemic* (New York: Vintage Random House, 1997), 53.

[9] Ibid., 45.

[10] Ibid., 111.

[11] Ibid., 52.

[12] Elijah Anderson, *The Code of the Street: Decency, Violence and the Moral Life of the Inner City* (New York: WW Norton and Co., 1999), 205.

[13] Gilligan, 112-113.

[14] Ephesians 4:26

[15] Matthew 18:15

[16] James 5:12

[17] John 16:33

[18] Matthew 10:16

[19] John 13:14

[20] Lincoln, 367. As quoted in Bruner, 762.

[21] Barbara E. Reid, "The Cross and Cycles of Violence," *Interpretation* 58, no. 4 (2004).

[22] Bruner, 766.

Chapter 8: Digging Deeper

1. Using a good Bible dictionary and commentary, explore what Scripture says about employees and employers. In some translations, you'll need to look up "servant" and "master."

2. Study the word "humble" and read John 13:1-17. How do these inform the employee/employer relationship?

Chapter 8: For those Digging a Well

1. Design the smallest details of your product and work space. For example, if you are going make greeting cards with women in a prison facility, gather every item you will need and make copious notes. (If you forget the glue, you will be out of operation). Practice taking supplies to a focus group and get their feedback. What did you forget? What would make it easier? Your organization and attention to detail will create a healthier atmosphere in which to work.

2. Consider "stress" in your product design, work environment, and workers. How technical is the process? Can workers ruin the product easily (and feel terrible about themselves)? Is it hard to assemble? Do they need a level of expertise in order to feel they've accomplished the work?

3. How will you and your project "wash the feet" of the people you serve

Chapter 9: Notes

[1] 2 Samuel 11:5

[2] Eugene H. Peterson, *Leap Over a Wall: Earthy Spirituality for Everyday Christians* (San Francisco: Harper Collins, 1997), 185.

[3] Bruner, *The Gospel of John: A Commentary*, 261.

[4] Isaiah 42:16

[5] Mark 1:35, John 5:19, Isa 50:4-5

[6] Peterson, 187.

[7] 1 Peter 2:24

[8] Chambers, *My Utmost*. February 9.

[9] Libronix Digital Library System 3.0d, 2000-2006. "Logos Bible Software."

[10] Lawrence O. Richards, *The Teacher's Commentary* (Wheaton: Victor Books, 1987), 740.

[11] Leviticus 19:18

[12] W.E. Vine, *Vine's Expository Dictionary of Old and New Testament Words* (Old Tappan, New Jersey: Fleming H. Revell Company, 1981), 109.

[13] Here are some of my favorite saints: Kit Danley is director of Neighborhood Ministries, Phoenix, AZ. See www.neighborhoodministries.org. Arloa Sutter is director of Breakthrough Ministries, Chicago, IL. See www.breakthroughministries.com. Ray and Corean Bakke: For a good example of Ray Bakke's writing, see Ray Bakke, *A Theology as Big as the City* (Downers Grove: InterVarsity Press, 1997). Wayne Gordon Pastor, Lawndale Community Church: See http://www.lawndalechurch.org/bio.html. Danielle Riggs is medical director at Christ Clinic along with incredibly dedicated medical volunteers at Christ Clinic. See www.christclinic.org.

[14] Kevin Finch with Big Table Ministry. See www.big-table.com.

[15] Mark and Rachel Terrell with Cup of Cool Water Ministry. See www.cupofcoolwater.org.

Chapter 9: Digging Deeper

1. Note how Jesus deals with the Samaritan woman's sin. Then read 2 Samuel 11-12 and 2 Corinthians 5:11-21. What do you learn about confrontation, confession, forgiveness, and reconciliation?

2. Make a list of verses containing "love one another." Hang it in your cubicle and on your mirror. Memorize one each day. How do they influence your day?

3. Compare "Love your neighbor as yourself" (Leviticus 19:18) with "Love each other as I have loved you" (John 13:34). What is the difference between them?

4. Investigate the word *agape*. Do you know love like that?

Chapter 9: For those Digging a Well

1. Assess how you will minister to sin. What are your strengths, weaknesses, and experiences with it?

2. Figure out how every part of your project can be restorative.

3. How will your project accommodate broken people?

4. How do you handle confrontation? You will be relied upon as the expert. The flow of daily activities, even the success of your project, will depend your ability to confront well, like Jesus did. Yikes! Get ready. Know your Scripture.

5. Gather a board of advisors on whom you rely for business expertise, personnel issues, spiritual matters, encouragement, legal expertise, community and donor relations, etc. Start meeting together and one-on-one, so that you establish strong, godly relationships with the people who will walk beside you.

Chapter 10: Notes

[1] Ephrem the Syrian, (303), cited in Bruner, *The Gospel of John: A Commentary*, 258.

[2] Calvin, Thomas Aquinas, and Keener, as cited in Bruner, 267.

[3] John 3:2

[4] John Perkins, Morning Bible Study: CCDA 2004. New Orleans, LA. November, 2004.

[5] Woolcock, (2000).

[6] Smyth, (2009).

[7] Jember Teffera, "Transformational Leadership" *Overture 1* (lecture, Bakke Graduate University, Seattle, WA. June 8, 2004).

[8] Chambers, *My Utmost*. June 19.

[9] Graft.

[10] Moriera.

[11] Smith.

[12] Siefert, (2000).

[13] L. Goodman, Katya F. Smyth, V. Banyard, "Beyond the 50-Minute Hour: Increasing Control, Choice, and Connections in the Lives of Low-Income Women," *American Journal of Orthopsychiatry* 80, no. 1 (2010).

[14] Ibid.

[15] "The Lifelong Effects of Early Childood Adversity and Toxic Stress," *Pediatrics* 129, no. 1 (2012).

[16] Jack P. Shonkoff, "Early Childhood Adversity, Toxic Stress, and the Role of the Pediatrician: Translating Developmentla Science into Lifelong Health," *Pediatrics* 129, no. 1 (2012).

[17] Nicholas Kristof, "A Poverty Solution That Starts with a Hug," *New York* Times, 2012.

[18] Tracie Afifi and others, "Population Attributable Fractions of Psychiatric Disorders and Suicide Ideation and Attempts Associated with Adverse Childhood Experences," *The American Journal of Public Health* 98, no. 5 (2008).

[19] Nena Messina and Christine Grella, "Childhood Trauma and Women's Health Outcomes in a California Prison Population," *The American Journal of Public Health* 96, no. 10 (2006).

[20] Sudie Back and others, "Early Life Trauma and Sensitivity to Current Life Stressors in Individuals with and without Cocaine Dependence," *The American Journal of Drug and Alcohol Abuse* 34, no. 4 (2008).

[21] Tammy Tam, Cheryl Zlotnick, and Marjorie Robertston, "Longitudinal Perspective: Adverse Childhood Events, Substance Use, and Labor Force Participation among Homeless Adults," *American Journal of Drug and Alcohol Abuse* 29, no. 4 (2003).

[22] Lawrence Bailis, "Job Training for the Homeless: Report on Demonstration's First Year. Research and Evaluation Report Series 91-F" (1991). http://eric.ed.gov/ERICWebPortal/custom/portlets/recordDetails/detailmini.jsp?_nfpb=true&_&ERICExtSearch_SearchValue_0=ED359359&ERICExtSearch_SearchType_0=no&accno=ED359359.

[23] See Dennis Bakke, *Joy at Work* (Seattle: PVG, 2006). Also see Raymond Bakke, William Hendricks, Brad Smith, *Joy at Work Bible Study Companion*.

[24] Ruby K. Payne and Don L. Krabill, *Hidden Rules of Class at Work* (Highlands, Texas: aha! Process, Inc., 2002), 62.

Chapter 10: Digging Deeper

1. Do a word study on "healing." How does it influence your understanding of the "free gift" Jesus offers?

2. Discuss the idea of having a Bible study in the work setting and paying employees to attend with people of various opinions. What do you learn?

3. Define your own "theology of work." Consider reading *Joy at Work* and its very helpful study guide, *Joy at Work Bible Study Companion,* with your boss or fellow employees. It might just change the whole work environment.

Chapter 10: For those Digging a Well

1. Find an underlying scriptural precedent for your project. At Christ Kitchen, ours is 2 Corinthians 5:11-21. It stands with distinction on every one of our brochures.

2. What are your yardsticks for success? Consider long-term indicators and daily gauges.

3. Do you need to generate income or will your project be voluntary? How will you attract donors to your cause? Talk with development specialists, particularly those with expertise in small Christian nonprofits. Their knowledge is invaluable.

4. Consider your personal skills. Are you a jack-of-all-trades or would it be helpful to recruit partners? How are you at sharing power?

5. Consider implementing into your business plan a means for people in your target population to move into managerial positions in the organization. This takes a great deal of prayer and preparation. Advancement too early in their development can be discouraging for both the worker and the project. Not planning for it can create a "top-down" atmosphere that leads to unhappy labor relations.

Chapter 11: Notes

[1] Bruner, *The Gospel of John: A Commentary*, 263.

[2] Daniel 10:12

Chapter 11: Digging Deeper

1. Do a word study on the word "stability" and list verses helpful to understanding what it means.

2. Discuss what "disputable matters" in Romans 14:1 means and how you
   might use the concept in deciphering what issues are important in Kingdom work.

3. What is the difference between grieving the Holy Spirit (Ephesians 4:30)
   and deliberately slandering God's Spirit (Matthew 12:31; Hebrews 6:4-6)?
   How would you have explained this to Nadia?

4. Do you have a good idea how Satan works? Find verses that explain it
   accurately. For starters, try: 2 Corinthians 11:14; 12:7; 1 Corinthians 7:5;
   1 Thessalonians 2:28; 1 Timothy 3:6; 5:11, 15; Luke 22:31.

5. Now make a list of assurances that we are not at the whim of Satan's
   work. For starters, look up the following verses: John 3:16; 16:33; Hebrews
   2:14, 18; 9:14, 24; 1 John 2:1-2; 3:8; John 12:31.

Chapter 11: For those Digging a Well

1. *Stability* is the word we use to describe the intention of our work with the women at Christ Kitchen. By it, we imply mental, physical, emotional, and spiritual health. What do you consider a "stable" life? Make a list of the characteristics you would like to teach, model, and inspire in your workers. How will each be accomplished?

2. Make a list of volunteer opportunities for all the people who will hear about your project and want to help. Bringing weekly, healthy meals is a favorite around Christ Kitchen! A Christmas party is also tops!

3. What are your expectations of volunteers? Will they be an integral part of the organization, working along side those you serve? Will you conduct volunteer training events that help them understand the population you're working with?

4. How will you decide where volunteers fit into your project? We believe God will use volunteers' particular gifts to advance our ministry. At Christ Kitchen, we ask new volunteers to join us for a whole workday on a Thursday so they understand how we operate. Then we ask them what tasks interest them most. It's wise to use volunteers in what they feel they can accomplish. Remember, God brings them to your project for his reasons, some of which you may never be aware.

Chapter 12: Notes

[1] Luke 6:45

[2] James 2:5

[3] Frank Anthony Spina, *The Faith of the Outsider: Exclusion and Inclusion in the Biblical Story* (Grand Rapids: Eerdmans Publishing Company, 2005), 155.

Chapter 12: Digging Deeper

1. Make a list of verses about encouragement and discouragement. Have it ready to read at a moments notice.

2. Job said, "Let God weigh me in honest scales and he will know that I am blameless," (Job 31:6). Can you say this along with Job? What areas of your life need work?

3. Oswald Chambers writes: Surrender is not the surrender of the external life, but of the Will; when that is done, all is done. There are very few crises in life; the great crisis is the surrender of the will. God never crushes a man's will into surrender; He never beseeches him, He waits until the man yields up his will to Him. That battle never needs to be re-fought. Have you ever had such a battle? Do you know a very trusted friend who you can talk to about surrender?

Chapter 12: For those Digging a Well

1. How do you handle interruptions? Perhaps you should consider getting good at it.

2. What kinds of things discourage you? How can you prepare for discouragement within yourself and others?

3. How do you imagine interpreting "the world" to the people in your project and "your people" to the world? At Christ Kitchen, we are called upon constantly to do this by questions from the community like: "Tell us about the women you work with. Do they ever "move on"? Do you feel safe? How do you know they are honest?" From the women, I am asked things like: "Why do they spend so much money on their homes? Why do they need that much space? Why do they care so much about exercising?" These are often expressions of class and you become an interpreter.

Chapter 13: Notes

[1] Isaiah 44:3-4

[2] Walvoord, Zuck, and Dallas Theological Seminary, *The Bible Knowledge Commentary : An Exposition of the Scriptures*, 287.

[3] M. Henry, (1994). *Matthew Henry's Commentary on the Whole Bible: Complete and Unabridged in One Volume* (Jn 4:27–42). Peabody: Hendrickson.

[4] Frances Taylor Gench, *Back to the Well: Women's Encounters with Jesus in the Gospels* (Louisville: Westminster John Knox Press, 2004), 129.

[5] Bruner, 273.

[6] 2 Corinthians 3:16–18 (*The Message*)

[7] 2 Corinthians 3:12 (*The Message*)

[8] Job 11:7

Chapter 13: Digging Deeper

1. The Samaritans only read the Pentateuch, the first five books of the Old Testament. How might that influence their perspective?

2. Consider the "instruments" the Lord uses to announce his Kingdom: a baby born into poverty and obscurity and twelve nobodies—fishermen, a zealot, a tax collector, a traitor. If you were the Savior of the world, would you have trusted them with the message? What assures you that these were perfect choices?

3. Look up verses on the words *leader* or *lead*. Notice *who* leads in the majority of verses. Now look up verses with *follow* or *follower*. Again, who is the subject of the sentence? What does this teach you about our culture's emphasis on leadership? Consider putting on a conference entitled "Followship." Do you think many would come?

Chapter 13: For those Digging a Well

1. How can you involve local churches in your project?

2. How might your employees begin to minister back to the church? Perhaps they can give their testimony at a fundraising luncheon, at a missions conference, or minute-for-mission during the service. I was told, "We in the church need to hear their stories to remind us of the radical love of our Savior."

3. What do your employees think about "church"? Consider attending various denominations and types of services together so they can get an idea of the varied ways people worship.

Chapter 14: Notes

[1] Barbara Tamialis, "Ten Years of Keeping the Faith," *Sojourners* 22, no. 8 (1993).

[2] Eugene Peterson, *The Unnecessary Pastor: Rediscovering the Call* (Grand Rapids: William B. Eerdmans, 2000), vii.

[3] Arloa Sutter, *The Invisible: What the Church Can Do to Find and Serve the Least of These* (Indianapolis: Wesleyan Publishing House, 2010), 103.

[4] Spina, 157.

[5] Deuteronomy 8:3

[6] 1 Timothy 6:17

[7] Bruner, 275.

[8] Jan Silvious, *The Five-Minute Devotional* (Grand Rapids: Zondervan, 1991).

[9] Kay Arthur, *Precept Upon Precept* (Chattanooga: Precept Ministries International 1993).

[10] Chambers, *My Utmost*. November 2.

[11] Walvoord, Zuck, and Dallas Theological Seminary. The Bible Knowledge Commentary: An Exposition of the Scriptures (Jn 4:35).

[12] C.S. Lewis, *God in the Dock* (Grand Rapids: W. B. Eerdmans, 1972).

[13] W. W. Wiersbe, (1996). *The Bible Exposition Commentary* (Jn 4:31). Wheaton, IL: Victor Books.

[14] See Acts 8

[15] Lawrence O. Richards, *Every Miracle in the Bible* (Nashville: Thomas Nelson Publishers, 1998).

[16] 2 Timothy 3:6-7

Chapter 14: Digging Deeper

1. How does Jesus look upon those who don't accept his message? See Mark 10:17-29 (verse 21 in particular).

2. Read the story of the sower in Matthew 13. What kind of soil are you?

3. Do you eat the same kind of "food" as Jesus does in John 4:34?

4. What percentage of time do you spend reading, thinking, and talking about the will of God compared to the time you spend *doing* it? Keep track of the time for one whole day. What do you come up with?

CHAPTER 14: FOR THOSE DIGGING A WELL

1. Lawrence O. Richards wrote a book listing every miracle in the Bible. (See Chapter 14 Notes.) There are hundreds of them! Do you expect to see miracles every day?

2. Prepare for employees or volunteers who don't accept or like what you're doing. Some will quit voluntarily and some you will need to fire. Consider writing an employment policy manual and conducting yearly reviews.

3. How will prayer be designed into your workday?

4. Count on miracles to sustain you!

Chapter 15: Notes

[1] Ephesians 2:15 (*The Message*)

[2] Joyce Hollyday, *Clothed with the Sun: Biblical Women, Social Justice, and Us* (Louisville: Westminster John Knox Press, 1994), 233.

[3] R. Jamieson, A.R. Fausset, and D. Brown, (1997). *Commentary Critical and Explanatory on the Whole Bible* (Jn 4:40). Oak Harbor, WA: Logos Research Systems, Inc.

[4] 1 Peter 1:18

[5] Ephesians 5:12

[6] Psalm 34:18

[7] Psalm 38:4

[8] Hebrews 10:22

[9] Psalm 23:3

Chapter 15: Digging Deeper

1. Pray over 1 Peter 1:18. How can your own redemption open your heart to someone raised very different from you?

2. Isaiah 66:12-13 says in part, "I will extend peace to you like a river . . . . As a mother comforts her child, so will I comfort you." Does your life reflect that assurance?

3. The balm of Gilead, spoken of in Jeremiah 8:22, was a valuable resin from trees in the Judean hill country that was used as an ointment for medicinal purposes. It had astringent, antiseptic, and other therapeutic qualities. Jeremiah so identified with his people's misery that he pleaded for a balm to heal the wound of his people. Might you consider *being* a balm to the destitute?

Chapter 15: For those Digging a Well

As you develop a community of disparate, desperate souls, pray for the grace
and wisdom to govern well, to hold out the key of life to all who venture in.
"Lean not on your own understanding, but in all your ways, acknowledge
him and he will direct your steps" (Proverbs 3:5-6). You are, or will be, the
balm of Gilead, an instrument of healing among broken people in a parched
land. Be strong and alert. Be gentle and forgiving. Allow the Lord to have his
way. Remember whose you are.

Bibliography

Achtemeier, P. J. *Harper's Bible Dictionary*. 1st ed. San Francisco: Harper & Row, 1985.

Afifi, Tracie, Murray Enns, Brian Cox, Gordon Asumndson, Murray Stein, and Jitender Sareen. "Population Attributable Fractions of Psychiatric Disorders and Suicide Ideation and Attempts Associated with Adverse Childhood Experences." *The American Journal of Public Health* 98, no. 5 (2008): 946-7.

Alison, James. *Raising Abel: The Recovery of the Eschatological Imagination*. New York,: Crossroad, 2000.

Anderson, Elijah. *The Code of the Street: Decency, Violence and the Moral Life of the Inner City*. New York: WW Norton and Co., 1999.

Anderson, Keith R., and Randy D. Reese. *Spiritual Mentoring: A Guide for Seeking and Giving Direction*. Downers Grove: InterVarsity Press, 1999.

Anderson, Lynn "Is Spiritual Mentoring a Biblical Idea?" *HEARTLIGHT® Magazine* (1999). http://www.heartlight.org/hope/hope990407mentoring.html.

Angelou, Maya. *Even the Stars Look Lonesome*. New York: Random House, 1997.

Arthur, Kay. *Precept Upon Precept*. Chattanooga: Precept Ministries International 1993.

Back, Sudie, Kathleen Brady, Angela Waldrop, and Sharon Yeatts. "Early Life Trauma and Sensitivity to Current Life Stressors in Individuals with and without Cocaine Dependence." *The American Journal of Drug and Alcohol Abuse* 34, no. 4 (2008): 1.

Bailis, Lawrence. "Job Training for the Homeless: Report on Demonstration's First Year. Research and Evaluation Report Series 91-F." (1991). http://eric.ed.gov/ERICWebPortal/custom/portlets/recordDetails/detailmini.jsp?_nfpb=true&_&ERICExtSearch_SearchValue_0=ED359359&ERICExtSearch_SearchType_0=no&accno=ED359359.

Bakke, Dennis. *Joy at Work*. Seattle: PVG, 2006.

Bakke, Ray. *A Theology as Big as the City*. Downers Grove: InterVarsity Press, 1997.

Bakke, Raymond, Brad Smith, William Hendricks, *Joy at Work Bible Study Companion.*

Bargeron, Kristen. "Fruit That Will Last." 19, no. 8 (2000). http://www.open-doorcommunity.org/fruit.htm.

Belsterling, Ron. "The Mentoring Approach of Jesus as Demonstrated in John 13." *Journal of Youth Ministry* 5, no. 1 (2006): 77-92.

Bettenson, Henry, ed. *Documents of the Christian Church.* London: Oxford University Press, 1963.

Bonhoeffer, Dietrich. *Discipleship.* Minneapolis: Fortress Press, 2003.

Boshers, Bo, and Judson Poling. "Jesus-Style Mentoring." *Group* 32, no. 1 (2005): 82.

Brown, Joel, Bonnie Benard, and Marianne D'Emidio-Caston. *Resiliency Education*: Corwin, 2001.

Brown, Waln K. "Resiliency and the Mentoring Factor." *Reclaiming Children and Youth* 13, no. 2 (2004): 75.

Bruner, Frederick Dale. *Matthew: A Commentary.* Vol. Volume 1: The Christbook; Matthew 1-12. Grand Rapids: Eerdmans Publishing Company, 2004.

_____. *Matthew: A Commentary.* Vol. Volume 2: The Churchbook; Matthew 13-28. Grand Rapids: Eerdmans Publishing Company, 2004.

_____. *The Gospel of John: A Commentary.* Grand Rapids: William B Eerdmans Publishing Company, 2012.

Burroughs, Esther. *A Garden Path to Mentoring: Planting Your Life in Another and Releasing the Fragrance of Christ.* Birmingham: Woman's Missionary Union 1997.

C. Brand, C. Draper, A. England, S. Bond, E. R. Clendenen, T. C. Butler & B. Latta, ed. *Holman Illustrated Bible Dictionary.* Nashville: Holman Bible Publishers, 2003.

Cagney, Mary. "Mentoring and Modeling Great Aspirations." *Christianity Today* 42, no. 4 (1998): 56.

Calvin, John. *John.* Vol. 2 vol. 3rd ed., 1564.

Carruthers, J. "The Principles and Practices of Mentoring." In *The Return of the Mentor*, edited by B.J. Caldwell and E.M. Carter. London: Falmer Press, 1993.

Chambers, Oswald. *My Utmost for His Highest: An Updated Edition in Today's Language: The Golden Book of Oswald Chambers*. Grand Rapids: Discovery House Publishers, 1992.

Chambers, Robert. "Rural Development: Putting the Lat First." London: Longman Group, 1983.

"Christian Community Development Association — Mission," Christian Community Development Association http://www.ccda.org/mission.

Davis, Murphy. "Breaking the Bread of Solidarity: Prayer in the Activist Community." *Hospitality* 27, no. 9 (2008).

Day, Dorothy. "Loaves and Fishes: The Inspiring Story of the Catholic Worker Movement." Maryknoll: Orbis Books, 1997.

Dinesen, Isak. *Anecdotes of Destiny*: Vintage, 1988.

Dorfman, Elana. "Ayelet Program: Mentoring Women Leaving the Cycle of Violence." *Journal of Religion & Abuse* 6, no. 3/4 (2004): 101.

Elliot, Elizabeth. *Through Gates of Splendor*. Carol Stream: Tyndale House Publishers, Rev Upd 1981.

Erickson, Millard. *Christian Theology*. Grand Rapids, MI: Baker Book House, 1983.

Freud, Sigmund. "The Question of a Weltanschauung." In *New Introductory Lectures in Psycho-Analysis*, 1933.

Friedman, John. *Empowerment: The Politics of Alternative Development*. Cambridge, MA: Blackwell, 1992.

Funk, Ken. "What Is a Worldview?" (2001). http://web.engr.oregonstate.edu/~funkk/Personal/worldview.html.

Gench, Frances Taylor. *Back to the Well: Women's Encounters with Jesus in the Gospels*. Louisville: Westminster John Knox Press, 2004.

Gilligan, James. *Violence: Reflections on a National Epidemic*. New York: Vintage Random House, 1997.

Gonzales, Justo L. *The Story of Christianity*. Vol. 1: The Early Church to the Dawn of the Reformation. 2 vols. San Francisco: HarperCollins, 1984.

_____. *The Story of Christianity*. Vol. 2: The Reformation to the Present Day. 2 vols. San Francisco: Harper, 1985.

Goodman, L., Smyth, Katya F., Banyard,V. "Beyond the 50-Minute Hour: Increasing Control, Choice, and Connections in the Lives of Low-Income Women." *American Journal of Orthopsychiatry* 80, no. 1 (2010): 3-11.

Gordon, Wayne, "The Eight Components of Christian Community Development," http://www.ccda.org.

Gorman, Tom. "Government's Role in Wealth & Poverty." *InfoPlease* (2003). http://www.infoplease.com/cig/economics/government-role.html.

Goulka, Jeremiah. Joining the Reality-Based Community or How I Learned to Stop Loving the Bombs and Start Worrying http://www.tomdispatch.com/blog/175590/.

Harris, Wendy. "Poverty Level Grim in Spokane County." *Spokesman Review*, Sunday, April 7, 2002 2002.

Henry, Matthew. *Matthew Henry's Concise Commentary on the Whole Bible*. Nashville: Thomas Nelson, Inc, 1997.

Hill, Daniel J., and Randal G. Rauser. *Christian Philosophy a-Z*. Edinburgh: Edinburgh University Press, 2006.

Hobbs, Timothy Wilson. "Solidarity with the Poor as an Expression of Faithful Discipleship to the Vision of Christ." *Colombia Theological Seminary* (1999). http://rim.atla.com/scripts/starfinder.exe/5500/rimmarc.txt.

Hollyday, Joyce. *Clothed with the Sun: Biblical Women, Social Justice, and Us*. Louisville: Westminster John Knox Press, 1994.

Businessdictionary.com. http://www.businessdictionary.com/definition/best-practice.html.

Institute, Asset-Based Community Development. 2009. School of Education and Social Policy; Northwestern University.

The Seeker-Friendly Purpose Drivien Church Growth Movement. http://www.thepropheticyears.com/comments/Seeker friendly.htm.

Kristoff, Nicholas. "A Poverty Solution That Starts with a Hug." *New York Times*2012.

Kuhatschek, Jack. *Self-Esteem: Seeing Ourselves as God Sees Us* A Lifeguide Bible Study. Downers Grove: InterVarsity Press, 2002.

Lewis, C.S. *God in the Dock*. Grand Rapids: W. B. Eerdmans, 1972.

Lewis, Oscar "Culture of Poverty." In *On Understanding Poverty: Perspectives from the Social Sciences*, edited by Daniel P Moynihan, 187-220. New York: Basic Books, 1969.

Libronix Digital Library System 3.0d. 2000-2006. "Logos Bible Software."

"The Lifelong Effects of Early Childood Adversity and Toxic Stress." *Pediatrics* 129, no. 1 (2012): e232-e246.

Lincoln, A.T. *John*. Nashville: Thomas Nelson, 2005.

Linthicum, Robert C. *Empowering the Poor*. Monrovia: MARC Books, 1991.

Martinez, Jan. "Discipleship with Women Living in Poverty." Bakke Graduate University, 2009.

McCallum, Dennis, and Jessica Lowery. *Organic Disciplemaking: Mentoring Others into Spiritual Maturity and Leadership*. Houston: Touch Publications, 2006.

McClanahan, Wendy S. . "Mentoring Ex-Prisoners in the Ready4work Reentry Initiative." *Public/Private Ventures Preview* (2007). http://www.ppv.org/ppv/pub-lications/assets/212_publication.pdf.

Messina, Nena, and Christine Grella. "Childhood Trauma and Women's Health Outcomes in a California Prison Population." *The American Journal of Public Health* 96, no. 10 (2006): 1842-7.

Myers, Bryant L. *Walking with the Poor: Principles and Practices of Transfor-mational Development*. Maryknoll: Orbis Books and World Vision, 1999.

Newsweekly, Religion and Ethics. 2003. "Perspectives: Jim Towey: Faith-Based Initiative," Current Stories, http://www.pbs.org/wnet/religionandethics/week635/perspectives.html.

Nocera, Joe. "Subprime and the Banks: Guilty as Charged." *New York TImes*, October 14, 2009 2009.

Noll, Mark A. *A History of Christianity in the United States and Canada.* Grand Rapids: Eerdmands Publishing Company, 1992.

Nouwen, Henri. *Reaching Out: The Three Movements of the Spiritual Life.* New York: Image Books, 1975.

Payne, Ruby K. *A Framework for Understanding Poverty (Revised Edition).* Highlands, TX: aha! Process, 1998.

Payne, Ruby K., Philip E. DeVol, and Terie Dreussi Smith. *Bridges out of Poverty: Strategies for Professionals and Communities.* Highlands, TX: aha! Process, Inc., 2005.

Payne, Ruby K., and Don L. Krabill. *Hidden Rules of Class at Work.* Highlands, Texas: aha! Process, Inc., 2002.

Peterson, Eugene. *The Message.* Colorado Springs: NavPress, 1993.

_____. *The Unnecessary Pastor: Rediscovering the Call.* Grand Rapids: William B. Eerdmans, 2000.

_____. *A Long Obedienc in the Same Direction: Discipleship in an Instant Society.* Downers Grove: InterVarsity Press, 1980.

_____. *Leap over a Wall: Earthy Spirituality for Everyday Christians.* San Francisco: Harper Collins, 1997.

_____. *The Message: The Bible in Contemporary Language* Colorado Springs: NavPress, 2003.

Peterson, Heidi A. "Clothed with Compassion." *The Christian Century* 118, no. 13 (2001): 11.

Pohl, Christine D. *Making Room; Recovering Hospitality as a Christian Tradition.* Grand Rapids: William B Eerdmans Publishing Co., 1999.

The Poverty and Justice Bible. New York: American Bible Society, 1995.

Pratt, Horace R. "Pastoral Strategies for Ministering to Poor Black Single Mothers." (1988).

Putnam, Robert. *Bowling Alone: The Collapse and Revival of American Community*: Simon and Schuster, 2000.

Reid, Barbara E. "The Cross and Cycles of Violence." *Interpretation* 58, no. 4 (2004): 376.

Richards, Lawrence O. *The Teacher's Commentary*. Wheaton: Victor Books, 1987.

_____. *Every Miracle in the Bible*. Nashville: Thomas Nelson Publishers, 1998.

Rosenberg, Tina. "A Payoff out of Poverty." *New York Times*, 12/21/08 2008.

Sample, Tex. *US Lifestyles and Mainline Churches*. Louisville: Westminster John Knox Press, 1990.

_____.*Hard Living People & Mainline Christians*. Nashville: Abingdon Press, 1993.

Schwartz, John E. . *Freedom Reclaimed: Rediscovering the American Vision*. Baltimore: G-University Press, 2005.

Shelton, Yonce. "Overcoming Poverty Is "Both/And"." *The Clergy Journal* April 2007 (2007).

Shonkoff, Jack P. "Early Childhood Adversity, Toxic Stress, and the Role of the Pediatrician: Translating Developmentla Science into Lifelong Health." *Pediatrics* 129, no. 1 (2012): e224-e231.

Sider, Ronald. *Rich Christians in an Age of Hunger: Moving from Affluence to Generosity*. Nashville: W Publishing Group, 1997.

Silvious, Jan. *The Five-Minute Devotional*. Grand Rapids: Zondervan, 1991.

Sittser, Gerald L. *Water from a Deep Well: Christian Spirituality from Early Martyrs to Modern Missionaries*. Downers Grove: InterVarsity Press, 2007.

Smith, Susan. *Women in Mission: From the New Testament to Today*. Maryknoll: Orbis Books, 2007.

Spina, Frank Anthony. *The Faith of the Outsider: Exclusion and Inclusion in the Biblical Story*. Grand Rapids: Eerdmans Publishing Company, 2005.

Spokane Regional Health District. *Facing Spokane Poverty - a Community Health Assessment Resource*. Spokane, WA: Spokane Regional Health District, 2002.
Sproul, R.C. "Who Are the Poor?" *Tabletalk* 3, no. 6 (1979).

Sutter, Arloa. *The Invisible: What the Church Can Do to Find and Serve the Least of These*. Indianapolis: Wesleyan Publishing House, 2010.

Swan, Laura, ed. *The Forgotten Desert Mothers*. New York: Paulist Press, 2001.

Tam, Tammy, Cheryl Zlotnick, and Marjorie Robertston. "Longitudinal Perspective: Adverse Childhood Events, Substance Use, and Labor Force Participation among Homeless Adults." *American Journal of Drug and Alcohol Abuse* 29, no. 4 (2003): 18.

Tamialis, Barbara. "Ten Years of Keeping the Faith." *Sojourners* 22, no. 8 (1993): 17.

Temple, William. *Readings in St. John's Gospel*, 1945.

the Syrian, Ephrem. 303.

Tucker, Ruth A., and Walter Liefeld. *Daughters of the Church: Women and Ministry from New Testament Times to the Present*. Grand Rapids: Zondervan, 1987.

Poverty: 2007 Highlights. http://www.census.gov/hhes/www/poverty/poverty07/pov07hi.html.

Vine, W.E. *Vine's Expository Dictionary of Old and New Testament Words*. Old Tappan, New Jersey: Fleming H. Revell Company, 1981.

Walvoord, J.F., R.B. Zuck, and Dallas Theological Seminary. *The Bible Knowledge Commentary : An Exposition of the Scriptures* Wheaton: Victor Books, 1983-c1985.

"Webster's Third New International Dictionary." Springfield, MA: Merriam-Webster Inc., 1986.

West, Gerald O. *The Academy of the Poor: Toward a Dialogical Reading of the Bible*. Sheffield: Academic Press, 1999.

Wilken, Robert Louis. *The Spirit of Early Christian Thought*. New Haven, Conn.: Yale University Press, 2003.

Wood, D.R.W., and I.H. Marshall. *New Bible Dictionary*. electronic ed. of 3rd ed. ed. Downers Grove: InterVarsity Press, 1996.

For Further Training, or to Launch a Christ Kitchen Enterprise in Your Area

If you are interested in additional training and communication with
the author, please visit:
www.christkitchen.org/training
This site offers self-paced interactive learning through video clips,
additional resources, journaling, and community development
with others interested in working effectively with the poor
and the Christ Kitchen model overall.